PLANNING CHICAGO

D. Bradford Hunt and Jon B. DeVries, AICP

American Planning Association
Planners Press

Making Great Communities Happen

Chicago | Washington, D.C.

Also available in this series
Planning Los Angeles, David C. Sloane, ed.

Copyright © 2013 by the American Planning Association

205 N. Michigan Ave., Suite 1200, Chicago, IL 60601-5927
1030 15th St., NW, Suite 750 West, Washington, DC 20005-1503

www.planning.org/plannerspress

ISBN: 978-1-61190-080-4 (pbk.)

Library of Congress Control Number 2013930970

Publication of this book was made possible in part by the generous support of the Land Economics Foundation and Lambda Alpha International (LAI), the Honorary Society for the Advancement of Land Economics. Additional in-kind support was provided by the Ely Chapter of LAI.

Printed in the United States of America

CONTENTS

Acknowledgments xii

Part 1: Introduction

Chapter 1:   Planning the "Chicago Way"   3

Chapter 2:   Chicago's Planning Context   11

Part 2: Chicago's Central Area

Chapter 3:   The Origins of Chicago's Postindustrial City: Planning Change,
              1955–1958   25

Chapter 4:   The High-water Mark of City-led Planning: The 1966
              Comprehensive Plan   41

Chapter 5:   The Growth Coalition Takes the Lead for Planning   57

Chapter 6:   Chicago's Equity Planning Moment   67

Chapter 7:   Planning in the Void: Redevelopment in the North Loop
              and Near South   79

**Part 3: Neighborhood Change and
      Planning Response**

Chapter 8:   Chicago and Community Planning Innovation   97

Chapter 9:   Englewood   111

Chapter 10:   Uptown   123

Chapter 11:   Little Village   137

Chapter 12:   Remaking Public Housing: The Chicago Housing Authority's
              Plan for Transformation   151

**Part 4: Industrial Policy in Chicago: City Planning for Industrial
      Retention and Growth**

Chapter 13:   Defending the Industrial Base: Sector and
              District Strategies   171

Chapter 14:   A Changing Employment Scene   185

Chapter 15:   The Calumet District: Planning for Brownfields   193

Chapter 16:   Planning for Global Freight in the Chicago Region   203

Part 5: Chicago in the Current Era

Chapter 17:   The Tourist City: Navy Pier, McCormick Place,
              and Millennium Park   215

Chapter 18:   The Era of Big Plans Is Over   229

Chapter 19:   The Disconnect Between Financing and Planning   247

Chapter 20:   Positive Middle-Range Planning   255

Chapter 21:   The Lost Decade   267

Chapter 22:   Conclusion: Restore Planning to Chicago   277

Appendix A: Planning Departments and Leadership, City of Chicago,
            1958–2013   282

Appendix B: Selected List of Plans and Reports, 1957–2012   284

Appendix C: Industrial Employment Tables   289

Endnotes   294

Notes on Interviews   225

Credits   326

Index   328

ACKNOWLEDGMENTS

A significant portion of Chicago's planning community has contributed insights, recollections, interviews, documents, photographs, and sidebar articles to this book. We thank them for their work in planning this city over the past half century and for sharing their wisdom with us.

Norman Elkin, Dean Macris, Dennis Harder, and Doris Holleb helped frame Part Two by explaining the importance of the new Department of City Planning after 1957. Similarly Miles Berger, Jack Guthman, and Reuben Hedlund described the changing roles of the Chicago Plan Commission, while Kirk Bishop elucidated zoning and regulatory changes. Part Three is indebted to Les Pollock for his perspective on neighborhood planning since the 1960s and to Jesus Garcia and Paul Roldan for recounting the struggles of the Little Village community. Part Four is influenced by Joel Rast's extensive research and by Rachel Weber's thoughtful and incisive feedback. Other conversations with Terri Haymaker, Lee Bey, Larry Okrent, Laurence Msall, Steve Schlickman, and Eileen Figel offered confirmation of broader themes and specific details.

In all, 23 individuals provided in-depth interviews (see page 325). Our hope is that their voices, not just ours, have come through in this narrative. In addition, nine contributors have written short articles on specific subjects to supplement our story. These people are involved in aspects of planning that will be particularly critical for the future of Chicago. We thank them for their contributions.

In researching this book, it was a challenge to find and identify key plans and reports. As an aid to the reader and future researchers, Appendix B lists plans, studies, and reports in chronological order that are referenced here. We would especially like to recognize Larry Okrent, who shared his extensive collection of plans, exhibits, and photos; Lee Bey, who opened the files of the Chicago Central Area Committee and also produced several original photographs; and Lyle Benedict and Shah Tiwana of the Chicago Public Library, who tracked down numerous archival requests.

Others also contributed materially to the success of this book. Helene Berlin provided valuable research assistance and wise counsel. Expert cartographer Dennis McClendon constructed two original maps, and Jane Hunt read several drafts. Numerous individuals helped secure data, images, reports, and plans, including Alissa Anderson, Gabriel Cortez, Tim Desmond, Suhail El Chalabi, Yonah Freemark, Jessica Herczeg-Konecny, Diane Legge Kemp, Nancy Kiernan, Gail Lissner, Jennifer McNeil, Leslie Martin, Luis Monterrubio, Paul Nowicki, David Phillips, Amy Russeau, Joseph Shacter, John Shuler, Mike Shymanski, Jeff Sriver, Peter Strazzabosco, Madilyn Strentz, Sherrie J. Taylor, Lawrence J. Vale, Christine Williams, and Christopher Winters.

We also gratefully acknowledge the support of Lambda Alpha International (LAI), especially Ian Lord, LAI president; Jordan Peters, Ely Chapter president, and Laurie Marston, Ely Chapter and LAI board member. We also thank the Ely Chapter and LAI for cosponsoring, along with the Illinois Chapter of the American Planning Association (APA), a book signing and reception on the occasion of APA's National Planning Conference in Chicago in 2013. Roosevelt University afforded a yearlong research leave to Brad to support this effort as well as research time and resources at the Marshall Bennett Institute of Real Estate for Jon.

Special mention must go to Timothy Mennel, senior editor at APA, who spent countless hours helping us refine our thinking and tighten our themes. He is an editor in the best sense of the word, and his contributions were invaluable. Moreover, we appreciate the foresight of APA in undertaking this series of books about the state of planning in cities across the United States. Our thanks as well to APA's Susan Deegan, Roberta Rewers, and Julie Von Bergen.

Finally, we are grateful for the encouragement and patience of our wives, Page Hartzell and Christine Williams. They understand firsthand the time and energy that is consumed in crafting a compelling narrative on paper. We cannot possibly thank them enough.

CHAPTER 1
PLANNING THE "CHICAGO WAY"

Between 1950 and 1983, Chicago's future was much in doubt. The rhetoric of planning explained some of the many forces that threatened the city's strength: "blight" and "slums" spread like tumors in the 1950s and 1960s; "white flight" and "deindustrialization" bled the city of people and jobs. Chicago lost nearly 22 percent of its population between 1960 and 1990, and poverty skyrocketed. In 1980, *The Economist* surveyed Chicago and labeled it "The City That Survives," taking a glass half-full approach, while the *Chicago Tribune* was less confident, running a 1981 series by Richard Longworth called "City on the Brink" that bluntly described the city's trajectory:

> The City of Chicago has become an economic invalid. The condition may be permanent—unless the people responsible for its economic future can reverse the long, steady, and seemingly endless slide. . . . Chicago's basic problem is that it is losing industries, stores and jobs. Because of this it is losing tax money. Because of this, it won't be able to support itself, to pay for the services of a going city. . . . Business moves away. So do the best young people. The population ages. The city becomes a backwater."

Longworth interviewed various urbanists and concluded, "The cycle has been going on for twenty years. . . .There is no reason to think it will ever turn around."[1]

Figure 1.1. *Chicago's skyline from the John Hancock Observatory, August 9, 2010*

But Chicago pulled out of the downward spiral that devastated Detroit, Cleveland, and St. Louis, among others. The city rebounded from the depths of the 1981–82 recession, embarked on a downtown office construction boom, and made the postindustrial turn. Business service sectors grew, resulting in a downtown office market that added one to two million square feet per year over extended periods and captured at least 50 percent of regional office growth, second only to New York. Highly educated "creative class" workers—to borrow Richard Florida's term—found employment in the city and had the income and inclination to live and play near downtown as well.[2] New housing sprouted, working-class neighborhoods gentrified, and a vibrant restaurant scene emerged. Expanded cultural institutions, universities, and convention facilities followed. Tourists from around the world flocked to Millennium Park, the city's eclectic, crowd-pleasing cultural playground. By any measure, Chicago's central area had staged a remarkable renaissance by the beginning of the 21st century. In 2006, *The Economist* offered an updated profile that glowed, calling Chicago a "Success Story . . . a city buzzing with life, humming with prosperity, sparkling with new buildings, new sculptures, new parks, and generally exuding vitality."[3]

By the early 21st century, Chicago had joined a short list of what are now known as "global cities." A 2012 survey by the consulting firm A. T. Kearney ranked Chicago seventh (after New York, London, Tokyo, Paris, Hong Kong,

and Los Angeles), on the basis of its capital markets, trade, human capital, and cultural experiences.[4] The city's commodity exchanges, transportation hubs, and top-flight universities contribute to the high ranking. Once a regional manufacturing powerhouse and center of a Midwest agro-industrial empire, Chicago had adapted to the postindustrial economy and become one of the "ports of the global age," as A. T. Kearney defines global cities, one that helps "run the global economy and influence its direction." From landing the Boeing corporate headquarters (2002) to building Millennium Park (2004) and despite losing an Olympic bid (2009), Chicago has arrived on the world stage in ways that its onetime Rust Belt peers Detroit, St. Louis, and Cleveland can only dream of.[5]

This is the dominant narrative of the state of the city over the past decades. But not all is well in Chicago. Deindustrialization had devastating effects on manufacturing employment and, by extension, working-class neighborhoods. When the city's giant steel mills closed, an entire way of life vanished. The loss of blue-collar employment, coupled with long-standing race and class divides, produced what sociologist William Julius Wilson called "the truly disadvantaged," a population of mostly poor, young, disproportionately African American residents disconnected from mainstream work and family norms. Without work opportunity, an underground illicit economy replaced the legitimate one. The crack cocaine epidemic peaked

Figure 1.2. Foreclosed homes in the Englewood neighborhood of Chicago, December 1, 2012

in the mid-1990s, as did the city's homicide rate. Large public housing projects became notorious, neglected spaces before being demolished and their residents largely dispersed into other poor neighborhoods. Even those who invested in their communities often struggled: a wave of predatory lending followed by a housing boom and bust in the past decade led to widespread foreclosures, housing abandonment, and demolition. The downtown experienced a renaissance, but many neighborhoods remain mired in poverty. This contrast continues to haunt the city—and the planners who seek to enable its future health and success.[6]

Planners have long sought to shape and reshape Chicago's built environment. Frederick Law Olmsted laid out a network of parks and boulevards in the 1860s and platted one of the city's first suburbs, Riverside. Daniel Burnham and Edward Bennett's 1909 Plan of Chicago represented the height of the City Beautiful movement and delivered to residents a useable lakefront and visions of expansive possibilities. Mies van der Rohe and Walter Gropius bestowed Bauhaus modernism on the city in the 1940s, designed a radically modernist campus plan for the Illinois Institute of Technology, and sketched out the wholesale rebuilding of Chicago's South Side. Planning and Chicago have a storied past.

But planning became more contentious in the second half of the 20th century. Deindustrialization, suburbanization, and racial change destabilized a city that had already seen its building stock and infrastructure neglected during a Depression and a world war. Chicago's future, like that of other cities, was unclear. Federal policy offered urban renewal funds and planning grants, and in 1957 Chicago responded with the creation of a new Department of City Planning, which wrote and implemented major plans that transformed much of the city—particularly the central area. These efforts laid the groundwork for the revival of the office market, the launching of new downtown residential communities, and the protection of the city's natural amenities.

A "growth coalition" also reorganized in the postwar years, as in most U.S. cities, to promote redevelopment, boost economic growth, and fend off decline. Chicago's coalition included a wide range of interests, including downtown corporations, real estate developers, cultural institutions, politicians, and professional planners. It sought to use the city's new planning and development tools to defend the downtown from various perceived threats, including rapid suburbanization, creeping "blight," and racial change. It latched on to public subsidies to jump-start urban rebuilding, and it promoted civic spectacles such as world's fairs and Olympic games as a way to boost the city's growth and enhance its global reputation.

The growth coalition's agenda often met resistance, however. Resentment among those displaced by highways and urban renewal in the 1950s and 1960s eventually led to the restraint of those programs. Community organizers criticized grand plans for the central area while neighborhood needs were left neglected, sparking an "equity planning" movement in Chicago in the 1980s. More recently, developer-led gentrification is seen as a threat by some, and the city's Tax Increment Financing (TIF) policies have become a lightning rod for debates about the distribution of resources. As will be seen, resistance from "the neighborhoods" against "downtown," as the conflict is often formulated, played a significant role in limiting the reach of the growth coalition. The neighborhoods, however, could not seriously threaten the political and market forces driving development.

Moreover, as the mayoralty of Richard M. Daley (in office 1989–2011) progressed, planning power increasingly centralized in city hall, with the mayor and aldermen becoming the arbiters of development. Daley certainly understood that growth was a political imperative, as only an enlarged tax base could fund the services—streets, sewers, libraries, police officers, schools—essential to reelection. But the direction of that growth, the boundaries around it, and the resources dedicated to enhancing it, were all negotiable.

This book explores these negotiations, wrestling with the plans, policies, and choices that shaped the outcomes we see today. It examines the context of planning decisions, the power wielded, and the alternatives not taken. It focuses on planning as an executive function in Chicago, one that came into the contemporary era with the creation of the Department of City Planning in 1957 and then expanded its reach and influence. We explore all scales of planning, from large-scale comprehensive plans to economic development initiatives to neighborhood improvement ideas. Civic associations, local foundations, transportation agencies, community groups, regional bodies, and the business community have all planned as well, but we pay the most attention to the pivotal role of city government in guiding, and often not guiding, the arc of public discourse and action in the planning of our shared environment. Our narrative is short on technical details but long on the actors, forces, and ideas in planning over the past 50 years in Chicago.

The book also elucidates how planning in Chicago is in retreat in the current era. This "Chicago way" of planning may surprise those who have taken note only of the global city renaissance. The city that once embraced Daniel Burnham and Edward Bennett's 1909 Plan of Chicago no longer plans confidently. When we explained the scope of our research to planners in this city, many responded skeptically: "We still do planning in Chicago?" Or as Laurence Msall, president of the Civic Federation, puts it, "If you are working on a book on long-range government planning in Chicago, it is going to be a short book."[7]

Astonishingly, as of January 2011, the city no longer has a department with the word "planning" in it. (See Appendix A.) Major plans from recent years have been largely ignored and "deal making" has replaced structured planning processes. The city has lacked a comprehensive vision or set of planning policies since 1966. After peaking in the early 1970s, planning has been in the doldrums ever since. Rather than a systematic understanding of current problems, forecasting of future needs, and crafting of policies to address both, planning has been too often demoted and replaced by one-off projects.[8]

Planning in the current era centers on funding sources, especially TIF and specialized federal grants. While not inherently bad, TIF has distorted planning and budgeting, enabling a lack of transparency and granting too much discretion to the mayor's office alone. Instead of a plan, Chicago now has a collection of more than 150 TIFs plus other ad hoc area plans, some of which are impressive but remain largely disconnected. The lack of coherent planning has, at times, led to some unfortunate and wasteful choices. Chicago and planning have long had a special relationship, but that pairing has frayed beyond recognition.

Within this framework, we have four major themes. First, plans and ideas from more than 50 years ago continue to have lasting influence on the city's trajectory. The growth coalition prophesized, planned, and pushed for a postindustrial downtown as early as 1958, a vision with staying power that emerged with remarkable prescience. Second, as planners well know, politics matters. Chicago's unique governance environment—featuring parochial aldermen, strong mayors, and numerous TIFs—has frustrated broader comprehensive planning. Third, race and class remain strong influences on the city, and planning has struggled to be effective in the face of those barriers, especially in the city's poorer neighborhoods. Finally, the city needs to restore planning to a place of prominence as a vital function of government essential to its future.

This book is divided into five parts. Part One continues with important contexts that constrained Chicago planning, including the city's political regimes, rapid demographic change, and railroad legacies. Part Two examines planning in Chicago's central area, the three-square-mile space that includes the central business district, known as the Loop.[9] Beginning with the 1958 Development Plan for the Central Area, this area received a great deal of attention from the growth coalition, and it figures prominently in the city's rise to global city status. While the growth coalition wielded influence, its occasionally extravagant plans were rarely completed as proposed and at times were stopped cold by resistance from various sources. Yet even partial implementation moved the city toward growth coalition goals.

Part Three turns to planning initiatives in the neighborhoods. Chicago has played a key role in the evolution of community development planning. It pioneered community "conservation" in the 1950s, enhanced the reach of the Community Reinvestment Act of 1977, and took to scale a Local Initiatives Support Corporation (LISC) model for community-based planning. We drill down into the experiences of three very different Chicago neighborhoods—Englewood, Uptown, and Little Village—showing the range of struggles facing community planning. Further, this part assesses the ambitious and controversial efforts to remake public housing in Chicago, a massive change in the social and physical landscape.

Part Four focuses on Chicago's industrial policy. In the midst of deindustrialization and in the absence of federal support, the city launched its own efforts. District-based strategies and sector-based initiatives merged into an ambitious local industrial policy. We profile success stories in the Lake Calumet area and with rail infrastructure. Still, even as industrial policy has retained and attracted new types of employment in certain corridors, it has only slowed the overall hemorrhaging of manufacturing employment. The need for new strategies is critical.

Part Five concludes with the recent era, and here the erosion of planning is most pronounced. While smaller plans have been promising, the city's major planning efforts have been neglected, with consequences for transit capacity, the key to its future growth. Ironically, Chicago reached global city status in the early 21st century, but recent data suggest a "lost decade" in terms of economic and demographic indicators. Much of its global city agenda has been built on debt, and the city's finances threaten to undermine its health. Now Chicago faces the problem of sustaining growth, addressing neighborhood needs in a comprehensive fashion, rebuilding its transit system, and planning for its post-postindustrial future. None of this bodes well for a city that today lacks a strong, confident culture of planning.

CHAPTER 2
CHICAGO'S PLANNING CONTEXT

Planning in Chicago has rarely been executed by professionals applying best practices to enhance the public good. Instead, planning decisions are filtered through the city's intense political culture, itself an evolving mix of actors competing for power. These include corporate-led civic boosters, risk-taking developers, rough-and-tumble machine aldermen, progressive community activists, and, often caught in the middle, professional planners. The city's most prominent mayors since World War II—Richard J. Daley (in office 1955–1976) and his son Richard M. Daley—exerted outsized influence but were hardly all-powerful. The playing field in Chicago planning, while never entirely pluralistic, is more diverse than might be assumed by those either enamored or appalled by its powerful mayors. Coalitions and ad hoc alliances organized to fund plans, push projects, or resist them, with mayors and aldermen often serving more as mediators than as leaders. More broadly, demographic change has influenced the city's trajectory, with immigrants providing essential energy to the city since its inception. Finally, the legacy of 19th-century railroads is a further context with which planning has to contend.

Machine Politics and Reformers
The city's professional planners are often at the mercy of the city's aldermen, who wield planning powers that are greater than those of their peers in nearly any other U.S. city. Each of the city's 50 aldermen (even female office holders

use this title) can invoke "aldermanic privilege" over development in their ward, meaning that city council members defer to their colleagues in return for deference over similar issues in their own wards. This allows aldermen to hold up approval of a zoning change—essential to any large-scale development—thereby giving them major leverage over land-use decisions in their wards. At times, aldermanic privilege is used to block or reshape unpopular proposals and at other times to reward friends. The system, which dates to the 1930s, invites abuse, and numerous aldermen have landed in jail for taking bribes related to planning approvals. Yet aldermanic privilege remains a mainstay of local Chicago politics and a deterrent to citywide planning. As Benet Haller, a longtime planner currently in the Department of Housing and Economic Development, declared, "Chicago is really 50 cities, each with its own power center," namely, the alderman. Elaborating on the theme, former deputy planning commissioner Eileen Figel argued: "In planning in Chicago, if an alderman says 'no,' then there is no honest debate about the issue before a public body because projects aren't allowed to proceed without a letter of support from the alderman. This is so entrenched it is perceived as normal. People think that is how it is done everywhere."[1]

Aldermanic privilege has coexisted with strong mayors in Chicago, including both Mayor Daleys, who tolerated the privilege in return for obedience on larger policy matters, a trade that worked to the advantages of both parties. The Daleys, however, retained the upper hand. Richard J. Daley perfected machine politics as chairman of the Cook County Democratic Party, centralizing the nominating process for political office and dispensing rewards such as jobs and city contracts to the party's army of political allies, starting with favored aldermen. Allegiance to the party and the mayor allowed aldermen to distribute political favors, retain their privilege over issues in their wards, and be assured of political support come election time.[2]

The Democratic Party machine, however, underwent convulsions after Richard J. Daley's death in 1976. After the city failed to clear streets following a 1979 blizzard, voters installed upstart reformer (but former Daley protégée) Jane Byrne in city hall. But Byrne floundered politically, unable to control aldermen or the city's bureaucracy. This opened the door to a more genuine reform movement, and in 1983 an unprecedented African American turnout elected Harold Washington mayor. Washington attempted to govern as a progressive, rainbow-coalition, anti-machine reformer, and he moved planning in unfamiliar directions, emphasizing "equity" in the distribution of resources, rewarding neighborhood groups over ward organizations, and elevating citywide economic development over growth coalition initiatives. But machine aldermen, led by Ed Vrdolyak and Ed Burke, resisted Washington at every turn, resulting in a legislative stalemate known as "Council Wars" from 1983 to 1986. Yet Washington's equity planning legacy endures.[3]

Harold Washington died of a heart attack in 1987, and when Richard M. Daley won the 1989 election, the machine he inherited was different from his father's. Unable to practice straight patronage politics, Daley pursued a relatively inclusive identity politics, developing a coalition of moderates in various communities, especially among middle-class Hispanics and African Americans. Critics, however, charged Daley with "pinstripe patronage," supporting the interests of wealthy contributors. Certainly, power again centered in the Mayor's office, and Daley brooked little opposition on matters large and small.[4]

Figure 2.1. Mayor Jane Byrne, Democratic Party mayoral nominee Harold Washington, and State's Attorney Richard M. Daley at a "unity" breakfast following Washington's victory in a hard-fought, three-way Democratic primary, April 13, 1983

By temperament, Daley had a keen interest in the built environment. Whereas his father accepted the high modernism of the 1950s and 1960s, the son sought to manage the city's aesthetic. He traveled widely and returned with numerous design ideas that were pressed upon the city. As Figel explained, "Mayor Daley came back from Paris, and a memo went out saying all new projects needed hanging flower baskets and decorative streetlights." Other ideas included regulations on wrought iron fences around gas stations and median planters for boulevards.[5] Still, these ideas fell into the realm of design, not planning. Daley was distrustful of large-scale plans and rarely attached himself to the kind of comprehensive planning that could carefully guide the city. As Lee Bey, former member of the Department of Planning and Development and then deputy chief of staff for Daley observed, "the mayor didn't like big plans that restricted how he did things."[6]

Yet even as he distrusted big plans, Daley liked planners. He consistently elevated his commissioners of planning into the inner circle as chiefs of staff, including David Mosena, Valerie Jarrett, and Lori Healey. In doing so, he created a de facto planning cabinet in city hall, a small group that allowed him to be heavily involved in individual projects while distancing planning department professionals from power. Daley saw planners as a useful resource but hardly central players: "I'll call you when I need you," is how Bey put it.[7]

Growth Coalition Actors and Challengers

As in most cities, Chicago's growth coalition has been the most significant planning force in the past half-century.[8] The members of the informal coalition each have had their own aims and goals: real estate developers want to build and profit; business interests want a growing economy and retail sales; politicians need a rising tax base; professional planners want to rationally shape growth. The coalition organizes itself into elite bodies. The Chicago Central Area Committee (CAC) captures a range of interests and dominated planning discussions until the era of Richard M. Daley. The Central Loop Alliance and the Greater North Michigan Avenue Association represent retail, while the Chicago Development Council and more recently the Building Owners and Managers Association (BOMA) of Chicago speak for commercial real estate interests. More recently, the nonprofit World Business Chicago, chaired by Mayor Rahm Emanuel (2011– present), has emerged as a business-oriented planning arm of the city.

From the opposite end of the planning system, community-based organizations and progressive "equity planners" have articulated an alternative agenda of neighborhood reinvestment and working-class job creation. Community organizing has a long history in Chicago, but a contemporary network of nonprofit groups emerged in the 1970s focused on affordable housing, workforce training, and economic development. The Chicago Association of Neighborhood Development Organizations (CANDO) lasted from 1979 until 2001, building nonprofit capacity and drawing attention to neighborhood needs. Community development corporations (CDC) and community-based development organizations (CBDOs) have matured in the past two decades but remain tenuously reliant on sources of public-sector funding. At times, community organizations have tried to counter the growth coalition's emphasis on downtown and gentrification. Equity planners in these organizations proposed targeting resources to the city's poorest areas and involving greater community input in planning processes. While ultimately unsuccessful at wholesale reform, the effort did produce lasting change in the area of industrial policy. (See Part Three.)

Between the growth coalition and the equity planners lay a handful of expert organizations that seek to provide respected planning perspectives on debates of the day. The Metropolitan Planning Council, founded in 1934 to advocate for housing reform, has produced influential studies that balance growth coalition and reform interests.[9] The Local Initiatives Support Coalition (LISC) has become a de facto planning organization by leading a community-based process to create detailed plans for some of the city's poorest areas. The MacArthur Foundation, the city's most prominent philanthropy, is also heavily invested in planning, especially in funding both LISC and elements of public housing reform. The perceived neutrality of these experts gives them a valued voice in planning debates. At times they have endorsed growth coalition ideas and at other times sided with the neighborhoods, allowing them to sway debate and, at times, to drive planning agendas by themselves.[10]

Professional planning consultants can be found across this continuum, though by disposition and business self-interest they have tended to side with growth. While numerous small firms and consultants practice in the city, the planning office at the architectural firm of Skidmore, Owings & Merrill (SOM) plays an outsized role in our story. Until the past decade, when competition and cost allowed others into the field, SOM was the de facto planning agency of the city, hired by the growth coalition and even the city to undertake planning. SOM has been the primary author of many major plans, including the Central Area Plans of 1973, 1983, and 2003, as well as the Olympic Plan of 2009.

Finally, there is the city's own staff of planning professionals. Mayor Richard J. Daley created the Department of City Planning in 1957, and it reached its heyday of influence in the 1960s and early 1970s. Funded by federal grants, the department produced the 1966 Comprehensive Plan of Chicago, the last serious citywide plan written by department professionals.[11] By the late 1970s and 1980s, the Department of Planning no longer took the lead on bold ideas. Instead, consultants wrote major plans at the direction of the department. While the city's professional planners continued to produce significant smaller plans, by the early 21st century much of its work centered on negotiating zoning approvals with developers and aldermen on a deal-by-deal basis, trying to keep one step ahead of a real estate boom. The decline in government-led planning is symbolized by numerous reshufflings that have left Chicago without a readily identifiable city department. The city's planners can be found in one of the three bureaus of the newly created Department of Housing and Economic Development, where overall staffing has been cut by 40 percent from the levels of the predecessor agencies.[12]

The city, however, still has the Chicago Plan Commission (CPC). This body, founded independently in 1909 with the hope of separating planning from politics, was eventually brought into city government in 1939 when it ran out of funds. In 1957, with the creation of the Department of City Planning, it lost most of its staff and its ability to plan. The CPC survives as the forum for reviewing zoning changes and considering major plans, but approval by its mayor-appointed commissioners does not carry the force of law. Unlike in most cities, plans in Chicago rarely receive a vote from the elected city council, leaving the CPC's endorsement merely advisory and unenforceable. This preserves flexibility for city hall to pursue its own agendas.

Demographic Change

Relentless demographic change has long marked Chicago's history. The city experienced explosive population growth between 1850 and 1930; the population ballooned from 1.1 million in 1890 to 3.4 million by 1930. A decade later war production brought a flood of migrants, largely African Americans, and swelled the population to its peak of 3.6 million people in 1950 despite little additional housing. From this point, however, a story familiar to other Midwestern cities took hold. Suburbanization, deindustrialization, and social change eroded the city's base; by 2010, Chicago held only 2.7 million people, while the metropolitan area, as defined by the census, had grown to 9.5 million (Figure 2.2).[13]

While whites often moved up and out, African Americans faced daunting discrimination. The "black belt" on Chicago's South Side was starkly defined through a combination of violence, intimidation, and real estate practices.[14] This ghetto expanded considerably in the 1950s and 1960s

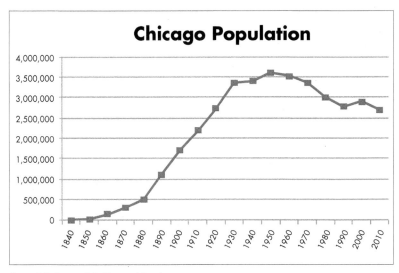

Figure 2.2. Source: U.S. Census of Population

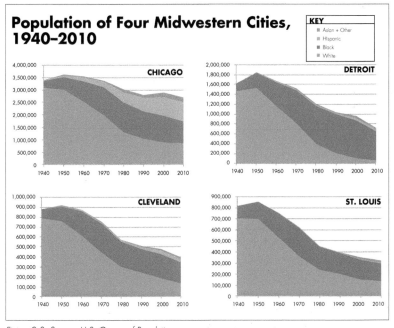

Figure 2.3. Source: U.S. Census of Population

and, when combined with white flight, transformed Chicago from a city loosely organized by white ethnicity into one starkly divided by race. The 1980 census showed a population that self-identified as 43 percent white, 40 percent black, 14 percent Latino, and three percent Asian and other. Moreover, the total population had declined by 11 percent, continuing a trend since the 1950 census.

Chicago's population would have continued to erode had it not been for immigration from Mexico, Central America, and Asia in the past three decades (Figure 2.3). Indeed, the untold story of Chicago's resilience is the role of new migrants in saving the city from even deeper levels of population decline and abandonment that often sent other cities into a downward spiral.

Compared to other cities, Chicago proved to be a magnet for Latinos at the end of the 20th century. By 2000, roughly 26 percent of Chicagoans self-reported as "Hispanic" and another seven percent as "Asian." Among Midwestern cities, only Milwaukee comes close, with 12 percent of residents Hispanic. For other cities, the Hispanic figures are meager: Cleveland, seven percent; Detroit, five percent; St. Louis, two percent.

Hispanic and Asian immigrants moved into thinning neighborhoods (mostly older white ones) and maintained the housing stock, created businesses, paid taxes, and sustained communities—as had waves of immigrants before them. Yet even as segregation indexes for the city as a whole have declined somewhat since 1980, whites, Latinos, and Asians have rarely moved into depopulating portions of the city's "black belt." Chicago's ability to keep and attract migrants of all types will be crucial to its 21st century health. (See chapter 19.)

Railroad Legacies

While largely invisible to the casual visitor to Chicago, the railroads have dominated the geography of Chicago's central area, and their influence in shaping the city's built environment cannot be overstated. Rail lines carved up territory and hemmed in the city's downtown on all four sides by 1860. Once laid, tracks were difficult to move, and train stations, depots, yards, and warehouses further constricted expansion of the central business district (Figure 2.4). These physical barriers had implications for development: with downtown land in short supply and demand for office space high in the late 19th century, Chicago engineers and architects pioneered "skyscrapers." Similarly, elevated rapid transit and freight tun-

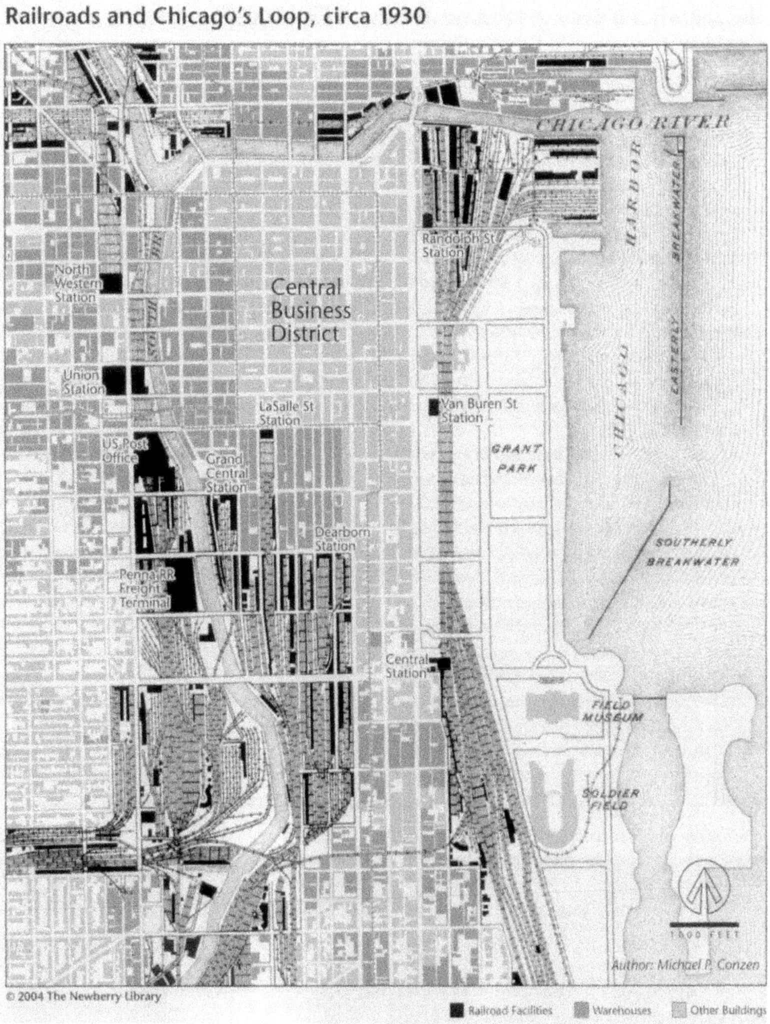

Railroads and Chicago's Loop, circa 1930

Figure 2.4. Map of Railroads and Chicago's Loop, 1930. Tracks, stations, terminals, and warehouses surrounded the central business district, creating a barrier to its growth.

nels became solutions to hopelessly congested streets.[15] The railroad's domination of space in the central area by 1930 is readily seen in Figure 2.5 (page 20).

Throughout the 20th century, planners have sought to break out of the box created by the railroads. Burnham and Bennett's 1909 Plan of Chicago dealt extensively with railroad relocation to allow expansion of

Figure 2.5. Aerial view of rail yards to the south of the central business district, 1929

the central business district, and the North Michigan Avenue Bridge, proposed even before the 1909 plan and completed in 1923, crossed over
not just the river but also rails to push development north of the Loop. Air
rights projects, including the Chicago Daily News building (1929) and
the Merchandise Mart (1930), showed the possibilities of building over
tracks. But the legacies of the railroads remained a key planning obstacle,
with Millennium Park (2004) the last in a century-long effort to reclaim
railroad space (Figure 2.6).

Chicago is not the only city with parochial aldermen, strong mayors, a
large growth coalition, a troubled history of race, or a legacy of railroad
development. But in many ways Chicago has these features in the extreme.
No other city has as extensive a tradition of aldermanic privilege. Few
have as troubled a history on race and redevelopment. None had as much
railroad land in such prime locations. Most cities *do* have a dedicated department of planning on their organization charts, and most enshrine major
plans in law. This context matters, and it helps explain how Chicago has
lost its once leading position in planning.

Figure 2.6. *Illinois Central rail yards to the east of the central business district, looking north toward the Wrigley Building and Tribune Tower, 1943. This space was later redeveloped into Millennium Park.*

As Chicago shifted from an industrial to a postindustrial economy, the central area, unlike manufacturing areas of the city, benefited. The path to a postindustrial future was spelled out in 1958, when a new Department of City Planning wrote a plan to protect the downtown core. This initiative took decades to play out, but the 1958 plan led by the 1980s to downtown residential development, office expansion, and civic improvements. Chicago's core did not hollow out, a practical achievement compared to other Midwestern cities.

Yet without strong pro-growth efforts, Chicago's development could easily have turned out more like that of its Rust Belt peers. Several strategic planning choices prepared Chicago for a postindustrial future. Chicago chose to defend a compact office core, sought to attract middle-class residents to the edge of downtown, pursued transit and airport investments, and proposed a new urban university campus—all ideas that ran counter to prevailing national trends. Many plans struggled to achieve these ends, and strategies were imperfectly executed. But the overall thrust placed ChicaSgo in a competitive position when a white-collar information-age economy prevailed. While the dramatic nature of this economic shift was difficult to foresee in the 1950s, Chicago's planning choices kept the central area attractive for investment. Into the mid-1990s, the Loop continued to capture nearly half of all new office construction in the metropolitan area—a figure exceeded only by New York City.[1] This growth, coupled with gentrification, sustained a solid tax base, allowing the city to invest not only in downtown initiatives but also in neighborhoods. While decentralization had not entirely halted, Chicago had not only avoided the deep contractions and austerity that plagued other cities but had emerged with significant strengths to carry it into the 21st century.

CHAPTER 3

THE ORIGINS OF CHICAGO'S POSTINDUSTRIAL CITY: PLANNING CHANGE, 1955–1958

Understanding Chicago's transformation requires stepping back to the mid-1950s. In the immediate postwar period, planners across the country prescribed clearance to excise "cancerous" slums and highways to appease the automobile. Chicago pursued these solutions aggressively in the 1940s and early 1950s. But beginning in 1955, the city's growth coalition worked with newly elected mayor Richard J. Daley to shift planning in different directions. Together, they initiated a major plan for the central area, updated zoning codes, and invested in transit to bolster the central area without massive demolition or autocentric thinking. Like most policy shifts and with easy hindsight, this remarkable burst of planning activity produced many prescient ideas but also several misguided ones. Still, the 1955–1958 period marked a pivotal transition for the central area's future.

Richard J. Daley Reorganizes Planning

The planning initiatives of 1955–1958 need to be understood in the less promising context of the previous decade. Chicago had seen little office investment, a decline of downtown retail, growing slum conditions, and the flight of whites to the suburbs. Decline was the dominant narrative, and revival required drastic solutions. Before 1955, Chicago, like many older cities, had already begun large-scale efforts to reconfigure the built environment. A major highway network was under way, displacing 6,000 families and 2,200 single people (mostly white) between 1948 and 1956. During

Figure 3.1. Chicago Department of City Planning staff at work, 1958

that same time, urban renewal on the South Side had cleared 101 acres, uprooting 4,600 families and 1,600 single people (mostly African Americans) to make way for modernist middle-class housing. Nine multistory parking garages were erected on valuable downtown land to serve shoppers and commuters. These massive, costly, and time-consuming efforts generated considerable resentments from displaced small businesses, property owners, and families.[1]

Mayor Daley and the growth coalition never explicitly acknowledged that these efforts could not be sustained, but they soon took steps to move planning away from grandiose efforts and toward direct support for the central area. First, corporate heads and developers organized the Central Area Committee (CAC) in 1956 to find consensus among competing Loop interests, creating a stronger forum and unified voice for growth coalition initiatives.[2]

Second, Daley brought several planning functions under his command. He pushed the Chicago Plan Commission (CPC), an outgrowth of the Burnham Plan, out of the day-to-day activities of planning and in its place created a new municipal Department of City Planning to make planning "an executive arm of government," according to the department's first report.[3] The CPC was thereby "freed of administrative responsibilities" and "reconstituted as a policy-making body." But in reality, policy would now emanate from City Hall with the CPC playing an advisory role. In a speech before the American Institute of Planners in 1957, Daley defended the shift: "I am convinced that the efficient use of staff planners is almost mandatory" for successful planning, and "the integration of such a staff into city government is an important phase today" in the evolution of the field. The move did

Figure 3.2. Mayor Richard J. Daley at a meeting of the Chicago Plan Commission to review the Basic Policies for the Comprehensive Plan of Chicago, with planning commissioner Ira J. Bach to his left, 1964

help professionalize planning, as Daley's first commissioner Ira Bach hired graduates of new planning programs, including the one at the University of Illinois. But Bach understood the deferential nature of his position, as Daley's reorganization consolidated new levels of planning power in City Hall.[4]

Other reforms modernized planning while also enlarging Daley's reach. The city initiated its first Five-Year Capital Improvements Plan in 1958, along with a Capital Improvements Program Committee (chaired by Bach) to centralize infrastructure decisions by various departments. Further, at Daley's suggestion, the State of Illinois authorized cities to form public buildings commissions with the power to issue bonds to finance new schools, police stations, and other improvements. Daley not only sat on the Public Buildings Commission of Chicago but also appointed the remaining commissioners. Likewise, the activities of the Chicago Land Clearance Commission and the Chicago Housing Authority (CHA) came under Department of City Planning review.

Finally, Daley benefited from the rise in federal funding for planning initiatives. To be eligible for federal urban renewal, public housing, and other grant programs, cities had to produce an annual "Workable Program" that documented basic measures of need and the capacity to use federal money wisely. One of the measures of capacity was the number of professional planners on staff. Dean Macris, FAICP, a member of Chicago's Department of City Planning from 1958 to 1968, recalled that planners in the late 1950s were in high demand: "You could walk out of planning school and into any big city in the country and get a job in the planning department."[5] Moreover, under the 1954 Housing Act, the federal government offered Section 701 planning grants to cities to fund planning, including the hiring of staff. Planning as an institutionalized element of city government came of age in the 1950s, and Daley rode this wave.

Zoning Reform and the Growth Coalition

Even before Daley's election, real estate interests in the early 1950s sought a more sophisticated yet predictable zoning code. The original 1923 ordinance had become an unintelligible patchwork due to a large number of amendments. Further, despite its reputation as the birthplace of the skyscraper, Chicago was not particularly hospitable to the form. Fearing the canyon effect of tall buildings on narrow downtown streets, the 1923 code limited building heights to 264 feet but allowed additional height in a smaller tower structure up to 600 feet if the tower remained within one-fourth the footprint and one-sixth the volume of the main structure. In 1942, an amendment removed the height limits and tower regulations and shifted to a volume restriction keyed to lot size. While not quite the modern floor area ratio (FAR) regulation, the change created a rough FAR equivalent of 12 in the central business district, about 20 percent below New York's basic restrictions.[6] Developers argued the code was excessively restrictive, pointing to the Prudential Building (1956), an air-rights project and the first office tower since the 1930s, and the Inland Steel Building (1957) as examples where the zoning code constrained development.[7]

Pushed by the growth coalition, Daley produced a rewrite of the zoning code and passed it through the city council. The new 1957 Zoning Ordinance proved friendlier to developers, making two significant changes. First, it included a true FAR system, with a limit of 16 for the central business district, 33 percent larger than before. Second, the ordinance added a Planned Development (PD) process which allowed property owners with parcels of four acres or more to negotiate directly with the Department of City Planning for comprehensive project zoning plans. Over time, this power was extended to any site larger than one acre, any building over 100 feet tall, or any development with more than 100 apartments. In theory, PD gave the Department of City Planning a great deal of influence to extract public amenities from large-scale development, such as public open spaces. But PD agreements, like all zoning issues, required city council approval, meaning aldermanic privilege often trumped the power of planning professionals in negotiations.[8]

The 1957 zoning rewrite hardly settled the myriad land-use debates in Chicago, but it did align with the growth coalition's desire to foster new development. Within a decade, several bold new buildings took shape in the heart of the central business district. The First National Bank Building and Plaza (1969; now Chase Tower and Plaza) rebuilt an entire block, as did two large public projects, the Federal Center (1964–1974) and the municipal Daley Center (1967), both designed by Mies van der Rohe or his disciples. The financial success of the private First National Bank building signaled to developers that office demand in the central Loop was back after a long drought. Moreover, the liberal interpretation of a FAR "bonus" system allowed buildings to reach new heights. In return for amenities including public plazas, step-back designs, and pedestrian-friendly ground-floor arcades, city planners awarded developers higher FARs. Such bonuses in Chicago became so generous by the late 1960s that density reached levels far higher than in other U.S. cities. The Sears Tower (completed in 1974), the tallest building in the world for 25 years, used a variety of negotiated bonuses to reach an FAR of 34.[9] By the late 1960s, the Department of Development and Planning had become completely aligned with the growth coalition agenda, facilitating the most permissive FAR and bonus system in the country.

The 1958 Development Plan for the Central Area

The new Department of City Planning's first effort, the 1958 Development Plan for the Central Area of Chicago, pointed the city toward a postindustrial future. Like most plans, it compiled a list of projects that had been under consideration, some for years. But its defining elements moved away from slum clearance and highways and instead focused on protecting, strengthening, and strategically expanding the downtown core with a mix of office, residential, and institutional development. In its choices, the 1958 plan differed from those of other cities and offered a vision with remarkable prescience and staying power.

Growth coalition interests pushed for the 1958 Development Plan for the Central Area, though they did not control it. The CAC urged Daley's Department of City Planning to produce a blueprint for downtown and rec-

Figure 3.3. Sketch from the Development Plan for the Central Area of Chicago, showing a proposed government center on the south bank of the Chicago River and residential housing on the north, 1958

ommended "a series of broad planning principles" developed by Frederick T. Aschman, the former CPC executive director and then president of the American Society of Planning Officials. First among those principles was maintaining a "compact, accessible, and attractive Central Area" especially given the "pressures that would tend to dissipate the strength of the commercial core." To do this, the CAC suggested residential and institutional "anchors" to the north and south of the Loop to avoid office expansion in those directions. The CAC funded several research studies to support the planning department in the latter stages of its work, and it eventually paid for construction of a room-sized model to help sell the plan.[10]

But the Department of City Planning did not need to be sold on a pro-growth, pro-downtown agenda. The congruence in thinking among planners, developers, and corporate interests was strong, with conflicts only over degree and details, not the broad outlines for the future of the city. The department's professional planners, now asserting themselves, went beyond the principles laid out by the CAC. The 1958 Development Plan for the Central Area envisioned an astonishing 50,000 new dwelling units close to downtown (Figure 3.3). Middle-class residents would bring their purchasing power to the Loop and reverse its retail and nightlife decline. This was a bold recommendation: at the time, the ring closest to downtown housed only 28,000 people, nearly all of them poor, living in rooming houses and small apartments interspersed among warehouses and railroads.[11]

The key to such development involved reclaiming underused railroad land immediately surrounding the central business district for office expansion and residential use. To the east, the 1958 plan proposed transforming the Illinois Central rail yards into a massive, mixed use office and residential complex, using air rights and track consolidation. To the north, further air rights along the north bank of the Chicago River would support residential development. To the west, railroad terminal consolidation and use of air rights would allow room for additional office construction, which had begun in the 1920s but then stalled. Finally, to the south, the city proposed transforming 130 acres of rail yards into a new University of Illinois campus. The plan strategically converted rail space into residential and institutional anchors that would limit office expansion to the north and south, instead directing it to limited areas on the eastern and western edges of the central business district. The "compactness" of the Loop would thus be protected. Moreover, the plan involved little displacement, since nearly all new growth would occur on former railroad land.

These strategic goals were not shared by all growth coalition members, and the 1958 plan could have embraced alternative visions for Chicago's future. Indeed, what is *not* in the plan is important to understanding its success. In the years before 1958, many developers believed the Loop was no longer a viable place for growth due to excessive land values, suburban competition, and racial change. Instead, these Loop skeptics, led by Arthur Rubloff, an ambitious real estate developer, proposed shifting the city's center of gravity to the north, closer to the Gold Coast and North Michigan Avenue, then establishing itself as an upscale retail district. To accomplish this, they unveiled the Fort Dearborn plan in 1954, a massive urban renewal venture involving the clearance of 151 acres of warehouses, rail yards, and rooming houses north of the Chicago River and just west of North Michigan Avenue (Figure 3.4, page 32).[12] Once cleared, the land would be rebuilt as a new government district surrounded by office and residential towers.

The Fort Dearborn proposal, however, divided Chicago's business interests. Within months, an ad hoc Committee for Government Buildings Downtown, comprising lawyers and Loop retail interests, opposed moving government functions north of the river. Equally important, owners in the proposed urban renewal area objected to confiscation of their property, while the Near North Side Planning Board argued, presciently, that land values in

Figure 3.4. Rendering of proposed Fort Dearborn Urban Renewal project by Skidmore, Owings & Merrill, 1954

the area would rise so long as the area was not condemned as a slum by planners. The fate of the roughly 8,000 poor residents of the area's rooming houses was apparently of less interest to Chicago's power brokers.[13]

With various interests divided over the plan, Mayor Daley listened to his planners and assumed a cautious stance, unwilling to commit to moving city government functions north of the river but not willing to squelch urban renewal for the area either. In the end, Daley and the 1958 Development Plan for the Central Area decided that government buildings and office development should remain firmly in the Loop, though the plan did not directly oppose clearance of the Fort Dearborn area for residential reconstruction, in keeping with the desire to increase the middle-class presence close to downtown. But without the government office piece, the idea of urban renewal north of the river died, and thus large scale clearance did not take place. The federal bulldozer would not have a presence in the 1958 plan.[14]

Nor did the 1958 central area plan call for much road building. A network of highways was already well under way and had plowed through some parts of the central area to reach downtown.[15] The 1958 plan, however, did call for one expressway extension, the Franklin Street Connector along a railroad right-of-way. But unlike early postwar plans, the 1958 document did not obsess about the automobile. Instead, it endorsed the

Chicago Transit Authority's plans for new transit lines, upgrades to stations, and replacement of the elevated Loop with tunnels—all of which were intended to strengthen the core through increased transit capacity. In his speech to the American Institute of Planners in 1957, Daley explained the investment in transit over additional highways: "High-speed, limited-access highways only attract more and more private automobiles. And unless some provision is made for mass transportation, the entire system would end up in strangulation."[16]

The lack of urban renewal and major new highways in the 1958 plan is significant. At the time, both were the planning tools of choice. Many cities emulated Victor Gruen's 1956 Fort Worth plan, which proposed ringing that city's core with a freeway and then providing access to parking garages from multiple points, treating the central business district like an oversize version of an outdoor shopping mall. Chicago had embraced a similar approach in the early 1950s, but the 1958 plan asked for no more parking garages. Most cities also used urban renewal funds to rebuild parts of the central business district or its fringes. These aggressive moves disrupted the urban fabric for years and built projects that did not restore confidence. Detroit, Philadelphia, and St. Louis, as well as smaller cities like New Haven, Connecticut, and Lancaster, Pennsylvania, wiped away working-poor residential districts and replaced them with middle-class modernist enclaves in an effort to "save" downtown. This activity removed perceived evils, but it did little to defend central business districts from diffusion. Instead of enhancing downtowns, urban renewal often sapped them.

Chicago was not immune from the attraction of these tools, and it, too, built highways and urban renewal projects, often to deadening effect. But the difference between Chicago and other cities is one of timing and location. By 1955, the city had mostly ended its large-scale slum clearance, except for a wave of public housing sites selected in 1955 and 1956 that would come to fruition—disastrously—between 1961 and 1964. Yet most clearance projects took place at considerable distance from the city center, often miles away, in areas beyond the rings of railroad and warehouse space (Figure 3.5, page 34). With one exception, few urban renewal projects disrupted Chicago's central area during the 1950s and 1960s.[17]

The Beginnings of Downtown Living

Numerous false starts, tactical errors, and even blunders occurred in the implementation of the 1958 plan. But as a long-term guide, the plan's chief goals of enticing middle-class residents to the central area and protecting

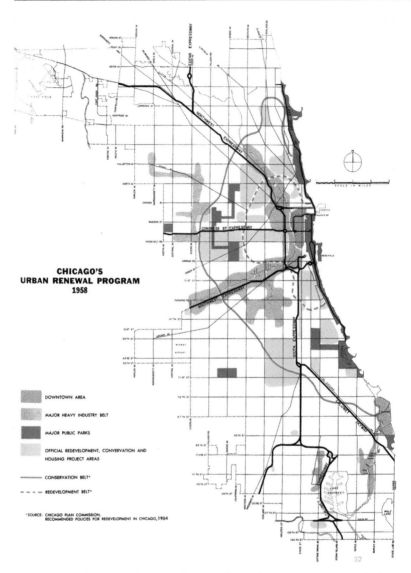

CHICAGO'S
URBAN RENEWAL PROGRAM
1958

DOWNTOWN AREA

MAJOR HEAVY INDUSTRY BELT

MAJOR PUBLIC PARKS

OFFICIAL REDEVELOPMENT, CONSERVATION AND
HOUSING PROJECT AREAS

CONSERVATION BELT*

REDEVELOPMENT BELT*

*SOURCE: CHICAGO PLAN COMMISSION,
RECOMMENDED POLICIES FOR REDEVELOPMENT IN CHICAGO, 1954

Figure 3.5. Map of Chicago's Urban Renewal program, showing "conservation areas" surrounding but at some distance from the central area, 1958

the office core remained remarkably durable. Still, it took a combination of federal guarantees, local infrastructure, and risk taking by developers to propel the plan forward. And difficulties acquiring railroad land forced the city into an urban renewal choice it soon regretted.

Bringing 50,000 new units to the central area took nearly twice as long as anticipated, but launching the plan would not have been possible without help from Washington. The Federal Housing Administration (FHA), widely known as the agency that helped build the suburbs, also ensured loans on multifamily apartment housing intended for middle-class renters, including high-rise development in urban areas. In Chicago, the FHA in 1959 backed the loan for Marina City, located on a half-block parcel on the Chicago River on the north edge of the Loop. Architect Bertrand Goldberg—one of the last students at the Bauhaus in 1930s Germany—proposed a highly sculptural design for two 42-story residential towers, the tallest apartment buildings in the country at the time (Figure 3.6). Equally ambitious, Goldberg planned a mixed use complex, incorporating a 16-story office building behind the towers and entertainment space, including a bowling alley, a marina, and a large, free-standing theater. Most of these buildings would be on air rights over the Chicago & North Western tracks. The FHA guarantee, its largest to date, allowed politically connected developer Charles Swibel (whose main business at the time involved skidrow flophouses) to secure a loan from the pension funds of Chicago unions. William McFetridge, the well-connected head of the Building Service Em-

Figure 3.6. Architect Bertrand Goldberg, labor leader William McFetridge, and developer Charles Swibel viewing a model of Marina City, circa 1960

ployees International, believed his members should have the opportunity to enjoy a more urbane life. Although the guarantee brought down interest rates and rents, the resulting one- and two-bedroom apartments attracted middle-class professionals, not union workers.[18]

Boldly conceived, Marina City filled rapidly but failed financially after Swibel mismanaged the property, drove away tenants, and defaulted on the mortgage. Yet Goldberg's "corn-cob" towers quickly became an architectural icon, delighting Chicagoans with its sculptural forms in ways that Mies van der Rohe's modern boxes did not. Ironically, a project financed by union members, deeply subsidized by federal taxpayers, and developed by an unethical Daley insider emerg ed as a symbol of Chicago's architecture-led downtown rejuvenation. Soon after, a handful of other FHA-backed residential buildings ventured downtown, including Outer Drive East (1963), another air rights project on railroad land, at the time the nation's largest single apartment building with 900 apartments. These projects were so new that the 1957 zoning reform had not imagined the possibility of residential towers so close to downtown; after some study, the code was amended to allow high-density residential zoning for the area.[19]

The early FHA projects had entered new territory within the central area and attracted a professional, white middle class to downtown. But a second wave of residential investment did not immediately follow, and progress toward 50,000 units was halting. Race and class fears kept developers wary about whether a market existed for downtown housing on a substantial scale. Much of the Loop appeared uninviting after dark, with entertainment options consisting largely of State Street movie houses, many of which had drifted toward seedy adult fare. A vibrant, pedestrian-friendly, entertainment-rich city appealing to the middle class had yet to emerge. Developers in the 1960s and 1970s clung to low-risk sites to the north of the Loop, around the Gold Coast and the lakefront, leaving the promise of the early downtown developments unfulfilled. It would take not just new apartments but a transformation to an information-age economy beginning in the 1980s to truly spark the creation of the 24-hour city.

The Struggle for a New Urban University

The 1958 central area plan strategically positioned a new University of Illinois campus on 65 acres in the South Loop. The institution would serve as an anchor to contain office expansion and would also block the encroachment of blight and much-feared racial change from the South Side. Pressure for a new campus was acute; improvised facilities on Navy Pier were sub-

Figure 3.7. Clearance of the Harrison-Halsted community to make way for a new university campus, circa 1963. The two buildings to the right were part of the Jane Addams Hull House complex and were preserved. Figure 3.8. (below) The high modernist University of Illinois–Chicago Circle campus (today the University of Illinois–Chicago), designed by Walter Netsch, circa 1970

standard and overcrowded. University trustees preferred a vacant land site in the Cook County suburbs, but Chicago's business and planning interests lined up behind a campus close to downtown.[20] The South Loop site seemed ideal—close to the city's core, connected to transit, and with potential room for growth. Mayor Daley agreed, but extracting the site from myriad railroad companies expecting inflated valuations proved daunting. Neither condemnation powers nor federal funds could be used; only residential blight relief could be obtained through the urban renewal program.[21]

Unable to finance a reasonable negotiated sale with the railroads, Daley reluctantly abandoned the site in 1960. In a fateful decision, his planners turned to an urban renewal area already in the planning stages known as "Harrison-Halsted," just outside the central area. The city had been working with white, working-class Italian and Greek residents hoping to "conserve" their neighborhood with only spot clearance paid for by urban renewal funds. But now Daley reversed course and rammed a university plan for the site through the city council a month after announcing it. More than 8,000 residents and 630 businesses would be displaced in a massive clearance (Figure 3.7). They quickly rebelled, led by housewife-turned-activist Florence Scala, and sponsored a sit-in strike at City Hall, while lawyers fought clearance in court. But the U.S. Supreme Court declined to hear the case in 1963, and by 1965, the new campus had opened (Figure 3.8).[22]

Chicago turned to urban renewal to solve its university problem out of an expediency fed by the lure of federal dollars. The rail yards would have been a better choice from a planning perspective and a neighborhood one. The protests embarrassed the mayor; the residents picketing city hall were neither "good-government" liberals nor slum-dwelling African Americans who could be ignored but white ethnic, working-class families trying to protect their homes. Miles Berger, a Daley confidant and member of the Chicago Plan Commission from 1965 to 1986, recalled: "Building the university took its toll on Daley personally—fighting all those people wore him out—and it made him wary of other big fights."[23] Had there been more time and had condemnation resources been available, the mayor might have been able to use his considerable political skill to extract the railroad site, and Chicago might have avoided the pain of ripping apart a viable neighborhood. Equally important, the railroad site remained a stagnating space in the South Loop, foiling an important goal of the 1958 plan.

After a decade, the 1958 plan remained a work in progress. Reclaiming railroad land for residential and institutional use had proceeded at a snail's pace. Downtown living—by the middle class and the affluent—had begun only tentatively. Vast tracts in the 1958 plan, including the Illinois Central rail yards to the east and south of the Loop, would take decades to develop. The South Loop rail yards were still a blight. The new University of Illinois–Chicago Circle campus offered expanded educational opportunity to working-class and middle-class students—a significant gain—but at high cost in terms of a lost neighborhood. Having learned its lesson, the city avoided large-scale urban renewal displacement in the future, though small-scale clearance remained a tool in its kit.

Still, the pieces were in place for downtown growth to resume after a 25-year drought. The 1958 plan made clear the city's interest in defending the core and preventing it from dissipating its density through reckless expansion. Zoning now favored development, and soon office towers in the Loop signaled market strength. Similarly, government remained planted in the Loop as an anchor. The reorganization and professionalization of planning had created a strong and active department.

The 1958 plan would have remarkable durability, yet it is hardly mentioned in the city's planning past. It lacked a glamorous centerpiece project, one that could easily be pointed to by future generations, unlike the many amenities of the 1909 Plan of Chicago. It also lacked a color publication and a public program to sell it. Instead, the 1958 plan quietly cemented the parameters of a downtown development agenda, one influenced by the growth coalition and one the city would continue to follow for the next four decades.

CHAPTER 4

THE HIGH-WATER MARK OF CITY-LED PLANNING: THE 1966 COMPREHENSIVE PLAN

While it would take years for the 1958 Development Plan for the Central Area to take hold, the Department of Planning soon entered a period of remarkable productivity. The high-water mark for planning in Chicago came from 1966 to 1974, when a confident department produced a series of major policy plans, many of which had lasting influence. This department offered the kind of fundamental guidance in the public interest that is the essence of good planning. City agencies, however, never fully embraced the plan or the process, a missed opportunity to embed planning in Chicago's governmental culture. Moreover, the moment passed, and the department receded as a leading force for an active planning agenda.

The 1966 Comprehensive Plan of Chicago

In the early 1960s, Mayor Richard J. Daley asked his Department of Planning for a comprehensive plan. According to planner Dean Macris, hired in 1958, Daley wanted a "Burnhamesque" document to show that he could "think big." Other cities, like Philadelphia under progressive mayor Richardson Dilworth and head planner Edmund Bacon, had won accolades for their recent city plans (Bacon would appear on the cover of *Time Magazine* in 1964). Daley liked the *idea* of planning perhaps even more than the process or its results.[1]

The planning department took Daley's request and ran in new directions. Previous plans had been designed to appeal to the public or to bureaucrats. Burnham and Bennett's 1909 Plan of Chicago offered grand drawings of large-scale redevelopment—a "project plan" to dazzle opinion makers. The Preliminary Comprehensive Plan of 1946—the previous large-scale plan in Chicago—mapped out land-use and transportation choices on a block-by-block scale, a "master plan" attempting to control city development for the next 20 years.[2]

But the 1966 Comprehensive Plan of Chicago followed a "policies plan" approach, an idea borrowed from Philadelphia and then expanded upon under the leadership of Louis B. Wetmore, a planning professor from the University of Illinois hired by Daley. Rather than a visionary roadmap or a static document, the policies plan offered "a series of broad guidelines for the city's development, with specific details shown as illustrative examples rather than as fixed decisions." The city would produce a set of goals that would guide specific development plans. By intent, the goals would be construed far more broadly than in the past, covering not just land use but a wide range of quality-of-life issues including health, education, industry, and even racial integration. Strategic objectives included "the proper allocation of land," "unified city development," and, more progressively, "expanded opportunities for the disadvantaged."[3]

In line with federal policies of the time, the plan was also designed to cover the entire city, not just the central area. In addition to wanting to produce a "Burnhamesque" plan, Daley understood that the Comprehensive Plan was a route to federal dollars. Accordingly, the plan proposed a 15- to 20-year citywide capital improvement plan that would nearly double the level of capital spending. The plan specifically expected "substantial increases in the federal share of costs," as had been the recent policy trend.[4]

While not an explicit strategic objective, racial change was discussed in the plan with unusual candor. A 1964 draft of the basic policies said that the city would seek "to achieve harmonious, stabilized neighborhoods attractive to families of all races and needs."[5] Two years later, marches led by Martin Luther King Jr. led to a fair housing ordinance, albeit one without much teeth. Navigating this shifting ground, the final 1966 plan charted a policy that was both progressive but acceptable to City Hall. The plan called for efforts to "reduce future losses of white families while accommodating the growth of the non-white population under the fair housing policy adopted by the City Council." More provocatively, it proposed policies to actively manage racial integration:

The city's policy is to seek to change the pattern of massive racial transition, neighborhood by neighborhood, which has in the past characterized the expansion of housing opportunity for non-whites. Involving human values, and attitudes as well as housing economics, the achievement of this change will require a combination of programs. Redevelopment and conservation programs would be used to achieve better racial balance in neighborhoods threatened by massive transition.[6]

At the time, this was a liberal stance for a city still deeply divided by race. However, the policies were never fully translated into proactive programs that might end white flight or achieve racial integration.[7]

Other policies in the 1966 plan went well beyond the built environment. Policies called for an expanded community college system, improved police-community relations, a network of local health centers, creation of special service areas for certain business districts, and new parks for neighborhoods with fewer than 1.6 acres per 1,000 people (Figure 4.1, page 44). Specific locations and quantitative goals were not included. Rather, the plan created an agenda for further work, including "key studies" on specific problems, including the lakefront. It also established a process for creating 16 development area plans covering subareas of the city.

The department promptly produced 15 of the 16 development area plans between 1967 and 1968, each a careful study in the overall needs of a broad but manageable section of the city. (Only the 16th plan, for the central area, was not written by the department; see chapter 5). Each development area plan was fewer than 20 pages long but included a profile of existing conditions and benchmark recommendations for projects in residential, recreation, education, libraries, social programs, public safety, health, business development, industrial retention, and capital improvements to support these efforts. These documents were intended not as "point to" pieces—as in "the library will go here and look like this." Instead, they were guidance documents for the school board, park district, community colleges, aldermen, and community leaders. They were expected to be updated regularly.

Despite a clearly written text and a high-quality production with color photographs, the 1966 Comprehensive Plan was neither popular nor particularly well understood. Daley struggled with the concept of a policy plan, as did other politicians. Norm Elkin, a member of the planning department, explained, "In Chicago, planning meant projects and proj-

Recreation and Park Land Improvement Plan

Existing Local Park Space in Residential Areas:

2 or More Acres Per
1,000 Persons

Less Than 2 Acres Per
1,000 Persons

Residential Area with Special
Social Program Needs

Existing Major Park

Lakefront Recreation
Land Addition

Figure 4.1. Recreation and Park Improvement Plan from the Comprehensive Plan of Chicago, 1966

ects meant contracts, something the machine could understand."[8] Polices, however, were vague and theoretical. Similarly, the graphics were general, making it hard for aldermen to discern concrete proposals for a given ward. As would become standard practice, the city council never formally approved the plan. Further, the plan declared "a new approach to planning for major cities" that included "citizens in the process of formulating goals and arriving at policies and programs to accomplish them."[9] But little evidence of extensive community input exists, and the plan was not a bottom-up exercise by any measure.[10]

Still, the 1966 Comprehensive Plan was "ahead of its time," as Dean Macris maintains. (In 1968 he took the idea to San Francisco, where it became the model for that city's General Plan of 1970).[11] It created a document that established a vision of a more progressive, healthier city with higher quality of life for all residents. The 1966 plan had staying power, especially in several key regulatory studies that developed in its wake. "The 1966 plan was the first and really the last comprehensive plan in the modern sense," longtime Chicago planner Les Pollock, FAICP, argues. "It treated the city as a whole but also created actionable subarea plans. It was a high point in Chicago planning and is underrecognized." Its themes were subsequently picked up in the equity planning movement of the Harold Washington era, the Model Cities program, and the LISC New Communities Program. Here was the translation of broad policies into specific recommendations that solved problems, enhanced public interests, and moved planning forward. As the city entered the 1970s, however, the anticipated federal dollars dried up. According to Dennis Harder, a member of the city's planning department, efforts shifted "into more of a regulatory mode."[12]

The Illinois Center Guidelines

The first regulatory study engendered by the 1966 plan centered on a crucial component of the unfinished 1958 Central Area Plan: the redevelopment of 60 acres of Illinois Central Railroad yards just east of the Loop. This was a valuable piece of real estate, bordered by the Chicago River, Lake Michigan, Grant Park, and the Loop. The 1958 plan anticipated dense office and residential towers over air rights, an idea already tested with completion of the Prudential Center in 1956 on the site's southwest corner. But a legal battle raged over the remaining valuable air rights until 1966, by which time they were worth more than the rest of the Illinois Central Railroad's assets combined.[13]

Planning for what became known as Illinois Center (and much later, a residential phase called Lake Shore East) began that year. With the 1966 Comprehensive Plan not completed until December and few policies in place, SOM produced a scheme for the area that reflected the high cost of the site and the need to maximize density to make development economical. It proposed packing the area with 35,000 residents (a density of over 400,000 residents per square mile) plus another 80,000 office workers. To manage this many people, SOM designed a three-level roadway system, including a lower level for rail, a middle level for trucks, and an upper level for autos and pedestrians. The SOM plan also reconfigured Lake Shore Drive and added additional lakefront park space through landfill.[14]

Two years later, in May 1968, the Department of Planning weighed in with the "Illinois Central Air Rights Development Guidelines," the first-ever extensive plan issued for a large-scale residential or office complex in Chicago, signaling an assertive approach by a planning department that not merely reviewed Planned Development (PD) proposals but led with policies, concepts, and regulations to guide development. Yet, eager to bring middle-class residents to the city, the department embraced the SOM scheme—perhaps too closely. It accepted the residential densities without extensive analysis, along with the massive roadways those densities implied, though it scaled back the office development. The department's guidelines did focus extensively on "the quality of development," discussing in detail the pedestrian experience and the need for esplanades, plazas, and access points (Figure 4.2).[15]

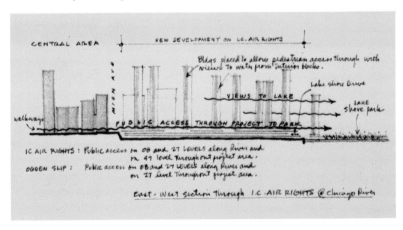

Figure 4.2. Sketches from the Illinois Central Air Rights Development Guidelines showing view corridors, walkways, and pedestrian access, 1968

Figure 4.3. Construction of Wacker Drive Extension, looking east, 1974. This three-level roadway dominates the south bank of the Chicago River.

The Illinois Center guidelines set in motion a complicated negotiation over the costs of the pricey infrastructure—especially the three-level roadways. After Planning Commissioner Lewis Hill struggled to find common ground with developers and other departments involved, Richard J. Daley called in Miles Berger of the CPC to mediate a contentious negotiation with high stakes, given the extraordinary infrastructure and potential for profit. Berger says Daley told him to "get to the point to where the developers make money but don't screw the city." Once Daley made it clear to other departments and the developers that Berger was his man, the pieces fell into place. The CPC reestablished its relevance after a long period of limited reach. Innovatively, the ordinance included PD clauses that allowed for flexibility in shifting programming from office to residential or hotel as market demand suggested.[16]

The Illinois Center plan, however, had two flaws. Unrealistic projected densities, coupled with autocentric parking and traffic requirements, resulted in a vastly overbuilt road network. As a result, Illinois Center today has excess vehicle capacity at all levels at high cost to the pedestrian experience.

Second, the department and plan commission did not do enough to protect the Chicago River. The multilevel roadway is only 50 feet from the river in most places, creating a poor riverwalk experience (Figure 4.3). In the hands of city engineers, the roadway—Wacker Drive between Michigan Avenue and Lake Shore Drive—was built with highway aesthetics, producing the type of ugly structures now being torn down across the country. *Chicago Tribune* architecture critic Paul Gapp called the road a "blunder," explaining: "By hugging the river's edge, the elevated street extension forever precludes creating a large and sunny pedestrian promenade next to the water." SOM planners, he noted, had "recommended that Wacker Drive [extension] be canted away from the riverfront. The city dismissed the idea."[17]

The north bank of the Chicago River, also a former rail yard but redeveloped in the 1980s, suggests the extent of the missed opportunity at Illinois Center. The Dock and Canal project (now Cityfront Center) engages the river with substantial walkways, a park, and a handful of restaurants. The city's planners either had not thought carefully enough about the river's relation to Illinois Center or were unable to coordinate with the city's traffic engineers, one of the goals of the 1966 Comprehensive Plan.

The Lakefront Plan

A second regulatory plan advanced strong and clear policies to protect the lakefront. Since the 1909 Plan of Chicago, planners had recognized Lake Michigan as the city's most notable natural asset. Burnham-era improvements framed a useable lakefront with parks, lagoons, and beaches—an enormous achievement. But in the postwar period, the lakefront became a less protected space. In 1947, the park board carelessly leased Northerly

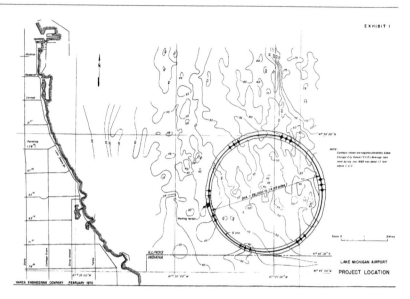

Figure 4.4. Engineering diagram showing location and circumference of a proposed airport in Lake Michigan, to be connected by causeway to the city, from "A Lake Michigan Site for Chicago's Third Major Airport: Summary of Engineering Studies," 1970

Island for $1 to the Department of Public Works for an airport, Meigs Field. A year later, the CPC passed a "Lakefront Resolution," declaring that the lakefront should be used only for recreational and cultural purposes. But that edict carried little weight when Colonel Robert McCormick of the *Chicago Tribune* bullied the city into building a convention hall on prime lakefront property in 1956. Daley himself proposed a giant airport built on landfill in the lake, a potential environmental nightmare that thankfully died due to its cost (Figure 4.4). In 1965, developers took possession of an unprotected tract near Navy Pier to build the 70-story Lake Point Tower, the first high rise east of Lake Shore Drive. The possibility of a rash of high rises along the lakeshore—already under way on the city's far north side—became a rallying point for those calling for a stronger ordinance. Without a plan or zoning protection, the lakefront had become vulnerable.[18]

Momentum for action accelerated with a variation of the "freeway re-volts" that stopped highway construction across the country in the 1960s. In 1965, the city and park district intended to widen South Lake Shore Drive to eight lanes from 47th and 67th streets and to reroute it directly through Jackson Park. Local protest from the nearby Hyde Park community was vo-ciferous. After roughly 500 trees had been cut down to make way for the

Figure 4.5. Panoramic drawings of proposed barrier islands, Lakefront Plan of Chicago, 1972

road expansion, women clung to remaining ones in the face of park district chain saws and bulldozers. Daley, uncharacteristically, halted the work and asked for a better plan.[19]

The park district commissioned a lakefront master plan by the Ann Arbor firm of Johnson, Johnson & Roy. In 1967, it completed a modestly sensitive plan that scaled back the road to six sunken lanes running closer to the lakefront rather than bisecting the park. But the park district refused to release the plan for several years; a political fiefdom for the machine, the park district lacked a strong planning culture and had little interest in complaints from Hyde Park liberals. Nonetheless, a chorus of citizen groups from the neighborhoods eventually produced a call for action.[20]

The Department of Planning stepped into the fray and wrote its own plan that extended the basic policies of the 1966 Comprehensive Plan into a remarkably strong new Lakefront Plan of Chicago, released in December 1972. The strength of the plan was its 14 strong policies, including: "in no instance will further private development be permitted east of Lake Shore Drive," preventing another Lake Point Tower. But the plan also called for "urban edge communities"—those adjacent to the lakeshore park—to be "compatible with the character of the lakefront." Here was a new level of protection for the city's front yard. A second policy was to "strengthen the parkway characteristics of Lake Shore Drive and prohibit any roadway of expressway standards," recommending a speed limit of 40 to 45 mph. Beyond the regulatory framework, the plan also emphasized maximizing public use along the entire 30-mile length of the lake in the city of Chicago and included widely publicized drawings of offshore islands to enhance recreational opportunities and prevent erosion (Figure 4.5).

Most important, the plan called for the adoption of a new ordinance that would give the city a "formal process . . . for testing proposals for development" along the lakefront. That process extended to "the issuance

of building permits and all acquisition and disposal of land."[21] These provisions would be championed by the CPC and enacted into the Lakefront Protection Ordinance passed in 1973. The ordinance created zoning overlays along the lakefront, protecting not just the shoreline and the parkland along it, but also defining a "private use zone" that stretched well inland. Development in this zone required an environmental study, departmental approval, and CPC review. The latter power "returned the Chicago Plan Commission to prominence," according to member and future chairman Reuben Hedlund.[22] Citizen activism, coupled with a vigorous Department of Development and Planning effort, had produced a far-reaching reform.[23]

The Riverfront Plan

A third regulatory study focused on the Chicago River, perhaps the most neglected of the city's natural assets. The 1909 Plan of Chicago sought to beautify the riverfront, and the city eventually produced a two-level Wacker Drive along the south bank to accommodate freight unloading on a dock level and automobile and pedestrian traffic on an upper level. The 1958 central area plan included a rendering suggesting more public amenities along the river, and developments such as Marina City (1963) fulfilled some of its potential. But little to no coordination existed among new buildings along the north bank. It was impossible, for example, to walk along the north side of the river at dock level for more than a block in the 1960s, and even Marina City lacked pedestrian access to the riverfront. Mayor Richard J. Daley told reporters that he dreamed of Chicagoans fishing for coho salmon on the river.[24] Yet as late as 1973, less than one percent of the nine highly polluted miles of riverbank in the central area had been developed for park or recreational purposes. That year, the Central Area Committee (CAC) called the river "one of the greatest opportunities for significant environmental improvement anywhere in

The Riveredge Plan of Chicago

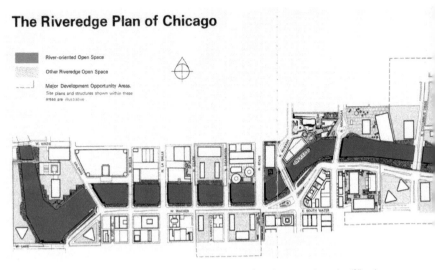

Figure 4.6. The Riveredge Plan of Chicago, showing open space along the river and new landfill at the river's mouth, 1974

the Central Communities" and proposed an ambitiously long river park, never realized.[25]

Following the CAC's lead, the Department of Development and Planning completed the Riveredge Plan in December 1974, a major step toward managing the river as a public space (Figure 4.6). In its basic policies, the Riveredge Plan called for expanding recreation opportunities, preserving "the cultural and historical heritage of the river," and developing the south bank of the river "as public, river-oriented open space." The plan stopped short of zoning changes or strong design guidelines, as with the Lakefront Plan, suggesting only that the PD process be used "to reflect the policies and recommendations of the Riveredge Plan." The plan's cautious nature was evident in the many questions that remained unanswered, including, most obviously, "How can the private sector be encouraged to participate in the development of the full potential of the Riveredge?" Unlike the Lakefront Plan's unambiguous public good, the river required public-private cooperation, still a new idea in the early 1970s.[26]

The river also lacked a political constituency and a coherent voice to argue for its improvement. In 1979, an impassioned article in *Chicago Magazine* entitled "Our Friendless River" called for an organization to adopt the river as a cause and define its future. Several months later, Friends of the Chicago River formed, and the group soon allied with the

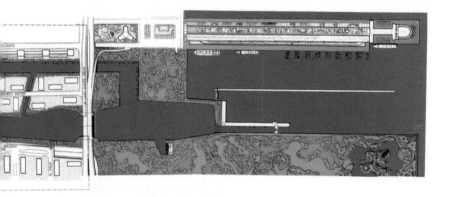

Open Lands Project and grew to 1,000 members. They faced numerous challenges, including making themselves relevant, prodding government agencies to prioritize river cleanup, and holding the city accountable to its own plan.

The Riveredge Plan experienced a high-profile test a year later at Wolf Point, a prized property at the strategic junction of the main branch and north branch of the river. The family of the late Joseph P. Kennedy owned the land (and had developed the adjacent Merchandise Mart in 1930). In 1973, they had promised to create a small park on the river's edge in exchange for zoning variances in a planned development for the rest of the site. But in 1979, the Kennedys asked to build a heliport on the point instead, with the intention of running a helicopter shuttle to O'Hare Airport. Mayor Jane Byrne approved the idea, and the CPC narrowly endorsed it. The Friends of the River, along with the Open Lands Project and the Metropolitan Housing Council, rallied against the heliport, saying it didn't abide by the Riveredge Plan. The project fell through because of opposition from Friends and others and because the state would not permit commercial flight operations on the small property. During the episode, the Department of Planning was largely silent, abrogating its role in policing its own plans. Three decades later, the Wolf Point site—one of the most valuable in the city—remains a parking lot. It is once more in a planning process, this time for a multitower project, and again the city has confined its role largely to a zoning review.[27]

Friends of the Chicago River eventually displaced the city as the main driver of planning for the entire river, and attempted to corral the Department of Planning and the Metropolitan Water Reclamation District into a comprehensive plan for the river, with various new parks, amenities, regulations, and guidelines. It was an ambitious effort, and the wide variety of existing land uses along the river made property owners nervous about detailed land-use restrictions. Cautious city planners scaled back the Friends' vision and recommended only that property owners with frontage along any Chicago waterway be required to use the PD process. Planning Commissioner Martin R. Murphy said he "wanted to avoid the 'cookbook' approach" and sought to limit the specificity of any ordinance. With Jane Byrne's backing, Murphy's modest approach passed the city council unanimously in 1983.[28] The city had retreated from an active stance along the river and settled for a defensive posture, and as a result riverfront development for the next 15 years would be negotiated one parcel at a time through the PD process, without comprehensive guidelines. Not until the late 1990s would the city reengage in assertive planning for the river. (See chapter 20.)

Between 1966 and 1974, the city's professional planners reached a high-water mark, producing a major body of work. A comprehensive plan, 15 area plans covering all of the city except the central area, and key regulatory studies installed the department in the center of the city's development process. This was structured, confident planning that gave the department a clear mission: to set policies that would benefit the city and to get developers and other city departments to live within those choices. The CPC, too, received a boost from its role in championing elements of the process, most prominently brokering the Illinois Center Planned Development and in championing the Lakefront Protection Ordinance. The city's planning agencies had never been stronger.

Implementation and enforcement of the policies, of course, was another matter. While the Lakefront Protection Ordinance offered rock-solid protections, much of the 1966 Comprehensive Plan was never institutionalized. Other city departments did not always follow the plan's policies, in part because the city did not receive the federal funding that it had hoped for and in part because Mayor Daley did not totally endorse or possibly understand all of its concepts.[29] Further, the plan's ambitious calls for addressing racial transition, housing opportunity, and white flight were ineffective given the racial turmoil of the time and the deep-seated fears of whites.

Planning historians have suggested that the comprehensive plan as a tool fell out of favor by the early 1960s, responding in part to trends in social science that argued for more limited, "middle range" theories rather than grand plans. Further, process issues have replaced the significance of plans themselves, especially in terms of citizen input. The 1966 Comprehensive Plan tried to meld these concerns, producing first a policy plan that could be translated to smaller and smaller spaces with increasing citizen input. But it still retained the authority of planning expertise, an idea that fell from grace as citizen-based, bottom-up planning came to be perceived as the only legitimate form.[30]

In today's planning climate, many see the comprehensive plan as the kind of large-scale exercise that sits on a shelf, while the real work of planning departments focuses on serving as a mediator and broker among interests and communities. But in Chicago in 1966, the Comprehensive Plan laid the basis for a long series of area development plans and regulatory changes. Its assertion of a policy role gave the Department of Development and Planning a strong voice in debates, one that eroded throughout the late 1970s and the 1980s as other players took on stronger roles.

CHAPTER 5
THE GROWTH COALITION TAKES
THE LEAD FOR PLANNING

The 1958 Development Plan for the Central Area laid out a basic strategy
for downtown growth, but progress was slow at best. To some in the growth
coalition, the national forces of decentralization, suburbanization, and racial change appeared unrelenting. Downtown retail continued to suffer,
while crime across the city surged. Development drifted north along North
Michigan Avenue and the Gold Coast, draining business from the Loop's
department stores. Decay in the Near South area threatened to engulf the
Loop as well. Race and class issues as much as deindustrialization were
driving these shifts: some developers suggested that the Loop's retail was
"too black" to be salvageable.[1] Fear of racial change and its impact upon
the central area was in the front of the minds of developers and planners
throughout the period.

Two of Chicago's largest towers suggested the divergent paths
possible for the central area in the late 1960s. In 1965, the John
Hancock Life Insurance Company selected a North Michigan Avenue
location for a 100-story mixed use tower including retail, office, and
condominiums. The location rejected the central business district and
indicated—as Arthur Rubloff had in the 1950s—that Chicago's center
of gravity would move north of the river despite limited transit capacity there. The John Hancock Tower quickly became an icon when it
opened in 1969, and a surge of investment followed along North
Michigan Avenue.

A second office tower, however, held out a future for the Loop. The Sears Corporation announced in 1968 that it would move its headquarters from the suburbs to the West Loop and build the tallest structure in the world, a reflection of the company chairman's ego and inflated estimates of the company's future space needs. The resulting 108-story, fortresslike Sears Tower (now the Willis Tower) cleared two blocks of the garment district and opened the West Loop to further development.[2] Perhaps the Loop was not yet dead.

The two skyscrapers symbolized the competing futures of the city, one north of the river and one in the Loop. In the early 1970s, however, the city's growth coalition threw its weight behind the Loop and stepped up its efforts to revive downtown. Ideas became bolder, even desperate at times, with business leaders willing to accept considerable risks to redevelop entire blocks in the Loop and build self-contained communities for the affluent near it. Chicago's corporate heads played a more prominent role than in previous decades, filling a void left by the increasingly disengaged planning department. The results were one transformative project and one outright debacle.

Chicago 21 and Dearborn Park

Under the rubric of the 1966 Comprehensive Plan, the Department of Development and Planning produced all but one the 16 plans covering the city—the final one for the central area. In a turning point for planning in Chicago, the city stepped aside and in 1973 let the CAC take the lead on this plan. In turn, the committee hired SOM to handle the planning and vision for a dramatic plan called Chicago 21: A Plan for the Central Area Communities, acknowledging its ambitions for the 21st century. Sheathed in a silver cover, the lavish published version of the plan brimmed with glamour and confidence, much like the Hancock and Sears towers, both designed by SOM architect Bruce Graham. Beginning with Chicago 21, SOM became the de facto planning arm of the city for formal plans, preparing not just the 1973 plan but also the 1983 Central Area Plan, the 2003 Central Area Plan, and the 2009 Olympics Plan. After its expansive efforts to establish a comprehensive plan in 1966 and produce key frameworks, the city had disengaged, mostly because Mayor Richard J. Daley wanted the growth coalition to "own" any downtown plan and pay for much of it. But by leaving the field to consultants, the city diminished its leadership, beginning a downward slide in its public role for planning.[3]

Figure 5.1. Sketch of the proposed South Loop New Town, from Chicago 21, 1973

Chicago 21 continued the themes of the 1958 Development Plan for the Central Area, but the scale and ambition had grown considerably. Anticipating generous federal funding, planners drew new subway tunnels through downtown that would eventually allow the tearing down of the elevated CTA Loop transit lines, long considered a blight. New bridges and roadways would strengthen downtown connections, including extending Roosevelt Road to Lake Shore Drive, building the Franklin Street Connector to the Dan Ryan (as proposed in 1958), extending Columbus Drive to north of the Chicago River, and straightening the Lake Shore Drive "S-curve" near the river. Beyond infrastructure, the plan for the first time recommended districts for historical preservation, including Prairie Avenue and River North, both of which later anchored redevelopment in their respective areas.

The centerpiece of the plan, however, involved residential development. Chicago 21 proposed a massive "South Loop New Town" to remake the rail yards once earmarked for the University of Illinois campus. The "New Town" concept derived from British postwar initiatives that sought to build complete suburbs; U.S. planners imported the idea in the late 1960s.[4] In the hands of Graham and SOM planners, the proposed South Loop New Town was a high-density, high-modernist city, an enlarged and

Figure 5.2. Sketch of proposed new housing on former lumberyards adjacent to Pilsen, from Chicago 21, 1973

somewhat softened version of the brutalist high-rise towers of the Cedar-Riverside New Town project in Minneapolis, then under construction.[5] The Chicago *Sun-Times* called the design "futuristic," as high-rise towers rested on eight-story bases occupying entire blocks, complete with garages, an electric tram, and terraced town houses (Figure 5.1). SOM suggested that 40,000 apartments could cover the site, with aboveground walkways linking the superblocks to allow residents to avoid the streets nearly completely in their daily lives.

The design, however, had its critics. Norm Elkin saw the SOM scheme as "too big, too cold, and too dense," while Richard Babcock, a past president of the American Society of Planning Officials, called the designs "Fortress Loop," emphasizing that they sealed out the surrounding city. Security appeared to be the overriding planning principle, as the plan shunned most street-level activity, reflecting the perceived hurdles to attracting middle-class whites to an area still surrounded by warehouses, half-empty buildings, and, to the south, public housing projects. As Lawrence Okrent, an SOM planner at the time, recalled, the design "had to be fortresslike, in part because planners believed that the South Loop was simply too dangerous to do otherwise."[6]

Neighborhood activists in nearby Pilsen formed the Coalition of Central Area Communities to wage an intensive campaign against Chicago 21. The plan had singled out Pilsen, a working-class district with a mix of Latino and white residents, as a central area community showing "evidence of strength and improvement" and suggesting new town houses on abandoned lumberyards along the river with a riverfront path connecting to the South Loop New Town (Figure 5.2). While the plan was far more conceptual than viable, to Pilsen residents it signaled gentrification. Over time, they protested outside offices of growth coalition members, demanding that Chicago 21 be scaled back and that resources be redirected to address a host of community resentments, from garbage collection to redlining.[7]

Despite resistance, hopes were high when CAC leader and Commonwealth Edison CEO Thomas Ayers convinced civic-minded Chicago business leaders and high-profile real estate developers to form the limited-dividend Chicago 21 Corporation to build the South Loop New Town, accepting substantial risks without the prospect of significant returns.[8] But realities soon meant scaling back ambitions. As in 1958, site acquisition presented numerous problems; the corporation obtained 51 acres of former Baltimore & Ohio Railroad land at a bargain price, but this was a fraction of the original 300-acre proposal. With city subsidies only for basic infrastructure such as sewers and sidewalks, the corporation planned Dearborn Park, a mix of senior buildings, apartment buildings, and town houses at moderate density.[9] The plan retained elements of the fortress mentality, using a wall to limit pedestrian and auto access, but otherwise moved tentatively into the risky emerging real estate market in the Near South Loop.

While complex negotiations to secure capital and city approvals took time, Dearborn Park eventually achieved a modest success. Phase I (939 units) opened in 1979 with solid initial sales, though skyrocketing mortgage rates in the early 1980s dampened enthusiasm. Phase II (486 units) was delayed until 1988 and finished in 1994, producing exclusively town homes at even lower densities (Figure 5.3, page 62).[10] Throughout the development process, corporation leaders sought to "manage" racial integration by aggressively marketing town homes to whites.[11] As a result, Dearborn Park produced an interracial mix but not much of a class one. By the mid-1990s, the two phases were 58 percent white, 30 percent black, and 12 percent Asian or Hispanic. Only a small fraction of residents, though, had migrated back from the suburbs; most relocated from within the city and were college-educated professionals. Only 25 percent of families had children, and few placed them in the new South Loop Elementary School built as part of Phase II.[12] Despite the mixed results, most observers were surprised that a new community, integrated by race and attractive to at least some families, could be built at all in the South Loop, a sign of how low expectations had fallen.

The Chicago 21 Corporation was aided by the unexpected gentrification of the area immediately to the north known as Printer's Row, a dense

Figure 5.3. Dearborn Park, bisected by Roosevelt Road with Phase II (foreground) and Phase I (closer to downtown), 1995. The South Loop Elementary School sits in the center of the community, just below Roosevelt Road.

collection of tall but slender 19th-century structures that once housed a vibrant printing industry (Figure 5.4). In a quixotic buying spree, Chicago modernist architect Harry Weese fell in love with Printer's Row in 1975, and together with real estate developer John W. Baird began purchasing the underused and decaying buildings. He converted them into a mix of

Figure 5.4. Portion of Printer's Row neighborhood, including Dearborn Street Station (1885, left), the Franklin Printing Company building (1916, center), and the Rowe building (1892, right), circa 1970

relatively low-cost live/work spaces and residential lofts, attracting a new wave of urban "pioneers." The revival of Printer's Row preserved architectural gems that the city had believed would need to be condemned and demolished. By 1987, 15 large Printer's Row buildings had been saved and renovated, creating 1,260 apartments.[13] Equally important, Printer's Row gentrification served as a gateway to Dearborn Park, transforming an area that had previously frightened pedestrians into a desirable address.

Together, the two complementary changes had a catalytic effect on the entire central area residential market. Large-scale new developments sprouted, ranging from the West Loop's Presidential Towers, a complex of four 50-story towers set on a fortress base (1981–86, 2,400 apartments), to the South Loop's River City, a whimsical modernist complex designed by Bertrand Goldberg along the Chicago River. Similarly, developers began converting warehouses into lofts on all sides of the Loop. The North Side was no longer the only viable option for downtown living, and an explosion of development took place in the 1980s. While diverging greatly from the original New Town concept of Chicago 21, Dearborn Park plus Printer's Row ushered in new development and conversions that brought about the aims of planners since 1958.

The State Street Transit Mall

The growth coalition's eventual success with the South Loop was not easily repeated with retail on State Street. For decades, the city's longtime retail center had seen declining sales, first due to competition from neighborhood shopping districts, then from suburban shopping malls, and, in the 1970s, from North Michigan Avenue. State Street's department stores struggled to stay open, while downscale retailers moved into smaller spaces. Several large movie houses had lost their cachet by the early 1970s. As white buyers fled, State Street appeared on its way to becoming another symbol of the city's race and class divides.[14]

In an effort to change course, Chicago 21 proposed a transit mall for State Street. A narrow street available only to buses would remove unfriendly traffic, allow beautification of the streetscape, provide room for pedestrian-oriented sidewalks, and, hopefully, restore a stronger retail base. The idea of transforming streets into pedestrian corridors had become a hot topic among American planners in the late 1950s. In 1957 Arthur Rubloff had floated the idea for State Street, in part to offset criticism that his Fort Dearborn Urban Renewal project would drain retail from the Loop, and the concept gained credibility a decade later with the successful opening of the Nicollet Street Mall in Minneapolis in 1968. Chicago 21 planners included a sweeping sketch of State Street as a pedestrian-friendly space that would be sure to draw foot traffic.[15]

But the transit mall, which opened in 1979, was a planning disaster. Poor execution, misguided design, and inadequate funding led

Figure 5.5. State Street Mall, from Madison Street looking north, April 1981

Chicago Tribune architecture critic Paul Gapp to call the mall "an aesthetic failure" and a "civic embarrassment." The details were all wrong, Gapp explained, from the sidewalk pavers to the hulking modernist bus shelters (Figure 5.5). The mall gave State Street only a "characterless, lackluster face-lift that offers little in the way of beauty or comfort." Despite creation of the State Street Mall Commission funded by a special service area tax, efforts to make the mall attract greater traffic did not work. By the mid-1980s, five of the seven department stores—Goldblatt's, Montgomery Ward, Wieboldt's, Bond, and Baskin—had closed.[16] After several studies, the city reversed course, ripped out the transit mall in 1996, reopened the street, and constructed a more attractive streetscape with Beaux-Arts detail.

Soon after, State Street revived as a diverse retail environment, aided in part by a growing presence of universities in the South Loop. DePaul University, in a private-public partnership in the city, redeveloped the historically significant Goldblatt's building at the key intersection of State and Jackson streets in 1996. Columbia College expanded into an eclectic collection of South Loop buildings in late 1990s, and, more recently, Roosevelt University constructed a 32-story mixed use tower. Together, the three institutions built University Center, a 1,700-

bed urban dormitory on State Street, opened in 2004. By 2000, a survey found 50,000 students attending 24 higher education institutions in the Loop (employing 15,000 people), and by 2009, the figure had risen to 65,000. This population fueled a retail surge and a healthy 24-hour presence along State Street.[17]

Despite the State Street Transit Mall debacle, the growth coalition had grounds for optimism by the late 1970s. Dearborn Park had, belatedly, sparked a residential renaissance in the central area, one that would reach a critical mass in the 1980s. Over time, these residents—like the college students—would bring spending power to revive commercial life in entire districts around the central area. Still, Chicago would enter a storm in the early 1980s on several fronts. An economic recession battered manufacturing, and political upheaval further divided the city, generating the first real challenge to the growth coalition agenda.

CHAPTER 6
CHICAGO'S EQUITY PLANNING MOMENT

The postwar growth coalition aimed to reshape the city in a top-down fashion, aided by professional planners but not by much direct citizen input. A changing political landscape in the late 1960s, however, strengthened community voices, and by the 1970s an "equity planning" groundswell emerged to challenge the growth coalition in cities such as Boston, Cleveland, and San Francisco. Their goal was not only citizen participation in decision making but also a shifting of planning agendas from downtowns to neighborhoods.[1] Chicago's equity planning moment took place during the administration of Harold Washington (1983–87), triggering a fierce debate between his administration's equity planners and the growth coalition. "The neighborhoods versus downtown" became shorthand for a set of planning priorities, redistributive taxes, and economic development initiatives centered on directing investment into poor and working-class communities, implicitly at the expense of the central area. While overheated rhetoric and the divisive politics of race clouded issues at times, equity planning in Chicago produced several lasting reforms but could not dethrone the still powerful growth coalition agenda. However, the growth coalition eventually adopted important segments of the equity planning movement, especially in industrial policy.

The Rise of Equity Planning in Chicago
Equity planning ideas emerged from community-based frustration with orthodox postwar planning ideas that appeared exhausted at best or failed

at worst by the mid-1960s. Resistance surfaced on several fronts. In the 1960s, urban rioting by African Americans convulsed cities, calling into question a range of federal urban policies intended to improve poor neighborhoods. Some planners and politicians demanded greater citizen involvement in planning rehabilitation efforts, and the Model Cities program, a new urban initiative passed in 1966, called for the "maximum feasible participation" of neighborhood residents in community rebuilding. The "Freeway Revolts" of the decade began the backlash against expert planning, as opposition stopped additional highway construction from plowing through urban neighborhoods, especially in San Francisco, New York, Miami, and Baltimore.[2]

In Chicago, neighborhood groups revolted in the 1970s over the long-planned Crosstown Expressway, intended to divert truck traffic around the central area. The Crosstown threatened to displace thousands of homes in white, working-class areas along Cicero Avenue. Neighborhood organizations formed to resist the highway, and Daley, weary of a bruising fight, backed down, despite numerous efforts by planners to minimize neighborhood impacts. The city asked SOM to produce conceptual drawings of a carefully landscaped, sunken freeway, but these images failed to sway neighborhood groups. The eventual cancellation of the Crosstown is often cited by growth coalition members as a major loss, clogging the city's highways with traffic needlessly converging on the central area. But the voice of the neighborhoods was too powerful for politicians to ignore.[3]

Still, the question arose: could citizen input be sufficiently organized to be effective in broad-based city planning? Chicago had a long tradition of neighborhood organizing, much of it carefully monitored or co-opted by the Democratic Party machine. Before 1970, only a handful of groups—such as Saul Alinsky's Back of the Yards Coalition (chapter 8)—could operate effectively outside of machine politics. But in the 1970s, independent community-based development organizations (CBDOs) launched anti-redlining campaigns, built housing, pushed for economic development, and formed networks across the city. In 1979, they chartered the Chicago Association of Neighborhood Development Organizations (CANDO) to strengthen their political voice. Deliberately, most CBDOs remained political outsiders, mostly ignored by the Democratic Party organizations and even by Jane Byrne in her successful run against the machine that year.[4]

But Harold Washington embraced the CBDOs and invited them to frame the "Washington Papers," a document outlining his campaign's agenda to improve neighborhoods. Progress, the platform argued, should

Figure 6.1. Harold Washington at the Robert Taylor Homes, February 23, 1987

be measured in jobs added rather than square feet constructed, a definite challenge to a developer-led growth agenda. The community coalitions' anger at Byrne and City Hall proved crucial in generating the massive turnout of African Americans that propelled Washington's 1983 victory.[5]

The campaign carried over into governing, as Harold Washington attempted to break the power of the Democratic Party machine by working around it. The idea was to replace ward-level insider politics with a decentralized, community-based, inclusive politics. Instead of residents turning to precinct captains to ask for city services, they would work CBDOs and other neighborhood nonprofits demanding wholesale change. However, varying levels of capacity among the CBDOs, plus an entrenched civil service, made even basic reforms halting or incomplete. And at times, CBDOs struggled with the transition from outside reformer to inside implementer. Ultimately, ward-level politics survived, but the Washington years—coupled with legal rulings outlawing patronage—seriously weakened the machine.[6]

Two professional planners played key roles in Washington's campaign and subsequent administration. Kari Moe served as Washington's closest advisor during the campaign and then as chief of staff in his administration. Rob Mier, a planning professor at the University of Illinois–Chicago with a strong equity planning bent, organized neighborhood groups into the Community Workshop on Economic Development (CWED), which wrote much of the "Washington Papers." Mier wanted to "refocus policy on community" and no longer talk "about an urban policy but about a community policy." Critically, physical planning was to be directed toward the goal of employment growth: "Putting jobs on the agenda was our thrust, especially jobs for the most needy." Washington appointed Mier commissioner of economic development, turning the position into a powerful voice for a "neighborhood agenda."[7]

But to head the Department of Planning, Washington made a more moderate choice, Elizabeth Hollander. Formerly executive director of the centrist Metropolitan Planning Council, Hollander had long been supportive of downtown development and had allies in Chicago's business community. Hollander later confessed that she was "skeptical about the prospects for investment in poor communities and impatient with the anti-gentrification forces." Washington cared more about community development in the neighborhoods than about formal planning, she added. Eventually, however, she came to share much of Mier's thinking on economic development, job preservation, and the underestimation of Chicago's manufacturing sector. Still, Hollander insisted "on keeping downtown aesthetics and amenities on the agenda," albeit in an "open and participatory way.[8]

"Chicago Works Together" and a World's Fair

The break with the growth coalition was most apparent in the contrast between the 1983 Chicago Central Area Plan, authored by SOM and paid for by the CAC, and the Washington administration's Chicago Works Together plan, finalized in May 1984. Like earlier incarnations, the 1983 Central Area Plan sought to strengthen the city's core through residential growth surrounding the Loop. The plan also compiled small initiatives intended to enhance the downtown's appeal to business interests, affluent shoppers, potential residents, and tourists. Streetscapes, riverfront development, and upscale housing occupy much of the presentation. More than previous efforts, however, the 1983 plan contained Burnhamesque platitudes and did not hide its "expert" origins:

> As the natural expression of a vigorous new spirit, this plan represents the joint effort of a cross-section of our society—people who believe in the potential for a humane community and for a high quality of life for all people. Businessmen, government leaders, architects, planners, historians, and economists have worked together in preparing this plan. They have labored so that now these ideas for the future of our city can be placed before all

Figure 6.2. Model of the proposed World's Fair on Northerly Island and along the lakefront, from the Chicago Central Area Plan, 1983

citizens for public examination, in the hope that all will see fit to join in this endeavor.[9]

The growth coalition continued to ignore the planning zeitgeist of the 1970s in favor of noblesse oblige, a stance that did not sit well in the city's neighborhoods.

The crown jewel of the plan was a world's fair, whose expected 55 million visitors would not only elevate Chicago on the international stage but also pay for new infrastructure in the Near South area and catalyze the "development of a mixed-use community" on former railroad land. To design the fair, the CAC hired SOM's Bruce Graham, who led an all-star team of architects.[10] SOM's plan, both densely urban and postmodern, proposed not only a dazzling 575-acre fairground running along the lakefront from Grant Park south to 35th Street, but a wealth of new infrastructure as well (Figure 6.2). Lake Shore Drive would be relocated, a light-rail train would connect the Near South to the downtown, and a new "midway/canal" carved near 16th Street would "would enable the lakefront park system to penetrate deeply into the Near South area to encourage development." Expansion of the McCormick Place convention center and a "support zone of hotels, retail spaces, and specialty offices" was also proposed. Further afield, the 1983 Central Area Plan hoped a fair would catalyze completion of Grant Park by decking over Illinois Central tracks, a concept that later became Millennium Park.[11]

The committee saw a world's fair as the most feasible way to assemble funding, momentum, and energy to undertake massive infrastructure and community building in a time when urban renewal had largely been discredited and defunded. It was a gamble on a grand spectacle event intended to jump-start the Near South Side and bolster downtown. Thomas Ayers of Commonwealth Edison, Dearborn Park, and the CAC later argued that the fair was critical because "Chicago has slipped and in many people's minds. It's the dying capital of the Frost Belt."[12] Harold Washington signed the plan in May 1983 but called it a "draft" that would be "modified and completed after public discussion and feedback."[13] Moe and Mier were strongly opposed, as were neighborhood organizations, asserting that jobs would be temporary, the fair would do little for most communities, and costs and risks were high.[14]

A year later, the Washington administration's equity planners released Chicago Works Together, a plan which moved in another direction entirely. Ignoring the world's fair idea, Moe and Mier worked with the CBDOs to write a plan that in tone and substance critiqued the growth coalition. It criticized previous administrations for underemphasizing job creation, neglecting neighborhood development, withholding planning information from the public, and failing to leverage "publicly-subsidized projects for community development and local hiring." The plan then advocated five goals: increase job opportunities; promote "balanced growth"; assist neighborhood development "through partnerships and coordinated investment"; pursue greater public participation and openness in planning; and extract more from the state and federal governments. The plan was careful not to dismiss downtown, but it clearly pushed a new agenda: "Strong private market forces characterize the City's Central Area, while many neighborhoods suffer disinvestment."[15]

Chicago Works Together emphasized a new set of planning principles focused on outcomes and process. The document stressed "measurable commitments" and "responsiveness to citizen and business concerns," by which it meant the small manufacturers, local retailers, and service industries that accounted for two-thirds of Chicago employment. Chicago Works Together intended to plan "for the City as a whole, not just for the central business district and large-scale projects." Its appendix contained a detailed list of existing and proposed projects that could be leveraged to create employment in poor neighborhoods.[16]

But for two years, the CAC's fair dominated the planning conversation. The city and state created a joint Fair Authority before Washington took office to raise an estimated $1.1 billion for it. Nearly half this amount was expected to come from the private sector and one-quarter from the state of Illinois, along with an additional $220 million in state bond guarantees. The city hoped to spend only $28 million directly and add another $33 million in property tax abatements.

Harold Washington wavered on the fair, exasperating both the CAC—which expected him to line up behind civic projects—and his CBDO supporters, who expected him to oppose downtown-centered initiatives. Eventually, Washington said no, explaining, "The City of Chicago doesn't have the money. We don't need a fair or anything else to sell the city of Chicago. We have one of the greatest cities in the world."[17]

The growth coalition never forgave Washington, but the experiences of other cities suggested that the neighborhoods were right. Fairs in New Orleans and Knoxville proved disappointing financially, and promoters of a Chicago fair failed to offer a viable vision. As Howard McKee, an SOM planner who worked on it, later reflected: "The people who were charged with portraying the idea never got it off the ground. It was seen as a kind of tinselly party lacking in substance and lacking initially—I don't think this was true at the end—enough residuals to warrant the effort. And I think, frankly, that wasn't a bad assessment of it." [18]

Equity Planning in Practice

The neighborhoods had helped stop the fair, but pushing the Chicago Works Together agenda proved more difficult. Implementation of the plan required a city capable of shifting to new priorities. But the many bureaucracies, full of longtime machine members, struggled to meet the demands or dragged their feet.[19] Even extracting information was painstaking. As a Harold Washington appointee explained, "information was a source of power" within the old machine and was jealously guarded. Data on housing code violations or street repairs by ward could be used to reward friends or punish enemies. It was not for public consumption. Some departments created two sets of data "books"—one for external reporting of dubious accuracy and an in-house set, used for political purposes, with information exchanged "orally and informally." Bureaucracies feared the release of data might result in criticism or incur political wrath. In a city driven by machine connections, information had become subordinated to political concerns. Changing these patterns meant tedious reforms.[20]

Some changes, however, could be accommodated quickly, including Community Development Block Grant (CDBG) reform. Federal rules expected CDBG funds to be used to develop poor communities, but sufficient flexibility had allowed the Byrne administration to use the program as an all-purpose fund, aggressively earmarking it for political hires and political supporters in the neighborhoods.[21] The Washington administration transferred power over CDBG from the Department of Planning to Mier's Economic Development shop, even as Congress and the Reagan administration agreed to drastic cuts that would shrink the program from $158 million in 1982 to only $85 million in Harold Washington's first year. After much consultation with community groups, Mier imposed "standards of need" to target the scarce funds to low-income communities.[22]

These new priorities rankled white aldermen, whose wards were less likely to meet the new standard, and fueled their fear that Washington would dismantle the city's white political structure and hand it over to the city's long-neglected black community. Aldermen Edward Vrdolyak and Ed Burke controlled a block of 29 white aldermen that could stifle the Washington administration's progressive agenda. They amended the Washington administration's CDBG budget with ineligible activities, causing the mayor to veto the budget.[23] The council backed down, but CDBG awards became one more battleground in the "Council Wars."

Even basic planning and infrastructure initiatives became ensnared in the Council Wars. When Harold Washington proposed issuing general obligation bonds for sidewalk repairs and new sewers in the neighborhoods, Vrdolyak and Burke's block refused to approve them. After several months, Vrdolyak finally relented following a bus tour for white neighborhood leaders organized by the mayor's office that showed them the potential benefits from improvements being held up by the council.[24]

The Struggle for Linked Development

Nevertheless, it was often not difficult for the Washington administration to straddle the "downtown versus the neighborhoods" debate because the central area was booming on its own and didn't need city help. Massive private investment in new skyscraper construction and loft conversion began in the early 1980s as office demand boomed. A postindustrial economy centered on financial services accelerated in the aftermath of the 1981–1982 recession.

And yet, the progressive project of tapping downtown's wealth to redistribute it to poorer communities faced an uphill battle. Chicago

Figure 6.3. Mayor Harold Washington at the groundbreaking of an affordable housing project with leaders of the Kenwood-Oakland Community Organization (KOCO), November 25, 1987. Later this day, Mayor Washington died of a heart attack.

Works Together proposed "linked development" in an effort to extract more from Chicago's developers. Since the 1930s, communities had required developers to dedicate land or pay fees to accommodate suburban growth, and "impact fees" were in wide use across the country by the 1980s. But linkage usually involved a direct connection to the immediate development. The Washington administration pushed the boundaries of linkage, following the lead of efforts in San Francisco and Boston.[25] In return for support for downtown projects, developers would be pressed to "provide various types of development assistance directly to neighborhoods" and would be "encouraged to participate financially in neighborhood development."[26]

The administration investigated other avenues for reaping citywide benefits from the downtown boom. Late in 1985, it pressed through the City Council a six percent tax on all commercial leases to plug an $80 million budget hole, but it was repealed three months later even as the original ordinance was deemed unconstitutional by a Cook County judge.[27] Stung, the administration moved gingerly as neighborhood groups rallied behind a proposal to tax new office development downtown, an effort called the "exaction tax." The proposal emerged from white ethnic neighborhood groups on the Southwest and Northwest sides and was soon embraced by other community organizations. The idea was to tax new development at $5 per square foot to create a pool of money that could be used for neighborhood infrastructure and community development. The mayor expressed support, but his closest advisors were divided. As Elizabeth Hollander notes, the term "exaction" was termed "extraction" by downtown interests and redefined as "reparations" by some community organizers. In that deeply divided climate, emotions ran high.[28]

Washington formed the Mayor's Advisory Committee on Linked Development to debate the issue. Hollander observed that "the level of trust was low" on the committee, which included representatives of neighborhood interests and downtown developers. The developers vehemently opposed redistribution efforts and had the backing of the city's major newspapers. The developers—supported in part by professionals in Hollander's planning department—were eventually able to bury the idea, proposing a nearly worthless substitute to make linkage "voluntary." The administration, perhaps focused on reelection, never put its political weight behind a linkage fee, and the idea expired. Community activists were disappointed in the administration's lack of persistence on such a vital issue.[29] But Hollander believes that the mayor could not have passed the idea, given the deep divisions in the City Council, and that larger developers emerged from the battle "with a strong, organized, well-connected political voice."[30]

Harold Washington died of a heart attack on November 25, 1987, and the city's progressive community has mourned his loss for two decades. To supporters, Washington became an icon, a good-government progressive fighting the Democratic Party machine and the growth coalition with a neighborhood-centered politics that aimed to redistribute the city's growing economy to those left behind. To his detractors, redistribution felt like racialized payback. Further, Washington's stand against the Vrodolyak 29 during the Council Wars placed him in the way of one view of "progress," be it with the world's fair or other potential sizeable projects such as Navy Pier or a new central library, both delayed by infighting and not completed until the Daley years.

Criticism of equity planning was also voiced in a 1988 *Chicago Tribune* series "Chicago on Hold," by John McCarron, who had covered the city's urban development beat for 10 years. McCarron wrote a polemical critique of the lack of leadership over that time, including not just Washington but mayors Bilandic, Byrne, and Sawyer. He viewed the rise of community-based voices as just another "self-serving" interest group that had blocked development and created "paralysis" at the expense of the city's long-term health. Chicago had become "timid," unwilling to tackle large projects, and "inertia" had replaced bold action.[31]

Overheated rhetoric surrounded the Harold Washington years. Community activists felt elated at his election, then deflated by the limits of their power. Business elites were alternately frightened by change and frustrated at the loss of influence. Yet even as major efforts were made to refocus public investment on the neighborhoods, private development in Chicago's central area boomed. With high inflation and tax policy pushing commercial real estate investment, Chicago's downtown would soon be flooded with new office towers. Washington's critics—who assumed his stance would stifle development—were wrong.

Washington's legacy was more incremental and rhetorical than transformative. Most CBDOs continued to thrive after Washington's death and had the ears of City Hall and their aldermen. Washington's economic development policy survived under his successors, including Richard M. Daley, who kept several of his key appointments to implement an industrial policy. (See Part Three.) The central area, however, returned to a place of prominence in the Daley regime, and politics again centered on the growth coalition's efforts to defend downtown as the city's vital economic engine.

CHAPTER 7
PLANNING IN THE VOID:
REDEVELOPMENT IN THE NORTH LOOP
AND NEAR SOUTH

This chapter tells the story of two separate redevelopment efforts in the central area, both of which were defined by a void in planning leadership at the city level. First, urban renewal in the North Loop suffered greatly from a lack of planning, drifted aimlessly even as it cleared entire blocks, then, ironically, found a purpose through the voices of preservationists. Second, the Near South area, the last piece of the 1958 Development Plan for the Central Area, had the good fortune of strong institutional actors, privately produced plans, and a clearer vision, and thus produced solid outcomes. While the two episodes represent ends of a continuum, both reinforce the idea that urban development is precarious without a confident city voice in the process. Lacking a plan and at times guided purely by the market, the city continued a downward slide in its capacity and willingness to lead on major decisions and on vital spaces.

The North Loop
The North Loop project first emerged as a developer's dream in 1973 and ended with a planning nightmare in 2009. Along the way, it involved a messy political circus that dominated headlines and, worse, absorbed millions of dollars in public subsidies. In the absence of a coherent plan, deal making replaced clear thinking. The growth coalition strained to present a vision, and, in the chaos, the private market

Preservation and Historic Districts

Chicago enacted its 1968 Landmark Preservation Ordinance after a decade of public protest over the losses of 19th-century Loop skyscrapers. The demolition of Dankmar Adler and Louis Sullivan's Garrick Theater (1891) to make way for a parking garage proved a catalyst to citizen action, though the ordinance could not save another Adler and Sullivan masterpiece, the Chicago Stock Exchange (1894), torn down in 1972. The battle over the Stock Exchange building led to the formation of the nonprofit Landmarks Preservation Council of Illinois in 1971.

The ordinance created the Commission on Chicago Landmarks, which protected 35 buildings and historic sites along with nine historic districts in its first decade. Many early historic districts were prompted by neighborhood groups responding to development proposals, including threats to the industrial town of Pullman (1972), Gold Coast residences along Astor Street (1975), and workers' cottages in the Old Town Triangle and Mid North districts (1977). Progress soon slowed, however, and after 20 years only 17 historic districts had been given protection—a rate behind those of many other U.S. cities.

Designations increased during the 1990s and 2000s, when redevelopment pressures began to overwhelm many historic neighborhoods that had been zoned in 1957 for higher densities. Teardown threats to historic structures caused many community groups and their aldermen to petition for landmark protection. Between 1989 and 2009, an additional 36 historic districts were designated. Similarly, the city turned to focus on business districts, which had previously been avoided due to the potential opposition of property owners. Among the new districts were several historic downtown commercial areas, including Jewelers Row, the Michigan Avenue street wall, Motor Row, and Printer's Row.

Organizational changes facilitated these new approaches. In 1993, the small landmarks staff merged into the city's larger Department of Planning and Development, a budgetary move that nonetheless helped integrate preservation into overall community planning goals. Publication of the Chicago Historic Resources Survey (1996), a citywide study that identified potential landmarks, also aided preservation efforts. Local incentive policies contributed as well, beginning in the late 1990s. Mayor Richard M. Daley, sensitive to issues of preservation, proved decisive in advocating for residential tax "freezes," building permit fee waivers, and a new "Class L" tax classification aimed at promoting the rehabilitation of landmarks as well as buildings in historic districts.

The number of new designations began to slow in the late 2000s, in part due to a nationwide recession, which reduced teardown pressures in many of neighborhoods. Another factor, however, was a lawsuit filed by property owners in two districts in 2008. The plaintiffs maintained that the designation process undermined the value of their buildings; in early 2009, an appeals judge agreed with their claim that landmark language was "vague." The case has had a chilling effect, as no new historic districts have been pursued by the city since.

Other recent conflicts have roiled the preservation community as well. In 2012, Bertrand Goldberg's Prentice Women's Hospital (1975) became the center of a major battle over modernist structures. Northwestern University Hospital argued for demolishing the unusual cloverleaf building to make way for a new research facility, but architects and preservations rallied around Goldberg's innovations. Mayor Rahm Emanuel eventually sided with Northwestern and announced his opposition to landmarking Prentice. Then two days later the Chicago Landmarks Commission (appointed by the mayor) held an unprecedented meeting. First the Commission awarded the building preliminary landmark status per staff recommendations based on objective criteria, but then it immediately turned around—after a presentation by the Department of Housing and Economic Development—and rescinded its award based on economic considerations. The episode amounted to a bizarre twist of political theater, an unfortunate precedent for rescinding landmark status, and a signal that preservation will continue to be contentious in Chicago.

—James E. Peters, AICP

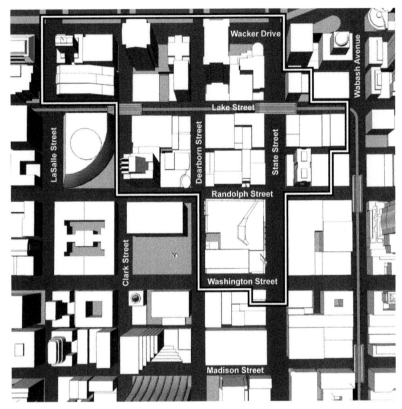

Figure 7.1. Schematic of North Loop area, showing boundaries of Tax Increment Financing district, 2012

struggled to sort out a use for the area. In the end, preservationists rescued the North Loop with a model that eventually succeeded.

The North Loop redevelopment area covered six city blocks in the heart of downtown along Lake and State streets (Figure 7.1). In the 19th century and early 20th centuries, these served as the city's retail and entertainment district, anchored by several large movie theaters. But by the 1970s, commercial space had filtered downward. Still, preservationists saw numerous examples of important 19th-century architecture and grand old theaters deserving restoration. Indeed, four buildings had already been placed on the National Register of Historic Places by 1973, and three more received that designation by 1982.[1]

The growth coalition's answer to State Street had been the Transit Mall, but its failures only accelerated the North Loop's decline. The growth coalition ran out of answers, except for real estate developer Arthur Rubloff who, beginning in 1973, initiated an effort to win public support for an idea to level six blocks for a hotel with convention space and new office construction. But Rubloff had no real plan, just a scale model and a potential deal with the Hilton hotel chain.[2]

Leveling six blocks downtown would be an enormous undertaking in any city, one that begged for the kind of careful planning that had defined the Illinois Center, the lakefront, and the riverfront. Yet the Department of Planning made only minimal efforts to guide the space or signal its intentions beyond a desire for redevelopment. Based on a slim study by the Department of Urban Renewal, the city established a Commercial District Development Commission in 1973 and gave it urban renewal powers but not much direction. In 1978, city planners applied to the Carter administration for a $25 million Urban Development Action Grant (UDAG), but was rejected. The commission used the sketchy UDAG application as the basis of a North Loop Redevelopment Plan, allowing it to proceed with condemnation of sites. The city had drifted into urban renewal in its central business district on the basis of real estate developer interest but little else and without much of a plan.[3]

Mayor Byrne pushed Rubloff out of the picture and chose her own real estate czar, Charles Shaw, to both participate in and manage the redevelopment, an obvious conflict of interest. Byrne and Shaw offered the Hilton hotel $50 million in tax abatement to produce a deal. The tax breaks, however, needed county approval and raised the ire of neighborhood groups who formed the Campaign Against the North Loop Tax Break in 1981. The deal fell through in March 1982.

But the North Loop needed more than a deal; it needed a vision, and the preservation community provided it. Preservationists had been critical from the start of the urban renewal idea and had campaigned for saving the theaters and a total of 14 out of the 52 structures to produce a Theater District. To quell their anger, Byrne appointed an Architectural Advisory Committee, which soon called for saving all the theaters in the district, programming them with "high-quality entertainment," and preserving even more of the office buildings in the area.[4] Byrne and her Department of Planning gradually came around to the idea of some preservation and a theater district, producing iterations of "guidelines" that shifted on the issue several times. Meanwhile, a few theaters had cobbled together financing assisted by preservation tax credits to begin rehabilitation work. A vision was being implemented in spite of the city's lack of leadership.

The Harold Washington administration inherited this mess in 1983. But with the help of Miles Berger at the Chicago Plan Commission, Wash-

Figure 7.2. Members of Friends of the Chicago Theatre line up to apply as volunteer ushers and tour guides in advance of the reopening of the theater, August 21, 1986.

ington's equity planners crafted the city's first tax increment financing (TIF) district to generate the flow of subsidy dollars needed to finance further preservation and land acquisition. Rather than federal dollars, which were not forthcoming, or tax abatements, which were politically dicey, the new and dimly understood TIF idea allowed the city to borrow against the future increase in tax collections in the six blocks of the North Loop. In all, $222 million was raised from TIF and general obligation bonds over a decade to finance redevelopment.[5]

Still, the Department of Planning remained unsure of how to proceed. Only concerted action by longtime residents in 1984 saved the iconic Chicago Theatre from destruction (Figure 7.2). The city had issued the owner a demolition permit, but the Department of Planning's Liz Hollander asked for advice from Norm Elkin, then head of the State Street Council. He counseled saving the theater at all costs, adding that if Harold Washington allowed it to come down, "then whites would say the Mayor didn't care about their memories and what was important to them," even as Elkin recognized that African Americans in the city thought the downtown already received too much attention. Privately raised funds plus TIF money restored the Chicago Theatre, today a major venue.[6]

Eventually a thriving theater district emerged. TIF funds were used to move the Goodman Theatre into two renovated spaces, and other historic buildings were preserved. Closer to the river, city blocks were cleared for modern office towers that poured tax revenue into the TIF. The influx of

Figure 7.3. Block 37, following demolition, 1990. This block, a key piece of the North Loop Redevelopment Project, remained vacant for over two decades.

funds greased solutions, even in the absence of a plan, though one block remained vacant for over two decades as numerous deals were made and then collapsed (Figure 7.3; see also chapter 18). Miles Berger called Block 37 "cursed," and its development saga has been told as extravagant political theater in journalist Ross Miller's book *Here's the Deal: The Buying and Selling of a Great American City.*[7]

The North Loop demonstrated yet again the difficulty of moving forward with urban development in the absence of clear planning. In an ad hoc manner, ideas eventually converged around a Theater District that proved successful. But if the Department of Planning had engaged in a careful, collaborative planning effort in the 1970s and early 1980s to think through land-use and public needs in the North Loop, this outcome might have been smoother, less costly, and more coherent.

The Near South and the Triumph of the Growth Coalition

Even as the growth coalition struggled with the North Loop in the 1980s, the Near South portion of the central area appeared even more problematic. Dearborn Park had catalytic effects around the Loop, but the rest of the Near South remained cut off from downtown by limited street access and rail yards. Moreover, three major cultural institutions in the area—the Field Museum, the Adler Planetarium, and the Shedd Aquarium—were similarly cut off from Grant Park and the Loop by the freeway-like Lake Shore Drive. Realizing the potential of the Near South Side would entail not only constructing roads and bridges but overcoming the area's stigma. The Near South lay south of Roosevelt Road, a racially coded border perceived by the real estate market as the start of the South Side. With rail yards, junkyards, and abandoned warehouses littering the landscape, the area appeared forbidding (Figure 7.4). The Near South's population—95 percent black—was itself isolated in the area's southwest corner, mostly in subsidized housing. The district's crime rate was the second highest in the city in 1982.[8] As Carl Grip of the South Side Planning Board stated in 1989, "There has [long] been a stereotype about the South Side. Only 10 years ago no developer went south of Congress [the south edge of the Loop]. Up until the beginning of Dearborn Park Phase II [1988], there was a stereotype that you didn't go south of Roosevelt Road."[9]

The widespread blight of the area begged for careful replanning, but the decline of the growth coalition and the inattention of the Department of Planning left a planning void. A coherent plan for the Near South was eventually crafted by a variety of actors, including developers, museums,

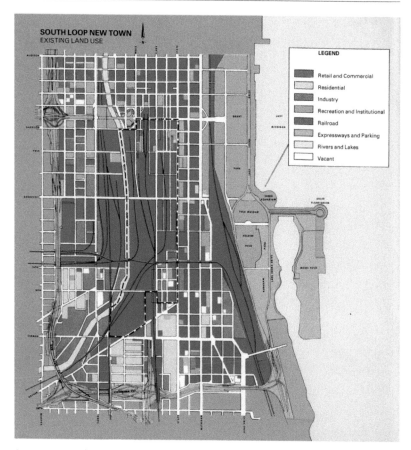

Figure 7.4. Map of conditions in the Near South area, from Chicago 21 Plan, 1973. Note the large rail-road spaces (a portion of which were redeveloped in the 1980s as Dearborn Park; see chapter 5) and the lack of road connections between the area and Lake Shore Drive, which hindered redevelopment.

McCormick Place, a TIF, and a task force that cobbled together a future for the area in a grand deal, consummated in 1990. Ultimately, the deal produced a positive improvement for the city. But the process demonstrated how unstructured and highly political Chicago's development had become.

In 1986, Chicago developer Gerald Fogelson and Cleveland devel-oper Albert Ratner purchased 42 acres of Near South rail yards from the Illinois Central Railroad, as well as 30 acres of air rights over functioning tracks. They imagined a project much like Illinois Center, combining office, residential, and hotel development, extending south from Roosevelt Road to McCormick Place. But the isolation of the site was extreme: the only access

Figure 7.5. The Near South lakefront before redevelopment, looking south, May 11, 1989. Note the isolation of both the Near South area and institutions such as the Field Museum (foreground) from the lakefront.

was from a narrow corridor on the west, and the site had poor road and pedestrian access to Grant Park (on the north) and the lakefront (to the east). Without a significant public infrastructure commitment, Fogelson and Rattner struggled to find financing.[10]

Around 1988, the lakefront museums were also looking for new infrastructure from the city. The Field Museum, Adler Planetarium, and the Shedd Aquarium had opposed a world's fair as too disruptive, but they liked the fair's proposals to relocate Lake Shore Drive, extend Roosevelt Road to the Drive, and rebuild adjacent Burnham Park. These ideas, especially the extension of Roosevelt Road, would also benefit Fogelson and Ratner's property. To resurrect these investments, the museums hired SOM's Adrian Smith to produce a new Museum Campus plan to unify the museums and link them to Grant Park.

But how could museums and developers get the city to pay for a costly reconfigured highway, a new bridge, and a new park? Enter McCormick Place, eager to expand its own facilities. The state-chartered Metropolitan Pier and Exposition Authority (known as "McPier"), which controlled McCormick Place, needed city approval for its own expansion plans. To bring together the various interests, newly elected Richard M. Daley created a Joint Task Force on Burnham Park Planning, headed by Chicago Plan Commission chairman Reuben Hedlund. "Suddenly, there was the clout and the resources to make things happen," a park district official told the *Chicago Tribune*. In

Figure 7.6. The Near South lakefront after completion of Museum Campus, the reconfiguration of Lake Shore Drive, the construction of the Roosevelt Road bridge (lower right), and the development of the Central Station community on former railroad land, July 9, 2008

a grand deal, the task force endorsed McCormick Place expansion in return for the state—via McPier's bonding authority—paying for the creation of Museum Campus, Burnham Park, and the relocation of Lake Shore Drive at a cost of $110 million.[11] For their part, Fogelson and Ratner donated to the city a portion of their land to make the rerouting of Lake Shore Drive work.[12]

Part of the reason for the grand bargain was the enthusiasm of all parties for the Museum Campus, which proved a planning and design success (Figures 7.5 and 7.6). Lake Shore Drive turned from a former expressway into a boulevard environment, and Roosevelt Road's extension connected the Near South to Grant Park and the drive. The museums ended their isolation with well-designed tunnels beneath roadways, creating a seamless pedestrian experience. The new Burnham Park reclaimed other roadway for open space and even Soldier Field access was dramatically improved.

As Museum Campus ideas were hatching, Near South developers Fogelson and Ratner advanced their vision for a large new community, now called "Central Station," after the old Illinois Central train station demolished in 1974. Lengthy negotiations with the city's Department of Planning produced the most complex PD guidelines to date, calling for rebuilding the street grid, protection of street walls and view corridors, and a mix of uses. The PD allowed a maximum of 19 million square feet of development, including 9,500 units of housing—a potentially enormous addition to the

city's fabric. But this time the mistakes of Illinois Center were not repeated; the road network was modest despite the density. Still, the developers
would not be able to get the project off the ground without city subsidies to
fund the extensive new infrastructure.[13]

This need created an opening for opposition to the project. During
hearings before the Chicago Plan Commission in 1990, the Chicago Affordable Housing Coalition (CAHC) demanded that no public funds be
expended, arguing that the central area "is experiencing its biggest boom
since WWII; it needs no further subsidies. Public needs are located in our
schools, our streets, our neighborhood commercial districts, our manufacturing sector, and our housing market." The CAHC focused on the $110
million figure for the entire project—mostly dedicated to Lake Shore Drive,
Roosevelt Road, and Museum Campus, not just the small portion to build
infrastructure for Central Station. That amount of money, the coalition said,
could "leverage the rehab of 12,000 units of affordable housing." The
Metropolitan Planning Council praised the negotiated planned development, but it too argued that public support "must also be considered in a
city-wide context, not just a downtown development context" and that "a
city-wide public financing policy" was needed to govern decision making
on infrastructure investment. Without a comprehensive plan since 1966,
neither the "context" nor the "policy" existed.[14]

In the absence of context and policy, the CPC assumed a more practical approach to the Central Station problem. It saw a need to "break the
perception" of the Near South as too risky for residential and commercial
development. CPC member Doris Holleb maintained in a public hearing
that the Near South Side was a fragile area and not a "hot market." But
Holleb admitted the difficulty in deciding exactly how much public subsidy
was required to jump-start a development: "We will look for that fine line as
much as we can find it. But we don't think this is quite the same hot market
area."[15] With strong support from the museums and other interests cultivated
by Fogelson and Ratner, the Plan Commission approved the Central Station
Development Guidelines in February 1990. Later that year, the city created
a TIF to support infrastructure improvements.[16]

Despite the careful attention to the site during the PD process and the
infusion of TIF-backed infrastructure, Central Station struggled to gain trac-
tion in the early 1990s. A turning point came in 1993, when Mayor Daley
announced he would purchase a town house in one of the development's
earliest phases. Even after the mayor and his wife moved in three years
later, the area remained a mostly blank slate and an untested proposition.

Yet Daley's choice signaled to potential buyers that the city had confidence in the area and would support its growth.

After Central Station's first phase was under way, its vast scope finally struck the city's equity planners and architects. In January 1995, the progressive Chicago Chapter of Architects/Designers/Planners for Social Responsibility (ADPSR) organized a one-day Community Planning Forum at which Near South residents expressed fears of potential newcomers and resentment that the area had been planned without their input. "The starting point of any improvement plan must be to preserve and build on the people and institutions that make this neighborhood attractive to those who already live there," wrote the ADPSR. "The notion that a plan can be developed in the interest of the neighborhood without the input of the neighborhood is at best naive and at worst manipulative."[17] The ADPSR called for planning to ensure the area became a "mixed-income community that is both economically and racially diverse."[18] But Central Station involved no direct displacement, and the fate of existing area residents, who were several blocks from Central Station, would be decided by public housing policy and not the effects of the new development. Still, the city, responsible for all its citizens, had not developed a broader plan for the Near South Side and its many impoverished residents.

Over time, Central Station rode the housing boom, and a wave of high-rise construction ensued that added an entirely new community where none existed before (Figure 7.7, page 92). The coffers of the Near South TIF rapidly swelled, and an astonishing $227 million was spent from the TIF between 1996 and 2008 on infrastructure, property acquisition, developer subsidies, and public improvements, much of it ad hoc after initial plans were complete. In recent years, the TIF has been so flush that the city has tapped it to build a new CTA station in a neighboring TIF and to rebuild a high school. In 2010 the city even returned $40 million to the city treasury to help balance the budget. But with the exception of a senior housing building subsidized through the TIF, Central Station made no provision for affordable housing, a missed opportunity.[19]

Yet the growth coalition had brokered an impressive deal in the Near South area, one that transformed the area from blight to an extraordinarily productive taxpaying space in less than a decade. In 1989, deep skepticism surrounded the idea of a new Near South community, but it became the largest submarket in the Central Area in the past deacde. Planning had mattered, as Museum Campus proved catalytic. By 2010, more than 14,500 new housing units had been completed in the area, includ-

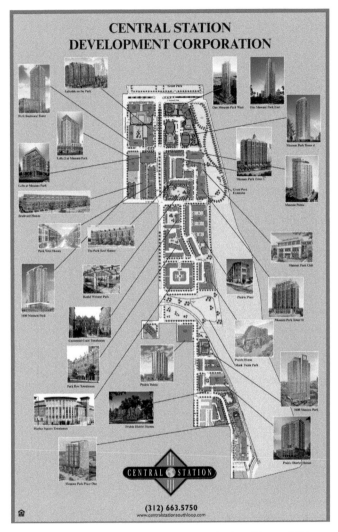

Figure 7.7. Marketing image showing developments within Central Station, 2006

ing 4,600 in Central Station.[20] The state's contribution, the city's TIF, and growth coalition and mayoral leadership had proved decisive.

Recovering railroad land and bringing residents close to downtown yielded a dramatic change to the central area, producing a more vibrant, 24-hour downtown. Fundamentally, Chicago solved the problem that had bedeviled it since the late 19th century: how to overcome the tight boundaries formed by

Figure 7.8. "Model City" on display at the Chicago Architecture Foundation, 2010

the railroads and expand the commercial downtown. Moreover, the growth coalition's choices, while not always productive or without controversy, allowed the central area to make the painful transition from a predominantly industrial economy to a largely information-based one. Along the way, there were winners and losers, successes and mistakes. But ultimately, the growth coalition preserved a substantial tax base that could be imperfectly redistributed to the city at large in the form of services and infrastructure.

Two Models

The room-sized model of the 1958 plan funded by the CAC displays a future downtown Chicago roughly doubled in size, with large new structures sprouting on all sides of the Loop. The vast expansion of high-density development contemplated by the plan is boldly illustrated, a prophecy that was eventually achieved five decades later. A 2010 model of the Loop created by the Chicago Architecture Foundation shows the prophetic nature of the plan (Figure 7.8). The defense of a compact central business district along with the attraction of residential development had paid dividends, fueled by a series of real estate booms. More than 181,000 people now live less than two miles from city hall (roughly the boundaries of the central area), living and working in the Loop and supporting a vibrant downtown.[21] Most bold city plans rarely reach this level of fruition, and the 1958 plan ranks with the 1909 plan as one that greatly influenced the vision of the city's growth.

NGE AND PLANNING RESPONSE

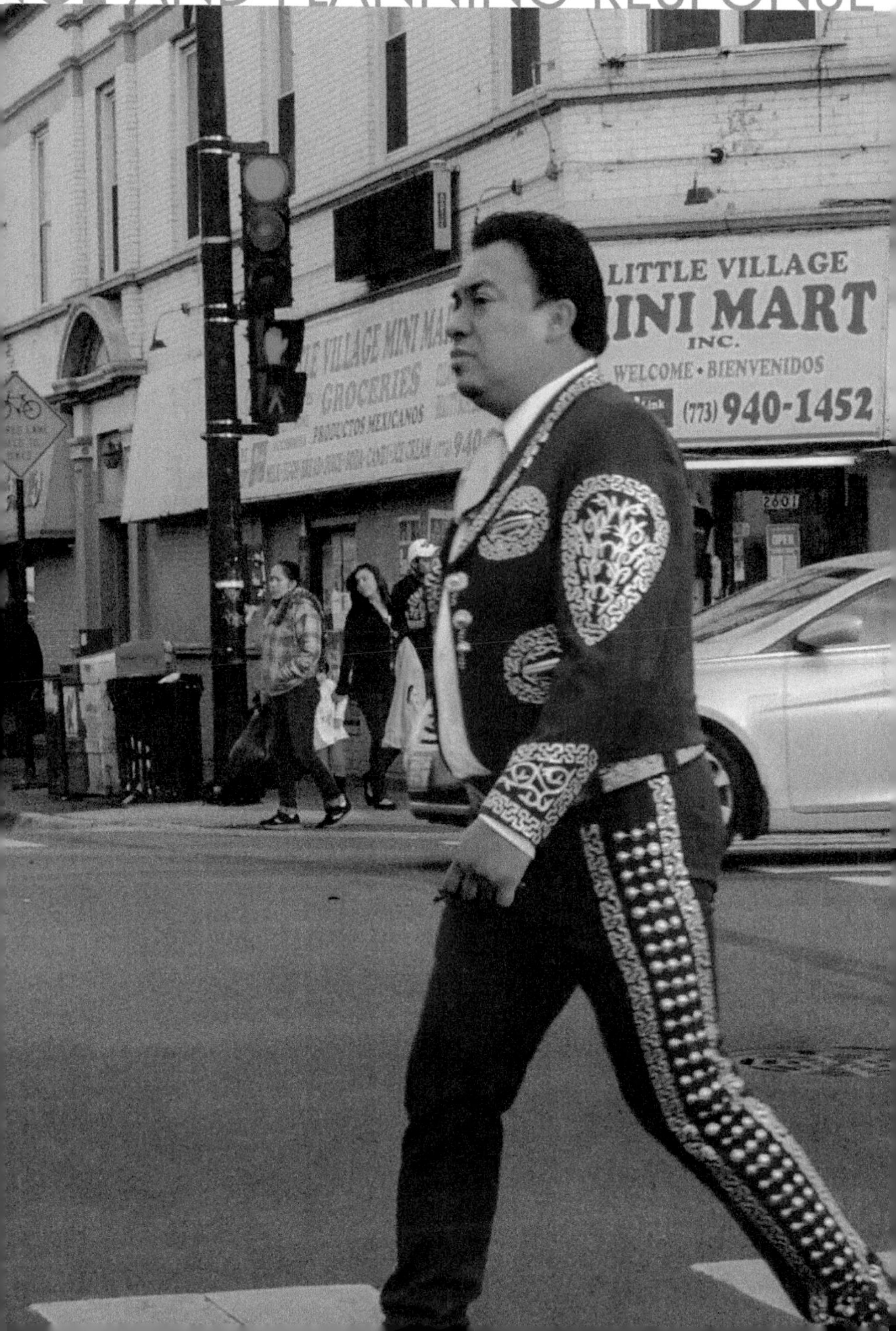

While a rift has long existed in Chicago between the needs of downtown and those of the neighborhoods, the neighborhoods are not monolithic and united. Stark race and class divides contribute to the creation and persistence of environments of extreme poverty and wealth alike. Addressing the problems of the city's low-income communities remains the city's most difficult and fundamental challenge.

Part Three covers planning efforts to rehabilitate and support the city's troubled neighborhoods. First, chapter 8 explores how planners have thought about neighborhood change in Chicago. Sociology and planning combined to use the city as a laboratory to examine neighborhood decline and test planning ideas to reverse it.

Chapters 9, 10, and 11 drill down to widely divergent communities and the planning strategies attempted in each over time. Englewood is a South Side community wrenched by a flawed urban renewal plan, racial change, depopulation, and decades of disinvestment. Its potential for recovery remains uncertain. Uptown on the North Side has a long history of community activism but remains internally divided. Political battles over affordable housing and gentrification have reached a stalemate that nonetheless preserves a surprisingly diverse community. Little Village on the Southwest Side is the city's entry point for Latinos that, until recently, has had to struggle to win the attention of city planners. Finally, chapter 12 looks at how the Chicago Housing Authority's Plan for Transformation has completely reconfigured many of the city's largest and most problematic public housing developments. This is perhaps the city's most dramatic—and most critical—community planning exercise in the past 30 years, and one fraught with controversy.

CHAPTER 8
CHICAGO AND COMMUNITY PLANNING INNOVATION

Throughout much of the 20th century, Chicago has been a space for theorizing cities, a laboratory for arresting decline, and a stage for community activism. This chapter reviews the city's innovations as well as some of its failures in community development planning, describing a range of ideas that have evolved over time into a blended approach that balances community-led planning and expert interventions.

The Chicago School and Community Conservation

The theorizing began in the 1920s and 1930s, when sociologists at the University of Chicago developed a model to describe urban change. Derived in part from ecology, the "Chicago School" posited that cites evolved naturally through a life cycle as "invasions" by successive groups resulted in the "decay" of the housing stock and the decline of neighborhoods. In turn, decaying neighborhoods led to pathologies such as juvenile delinquency and gangs, suggesting an environmental determinism whereby bad housing and slums cause social ills.[1] The Chicago School had crucial implications for planning. First, environmental determinism bolstered the Progressive-era slum clearance proposals of housing reformers; if good housing replaced bad, then social problems would abate. Public housing and urban renewal owed part of their intellectual justifications to the Chicago School. Second, for neighborhoods not yet in the grip of "blight," early signs of decay might be arrested or even reversed through planning interventions, an approach known in the 1950s as "conservation."

The city of Chicago pursued both slum clearance and conservation beginning in the late 1930s up through the 1960s, though the city is more famous for the former. Large swaths of the city's black communities were cleared for urban renewal and public housing, especially on the South Side (Figure 8.1). In 1947, the progressive and interracial South Side Planning Board hired architect Walter Gropius from Harvard and Walter Blucher of the American Society of Planning Officials to serve as consultants, and together they produced a sweeping plan for the total re-making of a three-square-mile area from 22nd to 39th streets and from South Park Boulevard (now King Drive) to the lakefront. Massive clearance and a modernist—almost Corbusian—landscape were to rise in its place. Gropius and Blucher recognized the "neighborhood unit" of planning that had guided the profession since the start of the century, with its desire to coordinate shopping, schools, and other community facilities. But the vast scope of the plan—much of it eventually realized through clearance over 30 years—created an uninspired and ultimately vacuous area with little sense of neighborhood or community.[2]

Figure 8.1. Urban renewal on Chicago's South Side, 1953. The cleared land was rebuilt with a mix of middle-income urban renewal developments and low-income public housing projects.

14

15

What has happened in these Conservation Areas?

TRAFFIC IS CONGESTED

DEPRECIATION THROUGH CONVERSIONS

OBSOLESCENCE ARE INCREASING

BUILDING TYPE ARE INHARMONIOUS

PLAY SPACE LACKING

LAND IS OVERCROWDED

CITIES ARE NEVER STATIC. THEY ARE SUBJECT TO CONSTANTLY CHANGING CONDITIONS. CERTAIN PARTS OF THEIR AREA ARE YIELDING INCREASINGLY TO PHYSICAL AND FUNCTIONAL DEPRECIATION! THIS

CHANGE IS TAKING PLACE SO GRADUALLY THAT IT IS SELDOM RECOGNIZED. FEWER COATS OF PAINT, MAKESHIFT REPAIRS, & INADEQUATE MAINTENANCE ARE CHARACTERISTIC FEATURES OF THIS TRANSFORMATION.

Figure 8.2. Pages from the Chicago Plan Commission report, "Woodlawn: A Study in Community Conservation," July 1946

Less well known, however, are the city's neighborhood conservation efforts from the 1950s through the 1970s. Conservation represented a different kind of planning from the top-down, heavy-handed variety at work in the urban renewal and public housing programs. Chicago and Baltimore pioneered the conservation idea, with both cities seeking an alternative to slum clearance for areas that were declining but not yet "blighted" in their presumed life cycles. The CPC labeled 56 square miles—nearly a quarter of the city—as needing conservation. To prevent further decline, it promoted deliberate planning in a case study of the Woodlawn neighborhood, including housing code enforcement, infrastructure upgrades, spot clearance of slums, changing traffic patterns, and even cul-de-sacs in an effort to resist the lure of the suburbs (Figure 8.2). In 1953, Illinois law approved the creation of Community Conservation Boards (appointed by the mayor) to carry out initiatives. Unlike the federal urban renewal program, however, the boards lacked a ready source of funds, and implementation of ideas lagged far behind plans.

Conservation ideas gained ground, however, as 1950s-style urban renewal projects came under criticism. In the 1960s, Chicago blended conservation strategies with urban renewal, especially in the Lincoln Park neighborhood. The Lincoln Park Community Conservation Board formed in 1955 to arrest blight and began charting the area's needs. Over a decade ideas evolved and were included in the 1966 Comprehensive Plan. By then small areas had been targeted for clearance and the construction of middle-income affordable housing. Further, the conservation board and the 1966 plan pushed for reclamation of Ogden Avenue, a diagonal boulevard included in the 1909 Plan of Chicago that plowed through the neighborhood in the 1920s. The wide avenue, largely unneeded as a traffic artery, was vacated then carefully replanned in ways that stitched the neighborhood back together before being sold to developers. These successful interventions propelled rapid gentrification in Lincoln Park.[3]

Chicago and Community Activism

Planning in Lincoln Park melded community ideas with expert planning from the city, but Chicago's long tradition of community-centered organizing tended to be wary of City Hall. Saul Alinksy (Figure 8.3) pioneered community organizing methods in the Back of the Yards neighborhood south of the stockyards beginning in 1938. He created a successful community council by overcoming the antagonisms that separated Catholic priests, labor leaders, and local merchants, even as he advocated sharp confrontation with Chicago's political machine. The Back of the Yards Council, guided by Alinsky, produced its own homegrown comprehensive program

Figure 8.3. Saul Alinsky in Chicago's Woodlawn neighborhood, February 20, 1966

that included youth activities, creation of a credit union, a newspaper, and a housing rehabilitation effort, all of it done with locally raised funds.[4]

The federal Model Cities program in the Lyndon Johnson years attempted to replicate elements of the Alinsky model, especially community-centered social programs designed with the "maximum feasible participation" of residents. In Chicago, however, Mayor Richard J. Daley sought to keep Model Cities on a tight leash, eventually centralizing control over program funds. Daley had little patience for political power outside the structure of the Democratic Party machine, and high-profile scandals—including the participation of the Blackstone Rangers street gang in the Model Cities' Community Action Program—soured local and federal officials. As such, Model Cities in Chicago became another machine-based service delivery program and not a vehicle for an independent community-based planning.[5]

The Alinsky legacy is more pronounced in the slow but steady rise of CDCs as primary vehicles for investment in low-income communities. While the CDC model emerged in New York in the 1960s, Chicago CDCs pioneered collaboration and networks, especially CANDO and the Rehab Network, both nurtured through partnerships with planners at the University of Illinois–Chicago, especially Rob Mier. Still, CDCs were often shaky operations, struggling for the capacity to influence trajectories in their communities. Economic ventures proved difficult to sustain, and many turned to housing development, which could readily attract subsidies through existing federal programs.[6]

Alinsky-like organizing by Chicago activists influenced other areas of community policy. Gail Cincotta, a West Side community activist, lobbied Congress to pass the 1977 Community Reinvestment Act (CRA) to require banks to loan in neglected neighborhoods, and then she was instrumental in transforming the law from a weak federal principle into an on-the-ground reality. Cincotta and the Woodstock Institute, a small local research organization, formed the Chicago Reinvestment Alliance, which brought together 35 active community groups. They used leverage from the CRA to pressure bank regulators—and hence banks—to invest more directly and systematically in declining Chicago neighborhoods, creating a national model.[7]

LISC and a New Model of Community Planning

Much of this new investment went to affordable housing development. Between CRA-induced private capital, state-supported Illinois Housing Development Authority (IHDA) loans, federal housing tax-credit deals, and Department of Housing and Urban Development (HUD) subsidies, CDCs

Saving Historic Pullman

The Pullman community on Chicago's far South Side is famous as a factory town constructed in the 1880s to build sleeping and parlor railcars. By 1960, much of the factory had become obsolete, and, although railcars continued to be built until 1981, the South East Chamber of Commerce recommended that a large swath be cleared for heavy industry expansion in the Calumet region. While this plan was never implemented, it served to catalyze a 50-year effort to preserve Pullman.

Residents of Pullman reacted by forming the Pullman Civic Organization (PCO), which demonstrated the viability of the neighborhood as well as the historic significance the nation's first planned industrial community. Through these efforts, the community influenced the Far South Development Area Plan (a component of the 1966 Comprehensive Plan) to call for the preservation of the Pullman residential neighborhood. Local advocacy resulted in Pullman's designation as a Landmark District by the City of Chicago, the State of Illinois, and the U.S. Department of Interior in 1972.

A year later, the Historic Pullman Foundation (HPF) was established to complement the efforts of the PCO and to broaden the support for preserving Pullman. The foundation saved threatened nonresidential buildings such as the Masonic Lodge, the Hotel Florence, and the fire-damaged shell of Market Hall. Concurrently, the city and the Chicago Park District made historically sympathetic improvements to Arcade Park and Pullman Park. With federal Urban Development Action Grant money, the HPF facilitated the adaptive reuse of a factory building into a 210-unit apartment complex. The program also stimulated the rehabilitation of original housing stock in the north part of the district (Figure 8.4). Throughout the early 1980s, CDBG funds were used for restoration projects at the Hotel Florence. Pullman had become a model for neighborhood historic preservation.

The recession of 1981–1982 closed the Pullman factory, and the entire Calumet region suffered, but preservation efforts persisted. In 1990, the Illinois Historic Preservation Agency (IHPA) purchased the factory site and the Hotel Florence. But just as the IHPA had contracted for stabilization of structures at the factory site in 1998, an arsonist set fire to several of the buildings, resulting in significant damage. The PCO and the HPF responded with a major campaign to save historic structures. The Pullman Factory Task Force formed to assess conditions and recommend a redevelopment concept for reuse as a history center and cultural tourism attraction, to be

Figure 8.4. Row houses known as the Arcade Row, built in 1881 along what is now St. Lawrence Avenue near 111th Street, Pullman neighborhood, 2009.

jointly developed by the IHPA and the National Park Service. Within a year the state appropriated $10 million for the reconstruction of the fire-damaged Clock Tower and Administration Building, while the Market Hall stabilization project received $1.2 million from the state and city. In the neighborhood, Pullman Bank started a program of residential rehabilitation using various city and federal funds to subsidize the purchase prices of housing units. Chicago Neighborhood Housing Service joined the effort, and the program has evolved into Chicago Neighborhood Initiatives.

In 2011, Pullman was designated as a Great Neighborhood in the American Planning Association's Great Places in America program, and efforts began the next year to make Pullman part of the National Park System. The effort has broad-based local and national support. With the combination of local and city cooperation, complemented by state and federal programs as well as the support of the philanthropic community, Pullman is emerging as a cornerstone in the redevelopment of the Calumet region and the far South Side of Chicago.

—Michael A. Shymanski

understandably gravitated toward housing as their primary community development tool. But building and managing low-income housing was often a challenge that swamped organizations. In 1995, three CDCs working on affordable housing went under, alarming Chicago's nonprofit world. Moreover, effort and attention on housing meant less attention to other neighborhood needs such as health care, job training, and job creation.

Concern with the stability and trajectories of CDCs led the MacArthur Foundation to fund an assessment of community development in Chicago. The Local Initiatives Support Corporation (LISC) organized the Futures Committee in 1998, consisting of neighborhood leaders from poor areas. It confirmed that poor neighborhoods needed more comprehensive community-building activities beyond simply building additional affordable housing. The committee suggested that larger and more experienced nonprofits be encouraged to partner with smaller CDCs to produce and manage housing, thereby freeing the neighborhood group to engage in a more diverse range of initiatives and improvement efforts.[8]

With MacArthur funding and LISC expertise, the two groups followed this recommendation with an ambitious New Communities Program (NCP). The NCP idea emerged from pioneering LISC efforts in the South Bronx, New York, in the 1990s that adapted 20 years of community-based planning dating back to Model Cities. LISC recognized that community planning had to be bottom-up to achieve legitimacy, but community-based planning was often too fragmented, unaccountable, and exhausting to produce high-quality results. LISC's primary innovation was to carefully blend bottom-up community participation with a strong structured planning process. That process was managed by a "lead agency," picked by LISC and often a strong CDC capable of working with other community partners. The lead agency received two funded positions—a director and an organizer—dedicated solely to the planning process.

Their job was to gain the trust of a wide range of constituent local groups—block clubs, churches, merchants, schools, and other community organizations—and walk them through a series of defined meetings to develop a Quality of Life Plan. Rather than free-flowing meetings that led nowhere, the LISC planning process laid out step-by-step meetings with specific goals (Figure 8.5). The process ensured that a broad range of community needs would be included in the plan, well beyond physical planning, among them employment, health, crime prevention, education, and community engagement. This broadened ownership of the plan, while still assigning responsibility for nurturing it to the lead agency. More-

Figure 8.5. The LISC/New Communities Program community-based planning process, from LISC's "Planning Handbook," 2003

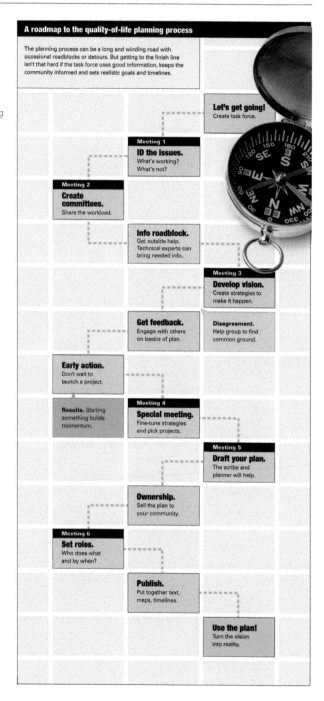

A roadmap to the quality-of-life planning process

The planning process can be a long and winding road with occasional roadblocks or detours. But getting to the finish line isn't that hard if the task force uses good information, keeps the community informed and sets realistic goals and timelines.

Let's get going!
Create task force.

Meeting 1
ID the issues.
What's working?
What's not?

Meeting 2
Create committees.
Share the workload.

Info roadblock.
Get outside help.
Technical experts can
bring needed info.

Meeting 3
Develop vision.
Create strategies to
make it happen.

Get feedback.
Engage with others
on basics of plan.

Disagreement.
Help group to find
common ground.

Early action.
Don't wait to
launch a project.

Results. Starting
something builds
momentum.

Meeting 4
Special meeting.
Fine-tune strategies
and pick projects.

Meeting 5
Draft your plan.
The scribe and
planner will help.

Ownership.
Sell the plan to
your community.

Meeting 6
Set roles.
Who does what
and by when?

Publish.
Put together text,
maps, timelines.

Use the plan!
Turn the vision
into reality.

Citizen Planning in Chicago

Citizen planning as we know it has its origins in the 1960s civil rights movement. That period saw the emergence of "advocacy" planning, in which neighborhood groups, often led by planners, sought to influence urban renewal and other top-down neighborhood plans. The federal Model Cities program of 1968 represented a major public-policy commitment to advocacy planning, as it required "maximum feasible participation" of citizens. In Chicago, however, citizen involvement was hampered by strong city control and limits placed upon public input. But Model Cities nonetheless established the essential elements of Chicago's public planning process, which continues in some form today.

In the 1970s and 1980s, advocacy groups often transitioned into economic development entities, which in turn became "delegate agencies" entrusted by the city to carry out neighborhood planning and economic development functions. These agencies became the vehicles for citizen-based neighborhood planning. However, each had its own agenda and expertise, and seldom was there any attempt at an integrated neighborhood plan.

Coordinated and focused citizen-based neighborhood planning received a boost in the mid-1990s via the federal Empowerment Zone Program, which offered substantial funds and tax credits to cities and private investors that produced comprehensive physical, social, and economic strategic plans, backed by strong public participation, for improvement of defined areas containing no more than 75 square miles and a population of 200,000. Chicago organized a committee of leading neighborhood-based planning advocates and provided them the professional assistance needed to prepare a plan that, using community input, met the program requirements. Three areas were chosen: Washington Park–Woodlawn, North Lawndale, and Pilsen–Little Village. The resulting program did provide coordinated improvement strategies, marking a major demonstration of the ability of citizen-based planners, but the program lost momentum and devolved into individual projects. The lack of a strong geographic base and the resulting competition among neighborhood groups appear to have doomed this effort.

In the late 1990s, the Local Investment Support Corporation (LISC) entered the advocacy planning fray, concluding that its investment dollars could have significant impact only if they were used in places where the root causes of poverty and endemic social conditions were addressed comprehensively and from a neighborhood-based perspective. Following a successful pilot program in the Bronx, LISC focused on Chicago, partnering with community-based "lead agencies" to develop plans. Using a strategic planning model, the lead agency established an outreach program to create community-based task forces, opened up the meetings to all interested neighborhood residents, undertook a process that comprehensively identified local issues and problems, formulated a vision for the neighborhood, and prepared strategies and projects that could be implemented by a host of neighborhood organizations, businesses, and the city. LISC has gone on to use its Chicago program as a national model. Thus, this Chicago form of citizen-based planning is now influencing comprehensive quality-of-life planning across the country.

The LISC program offers several key lessons for involving the community in planning for its future:

- Successful neighborhood planning is comprehensive.
- Neighborhood residents are good planners when professional resources are available to guide community-based visions and projects into implementable form.
- Strong neighborhood-based leadership is critical to keep the community focused on its end goals.
- Community organizers are an important component of citizen-based planning to keep people involved, as well as to assure that the process is not dominated by one group or certain personalities.
- Good citizen-based planning builds community pride.

Lessons learned from these efforts are now being put to use in the development of neighborhood plans and national programs.

—Leslie S. Pollock, FAICP

over, the process intended to build community capacity. The lead agency did not execute the plan but instead was its cheerleader, encouraging other community members and outside groups to get involved. [9] "The best way to have this program move from planning into implementation is that you have local people who are directly responsible and held account- able," LISC's Chicago director Andy Mooney told the *Chicago Tribune* in 2005. [10]

The LISC model included further innovations. LISC program officers trained, mentored, and gave technical assistance to lead agency staff, going well beyond the usual funder-patron relationship. LISC also encour- aged various lead agencies to share ideas, creating peer-to-peer learning as well as competition within the program. Most important, LISC carefully managed the communications effort, pouring resources into translating com- munity ideas into readily understandable language. LISC hired "scribes" to write up clear minutes of meetings and produce journalistic pieces for the LISC website. [11] Planners were hired to explain concepts at meetings and produce plans, drawings, and a community-friendly map. Both scribes and planners were directed to be faithful to the ideas presented in the commu- nity meeting while remaining positive in their presentation. Mooney directly managed the communications effort, insistent that the public face of LISC plans reflect community voices but also be accessible, professional, and not written in "planner-ese." [12] LISC also produced elaborate, yet clear "point- to" planning documents for each Quality of Life Plan that organizers could take to meetings to point out images to show community members and potential funders that careful thought, community input, and coordinated planning had taken place.

LISC's Chicago operation borrowed these ideas, combined them with findings from the Futures Committee, and successfully applied them on a large scale. Equally important, Mooney convinced the MacArthur Founda- tion to fund much of the effort. The first Quality of Life Plan was written for the South Chicago neighborhood in 2000. By 2006, 14 more of Chicago's most challenging neighborhoods had been named part of the NCP, includ- ing Englewood and Little Village. [13] While results so far are understandably uneven, for the first time since Model Cities and the 1966 Comprehensive Plan struggling communities have coherent plans that explain community de- sires and agendas for addressing them. Moreover, the community-centered process coupled with LISC and consultant expertise produces plans that have far greater community buy-in and understanding that those produced under the 1966 Comprehensive Plan.

The Continuing Significance of "Neighborhood Effects"

The importance of the LISC process is reinforced by the latest sociological work on neighborhood dynamics that contribute to renewal or decline. Bringing Chicago's role in the evolution of community planning ideas full circle, the city has been the site of the most extensive social-science study on neighborhoods in the country, the Project on Human Development in Chicago Neighborhoods, overseen by sociologist Robert J. Sampson. From 1994 until 2001, the project collected a massive amount of data, not just about individuals but about neighborhoods, seeking to understand the link between place and social outcomes. The data measured "neighborhood effects"—the social structures that organize life, the networks people interact with, and the strengths of local organizations. Data were compiled block by block on neighborhood characteristics ranging from land use to litter, while 343 neighborhood clusters were assessed on measures ranging from infant health to political organization. More than 8,700 Chicagoans were interviewed, and a smaller group was followed longitudinally.

Perhaps unsurprisingly to contemporary planners, Sampson found that neighborhoods' physical condition, social organizations, and institutional strengths form the crucial context in which individuals make decisions. Among the most important neighborhood measures is "collective efficacy," or the "social cohesion combined with shared expectations for social control"—namely, the willingness of neighbors to intervene and informally police their communities. Collective efficacy decreases with concentrated poverty and segregation, making it difficult for neighbors to agree on, or enforce, a set of norms. Further, Sampson also argues that organizational capacity is crucial—not just the willingness but the *ability* to intervene matters.[14] These findings align with the thinking behind LISC's NCP. Still, there is room for expanding the LISC agenda to specifically tackle not just capacity building but collective efficacy. For example, finding ways to enhance block clubs' reach, effectiveness, and perhaps training might improve collective efficacy.

More broadly, given the importance of neighborhood effects, Sampson and his colleagues argue for "community-level" interventions rather than "individual-level" ones. Topping this list is crime reduction efforts such as community policing and the work of Operation Ceasefire, which uses former gang members to intervene at the community level. Further, enhancing collective efficacy requires "increasing organizational opportunities for citizen participation in decision making" and "enhancing the legitimacy of governmental institutions that have eroded trust," such as the police. Rather than "designing escape routes" for residents to leave, we need to "repair or renew existing [social] structures."[15]

Sampson's arguments are a long way from the environmental determinism of the 1950s, which saw physical decay as directly linked to negative individual outcomes. Bad housing alone is not the issue here—it is the structure of the community, the linkages among its residents, its capacity for enforcing rules, and the strength of its institutions that matter. This is new territory for community development planning, which has made great strides in listening to residents' concerns, and improving cooperation among neighborhood groups and enhancing their capacity. But strengthening social order remains a distinct and ongoing challenge.

CHAPTER 9
ENGLEWOOD

Today Englewood is among Chicago's most severely troubled communities, suffering from high crime rates, concentrated poverty, limited economic opportunity, and a landscape with broad stretches of vacant lots. Planners from the 1950s on have sought to arrest the neighborhood's descent, but delays, incomplete implementation, and a lack of coordination have plagued the effort. Englewood has been the target of numerous postwar planning ideas, including community conservation, urban renewal, enterprise zones, TIFs, and most recently the LISC New Communities Program (NCP). Private investment and new populations, however, remain elusive.

Planners have faced an uphill battle against the historical forces that fostered Englewood's demise. The area experienced convulsive change during the peak of the Second Great Migration in the 1950s. Due to various forms of housing discrimination and the desire among whites to sustain segregation, arriving African Americans crowded into racially transitioning yet still decent housing stock on the margins of the black ghetto, in communities such as Englewood, Lawndale, and Woodlawn. Conversion of apartments, the concentration of newcomers, and housing exploitation, however, accelerated dilapidation, overcrowded the schools, and frayed the community.

Before 1950, Englewood had been largely white with significant pockets of African American residences that dated back to the 1850s. Between 1890 and 1910, transit-led development filled in most of the

Figure 9.1. Intersection of Halsted and 63rd streets, Englewood, looking north, 1955

area with Swedish, Irish, and German families, and by 1930 it was a white middle-class community of 89,000. Englewood's retail center at 63rd and Halsted streets evolved into a major regional shopping district (Figure 9.1). As Robert Bruegmann notes, "Englewood counted more retail sales than all but a handful of American cities, and it continued to be the largest retail center outside the Loop well into the postwar years, easily surpassing all the early postwar shopping centers in size."[1] This prosperity, however, had begun to fade during the Depression and 1940s, and in the postwar period Englewood business interests and Chicago planners alike were deeply concerned about stagnating sales and competition from modern shopping centers.[2]

The Perimeter Plan

Chicago planners proposed radical surgery to save Englewood's still thriving but threatened retail district. Their idea—likely the brainchild of CPC executive director Frederick T. Aschman and Real Estate Research Corp. executive Richard L. Nelson—was dubbed "The Perimeter Plan" in 1952. It involved plowing an entirely new ring road through the existing street grid to circumscribe the retail district at 63rd and Halsted, thereby directing traffic from this clogged intersection. Then "blight" behind the retail stores would be cleared to make room for parking lots. Some streets inside the

A TYPICAL SHOPPING DISTRICT AFTER REHABILITATION AND CONSERVATION
The Objectives of Rehabilitating Existing Shopping Districts should be to:
1) Provide parking.
2) Relieve traffic congestion and minimize hazards to pedestrians inside the center.
3) Eliminate non-shopping land use within the center.
4) Replace ugliness with beauty through cooperative action on redesign of signs, facades, and provisions of open space.
5) Protect adjacent neighborhoods by setting the center apart from residential areas, providing adequate trafficways into the shopping area, and providing ample parking space within the center.

Figure 9.2. The "Perimeter Plan" for Englewood's shopping district, showing ring road and interior parking lots, 1952

ring would become "pedestrian plazas" with covered walkways. In essence, the Perimeter Plan would turn an older retail junction inside out, creating a suburban-style pedestrian mall—a new concept at the time—with parking lots surrounding retail buildings (Figure 9.2). Halsted Street would carry only buses, and the elevated tracks at 63rd would bring shoppers to the core. The expectation was that older retail stores would be converted with rear entrances to accommodate the new parking lots behind them.[3] The idea received support from Victor Gruen, the premier planner of suburban malls in the mid-1950s, who later proposed a similar idea for Appleton, Wisconsin. "The main task of any corrective program should be the unscrambling of pedestrian, truck, and auto traffic. Automobile traffic has to be brought to the perimeter of the shopping area and stopped there so that a pleasant area for the pedestrians only remains," Gruen wrote.[4]

The Southtown Planning Association, formed in 1939, supported the Perimeter Plan but also hoped it would help resist racial transition. The organization had already tried to make offers on black-owned homes in Englewood and suggested the removal of Englewood's black community to

the poor black suburb of Robbins. They even offered legal advice to Robbins officials on how to obtain federal funds for a housing project.[5] Now
the association gambled that the Perimeter Plan might be attractive enough
to keep whites in Englewood.

However, converting an existing urban shopping district involved enormous costs and massive clearance; only the federal urban renewal program offered such resources. In 1956, Englewood received a "Community
Conservation Area" designation, and a series of planning studies dissected
everything from automobile traffic to racial transition. The influence of the
latter hovered over the entire enterprise, but by 1962 when the city publicly
released its plan for Englewood, no mention was made of race or the fact
that by then 69 percent of the community was African American. At the
same time, retail trade continued to erode at 63rd and Halsted, dropping
by half between 1945 and 1960.[6]

Englewood's 1965 conservation plan suggested a mix of street wid-
ening, retail consolidation, spot clearance, and "rehabilitation," as in other
parts of the city. Cleared portions would be rebuilt with modernist complexes,
financed by urban renewal funds. Owners of existing homes deemed salvageable would be encouraged to take out FHA home improvement loans to
make repairs, with the city Department of Urban Renewal undertaking "a vigorous program aimed at maximizing voluntary rehabilitation of properties."[7]

The most revealing section of the plan, however, centered on the
area's elementary schools, which experienced gross overcrowding, averaging 55 students per classroom. Unstated was the fact that elementary
schools in white areas were closer to the city's desired 35 students per
classroom, while schools in black neighborhoods labored under double
shifts to avoid 80 students in a classroom at one time.[8] Race remained an
unstated subtext to planning.

Urban renewal funds were belatedly dedicated to the project in 1963,
with little change in the planning logic.[9] By 1965, however, the Perimeter
Plan had been scaled back significantly. Instead of a complete perimeter
road, clearance was truncated into a partial perimeter, sparing the southeast quadrant. Further, the pedestrian mall was a shell of the original vision.
Covered sidewalks lined 63rd and Halsted, but the closing of interior streets
to create pedestrian arcades was never realized. When finally completed
in 1969—more than 20 years after its visualization in 1947—the new
Englewood Plaza did little to resurrect retail in the area (Figure 9.3). The effort felt incomplete, and establishments along 63rd and Halsted lacked the
resources or desire to reorient their buildings to provide convenient access

Figure 9.3. Englewood Mall, near Halsted and 63rd streets, showing the 1960s implementation of covered walkways, 2000

to the parking lots, which were far too large given the decline in retail. The combination of a half-executed plan and racial transition doomed Englewood Plaza, which suffered a slow descent, with the closing of Sears and Wieboldt's department stores in 1975.[10]

The Department of Development and Planning had placed its faith in the Perimeter Plan and conservation techniques, and its 1968 Mid-South Development Area Plan, one of the 16 follow-on plans to the 1966 Comprehensive Plan, reaffirmed this approach. The plan, however, identified other pressing problems, including overcrowding in schools, decaying housing conditions, and the lack of mental health facilities in Englewood. The plan offered the usual tools for addressing these issues—affordable housing, health clinics, light industry.[11] But as with other aspects of the 1966 Comprehensive Plan, coordination and follow through were limited. Englewood, with a conservation area and urban renewal money already had its share of resources, but a static plan that failed to recognize changing circumstances squandered them.

Development Without a Plan

Two decades of painful decline followed, with meager planning energy in Englewood. Larger structural forces overwhelmed the community, ranging from deindustrialization to housing abandonment to drugs (Figure 9.4, page 116). By 1987, the shopping center was near collapse. A report commis-

Figure 9.4. Boarded-up apartment building, 6400 block of S. Stewart Street, Englewood, November 28, 2012

sioned by the Department of Planning found that the mall attracts only "the lowest incomes and those with the least purchasing power." Most residents, the study revealed, patronized nearby shopping malls. The CTA elevated station at 63rd and Halsted was labeled "one of the worst" in the system, not helping matters.[12] That year, the area's alderman successfully petitioned to reopen 63rd and Halsted streets to traffic, effectively ending the Perimeter Plan. Some stores claimed a 20 percent jump in sales as a result.[13]

As Englewood decayed and depopulated, the city's response was an aggressive demolition of abandoned buildings, a move supported by many in the community who connected these properties with crime. The neighborhood lost 30 percent of its housing stock between 1980 and 2000, and its population plummeted from 97,000 in 1960 to 40,000 in 2000. Demolitions surged again in 1998 after the horrific rape and murder of an 11-year-old girl, whose body was found in a vacant lot.

This gruesome story and media attention to Englewood's dismal conditions likely spurred Mayor Richard M. Daley to action. In November 1999, he announced $256 million in investments in Englewood, including a new $150 million campus for Kennedy-King Community College at

Figure 9.5. Englewood looking east along 63rd Street, showing Kennedy-King Community College surrounding the rebuilt CTA train station, October 10, 2008

63rd and Halsted to replace the last remnants of the old shopping center (Figure 9.5). The surviving merchants would relocate to a new shopping center two blocks north. A police station, a library branch, and 400 affordable housing units were also announced. Funding came from community college bonding authority and a TIF district, created in 2001. At a press conference at Antioch Baptist Church, which ran the most important CDC in Englewood, Daley told the crowd, "We have seen the studies. We have seen the reports. What we are announcing today is a commitment to a neighborhood." Missing from Daley's announcement was a larger plan or acknowledgment of a planning process. No Department of Planning and Development study existed that examined Englewood's needs and where investment might be best targeted or prioritized. Most of all, there had been no community input beyond consultation with the alderman.

While not making a planning argument, critics soon questioned the new community college campus. The "old" Kennedy-King structure, less than a mile away, had been built only 27 years earlier, and estimates for its rehabilitation were $15 million. But Daley saw a new campus as another project, something that could be an achievement of his administration and that would end the blight at 63rd and Halsted. The new campus was expected to anchor growth, bring hope, and help rebuild a key intersection (Figure 9.6). A careful planning process might have affirmed this

Figure 9.6. Halsted and 63rd streets in Englewood, looking northeast, with Kennedy-King campus buildings visible, June 30, 2007

choice, but the city was being reactive rather than deliberate, enamored with physical rebuilding rather than weighing strategic investments. In the end, the Kennedy-King campus is attractive, is sensitive to its surroundings, and includes a new culinary institute, an important training opportunity for entry into a growing sector. But it is not an indicator of careful planning.

Similarly, the Englewood TIF has a redevelopment plan that is unobjectionable but underdeveloped, though it has more detail than most TIF plans. Its objectives seem reasonable: assemble sites for infill housing, add to the supply of affordable housing, enhance the neighborhood appearance, bring in light industry. But little thought is given to prioritizing and targeting resources. For example, what types of housing are needed—family, senior, supportive? How should the community balance affordable and market rate housing? What criteria should be used for funding infrastructure with the TIF rather than with existing resources? Policies and priorities are scarce because in Chicago TIFs are prized for their flexibility, not their plans. (See chapter 20.)

Englewood's Quality of Life Plan

In 2004, LISC selected Englewood for its NCP. But it struggled to find a lead agency to partner with and, in an unusual move, created a new organization, Team Englewood, in collaboration with a hospital, church, and a bank. By LISC's own admission, Team Englewood "got off to a slow start because it lacked a broad base of support and many community stakeholders did not clearly understand its purpose." LISC then found Wanda White-Gills, a talented organizer and director, to begin the 18-month "structured community planning process" with more than 600 residents participating in working groups, a planning task force, and a youth summit—the largest community participation of any NCP area.[14]

The resulting Quality of Life Plan, finished in December 2005, is an impressive document—the most nuanced, comprehensive, and creative in Englewood's history. Far more than the TIF plan, it lays out a vision for the future and strategies for getting there that are holistic and not focused simply on the built environment. Job strategies are first priority, with specific recommendations for helping residents train for health care, automotive, and urban agriculture work. Urban farming is a prominent strategy that crosses several goals: job creation, health, and land use. Improving police relations and reintegrating ex-offenders are prioritized as well. For each strategy, specific partnerships, approaches, and agendas are established. For example: "We will work with businesses and institutions to develop paid, year-round internship opportunities that expose youth to professional services, skilled trades and successful entrepreneurs in and outside the neighborhood."

Even in the built environment, the plan is innovative. It lays out policy recommendations to guide planning for vacant lots, many of them city-owned, noting that "Englewood has an opportunity to become a leader in creative and thoughtful reuse of vacant land. The best use for vacant lots depends on where they are located, how many are on a particular block and what types of uses are nearby." Vacant lots "sandwiched between adjacent homes should generally be conveyed to one of the adjacent homeowners for additional yard space." But two to four contiguous vacant lots "could be used for business purposes, community gardens or residential 'infill' development." Those near schools could be added to playgrounds; larger collections for "production scale housing."

Residents also asked to reestablish a new downtown called Englewood Center on an extensive vacant tract once part of the Perimeter Plan and now opposite Kennedy-King. A grocery store, a post office, retail, and a park are imagined, along with seating areas and performance space to create a community-centered environment (Figure 9.7, page 120). To help residents envision the possibilities, professional planners produced drawings, which are included in the plan.[15]

Figure 9.7. Sketch of proposed Englewood Center for vacant land on northwest corner of 63rd and Halsted streets, from Team Englewood's Quality of Life Plan, 2005

With the collapse of the housing market, these pretty pictures may not come to life anytime soon. At the time of the plan, subprime lending and easy credit were luring many residents into poor financial choices, and after 2007 foreclosures hammered the community. The plan is not starry-eyed, however, and acknowledges that the inventory of vacant land "represents a huge challenge. With more than 700 acres to fill, it could take 50 years to reclaim it all" (Figure 9.8).[16] But equally important, it strives to diversify economically, expecting that new housing development will not be entirely or even largely affordable. Deconcentrating poverty, then, is an implicit—though not explicit—goal of the plan. Englewood in 2000 already ranked fourth out of Chicago's 77 community areas in the supply of affordable housing and had high levels of poverty—39 percent of family households lived in poverty, fifth highest among the city's 77 community areas.[17]

The next step is implementation, with Team Englewood pushing, encouraging, and facilitating the plan. Per the LISC strategy, however, Team Englewood is not a lone agency trying to solve all of Englewood's problems. Yet community capacity in Englewood is weak. Antioch Baptist Church, which had utilized federal funds to build a considerable amount of housing, is

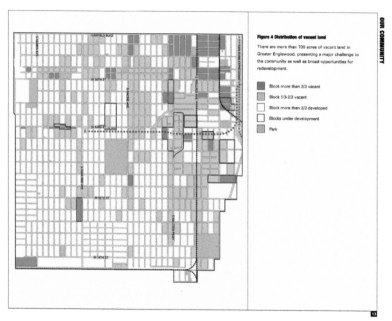

Figure 9.8. Vacant land in Englewood, from Team Englewood's Quality-of-Life Plan, 2005

perhaps the strongest community organization. At the neighborhood level, Englewood in 2010 had fewer block clubs than similar low-income African American neighborhoods.[18]

Further, Englewood's ability to attract private residential investment remains uncertain. Achieving at least some income mix is essential. Yet when Rebirth Englewood, a new CDC chartered by Congressman Bobby Rush and led by former congressional aide Vincent Barnes, proposed an ambitious housing program, the community pushed back. The plan included 550 units for a mix of incomes ranging in cost from $165,000 to $365,000, an enormous range for the struggling community that had gone nearly untouched by new private development during the housing boom. But John Paul Jones, leader of a local community group, told the *Chicago Tribune*, "Rebirth for who? Those who stuck with Englewood through all those bad times are losing out."[19] Barnes acknowledged that revitalization could make the neighborhood unaffordable, but he argued that "we want to make sure that individuals in the community presently are part of that development process . . . that they benefit from it."[20] This tension remains: Englewood wants new housing and new investment, and it desperately needs more people, but the community remains fearful of change.

Despite the enormity of its challenges, Englewood finally has a plan. It is ambitious, forward looking, and optimistic. It represents a strong community-planning process and has actionable goals. The plan came not from the city but from a careful process, and an argument could be made that the LISC process works precisely *because* the city is not heavily involved. But it would be a mistake to think that government is the problem here and that only nonprofits with deep funding are capable of intervening and partnering and following through. It is not difficult to imagine the city replicating this structured planning process. While intensive, and perhaps at times costly, this kind of planning is essential for achieving buy-in, ownership, and a sense of purpose for neighborhoods across the city.

CHAPTER 10
UPTOWN

The Uptown community is situated along Chicago's North Side lakefront, generally a zone of white affluence. But for the past five decades, Uptown has been a contested space, chiefly because it has served as an entry point for migrants, first low-income southern whites and later a racially diverse group of immigrants. Since the mid-1950s, the area has experienced the full range of postwar planning tools, including early conservation programs, urban renewal, Model Cities, "advocacy planning," affordable housing, CDCs, and TIFs. Unlike Englewood, where racial transition marked a seminal turning point, Uptown's planning conflict has been more about class than race, played out as an intense battle over gentrification. Property-owning whites resist concentrations of affordable housing and fight perceived social disorder; activist descendants of the 1960s New Left view upscale private development as an attack on the poor and an effort to homogenize the community.

Decades of conflict have produced a stalemate and perhaps an equilibrium: Gentrification has not overwhelmed the poor, nor have significant concentrations of poverty, affordable housing, and social service agencies led the community to a "tipping point." Uptown's trajectory does not fit with traditional patterns of urban change. Instead, urban policies have produced an imperfect and at times incomplete version of what equity planners call "development without displacement." Perhaps ironically, a high degree of conflict over planning has produced Chicago's most diverse community,

Figure 10.1. Uptown, Broadway, 1960

with extraordinary ranges of ethnicity, race, and income. That this outcome has not engendered more positive feeling among residents gives insight into how difficult it is to socially engineer a diverse yet harmonious community.

Figure 10.2. Uptown, Broadway, November 28, 2012

Uptown Tries Conservation

Like Englewood, Uptown's initial period of urban growth took place between 1890 and 1920, as developers built dense apartment houses and a substantial retail and office district. Banks and two national insurance companies established headquarters in multistory office buildings at major intersections, while large ballrooms and movie houses signaled the community's middle-class status. Neighborhood change—though not racial change—arrived during World War II, when a severe housing shortage encouraged landlords to convert large six-flat apartments into as many as 24 and even 30 one-room apartments. Uptown's density of small apartments—many for short-term rent—attracted new arrivals, and word-of-mouth led to a chain migration of white southerners looking for work. By the 1950s, Uptown elites expressed concern about the assimilation of "Appalachians" into urban living, deriding their "transient housing," frequent moves, and living habits as a "blight."[1] A 1957 report that found that "the southern white migrant did not join any churches, added to the problems of the schools, could not be reached, and generally seemed to contribute to the social disorganization of the area."[2]

Uptown elites organized and sought planning tools—both physical and social—to restrain these class changes. In 1955, they formed the Uptown Chicago Commission (UCC) under the leadership of community bankers, insurance executives, and prominent citizens including Ruth Bach, wife of Richard J. Daley's soon-to-be-named head of planning. Class concerns dominated the UCC's work in the late 1950s. In 1958, the UCC sought city funds to pay for a pilot project to "study and develop techniques" to "speed up the assimilation of rural newcomers into urban areas" and "stabilize the areas into which these newcomers move."[3] This earnest effort did not receive funding from the city's conservation program in the face of other priorities, and services remained scarce for newcomers in Uptown until the late 1960s.

The UCC also pushed for physical improvement in Uptown, targeting owners of buildings with poor maintenance that were "amendable to rehabilitation" through code enforcement and deconversion. Between 1956 and 1958, the UCC made Uptown "the scene of one of the most intensive campaigns of code enforcement in the city," according to the commission, and the city filed 101 court cases against owners in 1958 alone, though judges were more interested in "encouraging owners to make repairs" than fining them. Yet by the end of that year the UCC was unsatisfied with its effort, calling it "essentially a negative program." Enforcement brought properties to minimum standards but did not "ensure high standards of management." Moreover, it "encourages owners to postpone compliance until they are caught." For their part, owners complained that repairs and upgrades rarely resulted in higher rents. The UCC concluded that code enforcement would be a "necessary but not sufficient" part of neighborhood conservation.[4]

The UCC clamored for more planning powers, especially the tools and resources of the federal urban renewal program. Yet between 1957 and 1966, Mayor Daley's Department of Urban Renewal placed higher priority on stabilizing neighborhoods threatened with racial change, including Hyde Park, Woodlawn, and, to a lesser extent, Lincoln Park, though only Hyde Park had a stronger, better-connected planning commission than Uptown.[5]

In an effort to move up the city's urban renewal list, the UCC hired prominent planner Jack Meltzer, who had guided Hyde Park's effort. Meltzer's 1962 plan for Uptown mirrored his earlier work, suggesting small clearance sites to make way for middle-income housing as well as several small parks, street closures, cul-de-sacs, and pedestrian walkways, all in the service of upgrading Uptown's physical amenities in order to attract new, higher-income residents.[6] The Meltzer Plan represented the height of conservation planning thinking in the early 1960s, avoiding the tabula rasa clearance of the early 1950s but embracing limited strikes on "blight" in an effort to spur private investment and self-sustaining gentrification.

The Meltzer Plan edged Uptown higher on the priority list, and in 1966 the Department of Development and Planning began preliminary studies in advance of an application for federal aid. A year later, the city designated Uptown as one of four Model Cities areas, and in 1968 it sent to Washington an urban renewal plan that closely followed Meltzer's ideas, which was approved by federal officials a year later.

The People's Planning Campaign

The UCC had finally attracted attention and resources, but then the political ground in Uptown shifted dramatically. First, Uptown's poor had diversified. While white southerners were still more than half the community, significant populations of Latinos, American Indians, and African Americans had arrived. Second, youthful leaders of the New Left, including Todd Gitlin and Nancy Hollander from the Students for a Democratic Society (SDS), moved to Uptown in 1966 to build bridges between student radicals and the white working poor. Within a few years, multiracial, community-based radical groups including Jobs or Income Now and Voice of the People loudly protested the UCC's authority to plan community change.[7]

The Model Cities process—intended to address Uptown's social needs—had a rocky start in 1968. Richard J. Daley ignored the radicals and appointed mostly UCC members to the community boards overseeing the efforts. Still, the board conceded that "the voice of the Uptown community . . . is severely limited" by the lack of representation on the Model City board by "poor Southerners, Negro, Spanish-Speaking people, and American Indians." Moreover, four public forums "were hastily called, inadequately promoted, and poorly attended."[8] Nevertheless, Model Cities money attracted an array of social service agencies to Uptown, supporting a poor clientele that the UCC no longer had much interest in uplifting.

In urban renewal, the UCC's efforts to clear the area's worst housing met even stronger resistance. Eleven neighborhood groups joined in December 1968 to form the Uptown Area People's Planning Coalition to influence the plan. Uptown residents Rodney and Sidney Wright, he an architect and she a planner, facilitated a resident-led planning process funded by the Community Renewal Society, itself supported by the Ford Foundation. Several principles emerged from the sessions: plans should not displace residents, demolition should be kept to a minimum, and cooperative and nonprofit ownership structures should be instituted to keep rents

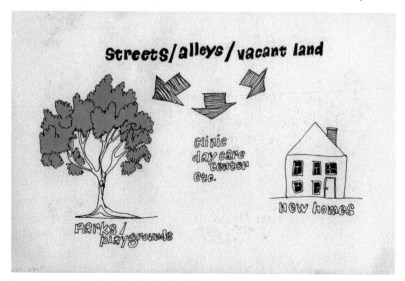

Figure 10.3. Selection from "Neighborhood and Community Planning," a citizen's planning guide produced by Rodney and Sidney Wright, 1971

low. A "town hall" with a "welcome center" would embrace newcomers; racial integration was also a commitment.[9]

The centerpiece of the People's Planning Coalition proposal was Hank Williams Village, named after the country music star, for a site scheduled for limited clearance under urban renewal. The village would close off streets, turn alleys into green space, and build parks on vacant lots. Other priorities involved calming traffic and making the area pedestrian and family friendly. Renovation, infill housing, and at least one tower for elderly residents were planned. The Wrights spent a good deal of time listening to Uptown residents and explaining concepts of land use in readily comprehensible ways. A year later, they gathered their ideas into an informal guide entitled "Neighborhood and Community Planning" (Figure 10.3).[10] Like LISC's approach with NCP, the Wrights served as scribes and planners for a community-based process, translating resident concerns into a viable plan.

The Wrights' physical planning was hardly radical. The city's professionals had included similar suggestions in the 1966 Comprehensive Plan. But Hank Williams Village did envision using federal programs in nontraditional ways, including building cooperatively owned apartments for rent and offering affordable condominium ownership to low-income families, all backed by federally insured mortgage programs.[11]

The UCC, which for 15 years had been the civic-minded voice of the community's property owners, resented the People's Planning Council's opposition to its plans for clearance and renewal. Urania Damofle, a UCC leader, wrote to a supporter in March 1970: "The Coalition is only a paper organization. . . . They attempt to create divisiveness in a community by playing the 'haves' against the 'have-nots.'"[12] Damofle was also chair of the Uptown Community Conservation Council, the mayor-appointed body with the power to make recommendations to the city's urban renewal program. Damofle and the UCC-stacked council rejected Hank Williams Village that year on the flimsy ground that it lacked an FHA commitment and instead pressed forward with the UCC vision of clearing 13 acres of Uptown's blighted, transient housing to make way for a community college campus.

The People's Planning Coalition did not fade away, and the fight surrounding what became Truman Community College marked the beginning of a long war in Uptown over community development policy, displacement, and gentrification. To Uptown's middle-class property owners, clearance, upgrading, and the establishment of new middle-class institutions like colleges were essential to stopping a downward slide and to "saving Uptown." To the People's Planning Coalition, clearance for the campus would unnecessarily displace 4,000 people (a high estimate) by destroying salvageable buildings.[13] More important, the coalition's alternative narrative of community ownership and programming for the poor—including community health clinics, welcome centers, halfway houses, and nursing homes—clashed sharply with the UCC's desire to attract new middle-class residents. Uptown already had more than its fair share of poor people, the UCC maintained, and the coalition's projects would merely attract more. Despite numerous protests and political twists and turns, the community college moved forward in 1971 on a shrunken site (displacing roughly 1,000 people) using urban renewal money.[14]

The Gentrification Debate in Uptown

The competing visions of the UCC and the descendants of the People's Planning Coalition have endured in the clash over Uptown development. The UCC evolved by the 1980s into a group of mostly white, middle-class professionals and home owners who accepted ethnic diversity but who wanted market-based gentrification to bring needed improvement to Uptown. They argued that excessive numbers of social service agencies, shabby retail districts, and vacant lots contributed to social disorder; only middle-class home owners could fill the vacant lots and provide the buying power needed to attract new retail. Since Uptown had enough facilities and organizations to aid the poor, additional services should be established in other white neighborhoods not doing their fair share.[15]

Figure 10.4. Slim Coleman, 1985

At the same time, activist supporters of the poor also evolved, and with greater political success. DePaul University political scientist Larry Bennett calls the inheritors of Uptown's 1960s New Left the "Coleman-Shiller movement," named after Walter "Slim" Coleman (Figure 10.4), a community activist with experience in the SDS, the Student Nonviolent Coordinating Committee, and the Black Panther Party, and Helen Shiller (Figure 10.5), a left-wing activist who later served as alderman of the 46th Ward from 1987 to 2011. Both worked for Harold Washington's campaign in 1983 after a decade as leaders of the Heart of Uptown coalition, formed in 1972.[16] Coleman-Shiller allies expanded social services for Uptown's poor in the 1970s and 1980s, forming the Uptown People's Health Clinic, the Uptown People's Law Center, and the Uptown People's Community Center, effectively branding their movement's social and political agenda. Most important, they battled for affordable housing and development without displacement, carrying on the work of the People's Planning Coalition. Coleman linked the planning and political agendas in 1983, telling a reporter: "We're interested in keeping poor people together as a power base. When you scatter people into isolated pockets, they remain powerless. If we can stay in Uptown long enough to empower the people, then we can do the same thing here that the Irish did in Bridgeport."[17] Nonprofit groups and service agencies were the base of the Coleman-Shiller movement's po-

Figure 10.5. Alderman Helen Shiller, 1987

litical organization. Resisting gentrification became the movement's central agenda and the key to its survival.

The movement faced an uphill campaign in the 1970s to stabilize Uptown's housing stock while avoiding gentrification. Some slumlords deliberately ran down properties, but most landlords struggled due to low market rents, rising energy costs, high turnover, and, at times, the destructiveness of tenants. In this context, it made sense for building owners to sell to developers who viewed Uptown as continually "on the brink" of large-scale gentrification. Over three decades, many of Uptown's buildings were rehabilitated and converted back into six-flats then sold as condos.[18] The Coleman-Shiller movement was up against a relentless market.

Yet Uptown never fully gentrified like other similar neighborhoods, including Lakeview, Bucktown, and Wicker Park. The Coleman-Shiller forces found new tools to resist, including a long, drawn-out lawsuit. In 1976, activists sued the city and a prominent developer on behalf of low-income residents displaced from an apartment hotel to make way for a luxury residential and commercial complex called Pensacola Place. After 14 years, the developer settled by accepting 50 Section 8 residents in the project. The suit against the city continued, but a proposed consent decree in 1981 for 600 new units of affordable housing was scuttled by protests from UCC members, who argued that too much affordable housing would tip the neighborhood into inevitable decline.

The lawsuit came close to settlement in 1987 when the Harold Washington administration proposed creating a land bank for city-owned vacant lots in Uptown. The land bank would be managed by a new Uptown Community Development Corporation, which would also receive financing to build additional low-income housing. But soon after Washington's death in November of that year, the city council voted down the idea. Eventually, the Coleman-Shiller forces won only a small cash settlement and some scattered site public housing.[19] Yet the antigentrification message of the lawsuit was clear, and the effect was to slow the pace—but never completely stop—private redevelopment.

These tactics were not what preserved Uptown's diversity in the long run. Instead, the construction of large amounts of privately owned, publicly subsidized affordable housing, financed by various HUD loan guarantees and subsidies (Section 221(d)(3), Section 235, and Section 8) ultimately allowed a significant number of poor to remain in Uptown and limited the reach of gentrification. Between 1965 and 1967, developers erected nine large, high-rise subsidized buildings in Uptown with 2,300 apartments. By

1976, total subsidized housing in Uptown reached 4,400 units—more than 15 percent of the community.[20] These were not public housing projects, though their sterile designs often made them readily stigmatized. Much depended on the level of subsidy, with modest Section 221(d)(3) loan guarantees labeled "middle-income" projects. More deeply subsidized Section 8 New Construction developments, however, often concentrated poor tenants much like public housing. Most of these buildings were located east of Sheridan Road, close to the lakefront, on land purchased through Uptown's urban renewal effort. Yet the unfinished nature of that plan resulted in an erratic built environment, with high rises occasionally located midblock and overwhelming surrounding walk-up buildings. As Larry Bennett notes, the human and physical landscape resulting from urban renewal "in no way corresponded with the UCC's desire to renovate existing buildings, reduce traffic, and de-concentrate the population." Concentration of poverty and inadequate maintenance meant many of the subsidized high rises soon "became home to the kind of intensive social pathology usually associated with public housing."[21] The UCC had begged for urban renewal in the 1960s, but the construction of large-scale subsidized housing did not produce the kind of "upgrading" they had hoped for.

The clash over Uptown priorities shifted in the late 1980s and 1990s when these affordable housing developments proved vulnerable. Building owners threatened to opt out of the federal programs and displace most residents. Coleman-Shiller allies organized a task force, rallied residents, and pressured HUD to "preserve" the properties, through additional incentives to owners either to remain in affordable housing programs or to sell to nonprofit corporations. One Uptown CDC, Voice of the People, agreed to take over a 499-unit subsidized building to keep it low income. Most of Uptown's largest subsidized buildings were preserved with additional HUD subsidies, a significant victory for the Coleman-Shiller movement and a defeat for UCC leaders, who argued that Uptown needed to shrink its affordable housing supply.

Wilson Yards

In 2000, a large proposed TIF in Uptown brought planning back to the forefront and revived the gentrification wars on new territory. The TIF came in the middle of the housing boom that abetted a slow but relentless conversion of Uptown buildings into condominiums. Vacant lots also became new housing for increasingly ethnically diverse professionals. When subsidies were available, nonprofit CDC housing continued to be built, though at nowhere near the pace of private investment. By the end of the boom in 2007, few vacant parcels were left for redevelopment.

The main purpose of the TIF was to develop the last large available site in Uptown, the six-acre CTA's Wilson Yards, an obsolete rail facility. But Shiller's independent stance as an alderman had made her persona non grata in the mayor's office, and she struggled to control the TIF. At the public hearing to establish the TIF in November 2000, consultant Steve Friedman, working on behalf of the Department of Planning and Development, made the unusual move of amending the original submission and downgraded a previous commitment to affordable housing, saying only the plan "could" rather than "will" include subsidized units, a revision that pleased the UCC.[22] Shiller did not gain control of the TIF until 2003, when, in a deal with Mayor Richard M. Daley, she agreed to no longer be a thorn in the his side at city council meetings. (She had routinely been the sole opposition to many of the mayor's proposals, including his budgets.) In return, Daley would stop supporting her opponents in elections and give her greater influence over the Uptown TIF. Critics called it a sellout, but Shiller was desperate to control the most important planning tool for Uptown since urban renewal.[23]

The community planning process had produced calls for a mixed use plan involving big-box retailer Target, a multiplex theatre, an Aldi (discount) grocery store, and a blend of market-rate and affordable housing. The movie theater fell through and Aldi moved north, leaving the Target—a clear nod to the demands of middle-class home owners. But Shiller changed the plans for the housing component. Instead of a mix, all the housing would be affordable, including 99 units of senior housing and 84 units of family housing. The project would be developed by the well-regarded Peter Holsten, whose early work on the CHA's Plan for Transformation had won much praise.[24]

The shift enraged home owner groups, which invoked fears that the subsidized units would become "another Cabrini" (Figure 10.6, page 134). Holsten had helped redevelop parts of Cabrini, but his new mixed income properties were entirely different than the public housing of old. Nevertheless, a "Fix Wilson Yards" group formed and filed a lawsuit, accusing the city of abusing TIF law, especially the "but for" requirement that without the TIF, the development would not happen. The group contended that development of the site could easily happen without a TIF. The lawsuit was thrown out—state law was simply too vague to enforce the "but for" clause, which some thought the city abused so regularly that this case was not special anyway.[25]

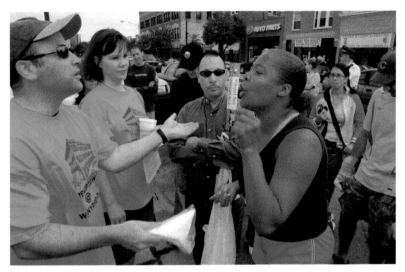

Figure 10.6. Uptown home owners protesting the concentration of affordable housing units in the proposed Wilson Yards development

After 12 years of negotiation, several lawsuits, and 18 layers of financing, the $151 million Wilson Yards project opened in March 2010 with not only the Target and the affordable housing but also a 400-space parking garage and 25,000 square feet of other retail (Figure 10.7).[26] Managed by the experienced Holsten, the project has become an asset to the community and an example of the positive possibilities for affordable housing development.

In Uptown, planning has been highly politicized. The Coleman-Shiller forces fought strategically and creatively to resist gentrification where possible, using the courts, HUD policy, and, after 1987, Shiller's aldermanic privilege to deny zoning changes. Uptown's nonprofit social service agencies received support though city grants and CDBG funds. Gentrifiers fought back, asking—not unreasonably but at times crudely—whether the community had excessive amounts of affordable housing that might be better distributed around the city. But this divide meant that little community planning—either top-down or bottom-up—took place between 1980 and 2000. Small scale neighborhood improvements—vest-pocket parks, street closings, pedestrian access, park improvements—occurred in the 1960s and 1970s under urban renewal, but modern planning concepts for improving streetscapes, encouraging transit-oriented development, and histor-

Figure 10.7. Wilson Yards development, with affordable housing in foreground and Target at far right, 2011

ic preservation could not take hold. Shiller did pursue the usual aldermanic tools at her disposal through the capital budget, including alley repairs, speed bumps, and stoplights—but broader livability questions fell victim to gentrification fears.

Shiller retired in 2009, and the current alderman, James Cappleman, has sided with the anti-Shiller forces. He is actively working for more social order in Uptown, a goal that, if managed through careful community organizing, would be positive. But Uptown today remains the most diverse of Chicago's neighborhoods, an entry point for immigrants from Africa and Asia, an intense blending of culture, making consensus on social order highly challenging. Given its badly divided politics, it is difficult to imagine a LISC Quality of Life planning process going smoothly in Uptown. Yet the effort would be worth it to begin to arrive at a compromise, or at least a truce, in this unnecessarily divided community.

CHAPTER 11
LITTLE VILLAGE

The Little Village neighborhood is an entirely different planning case than either Englewood or Uptown. Its story is neither raw urban decline nor gentrification-induced conflict. Instead, Little Village has been shaped by high levels of immigration, as the community has been a major entry point for Mexican newcomers since the 1970s. Overcrowding has been a fundamental problem, one that planning and public action should be well equipped to address. More housing, parks, schools and other public spaces are badly needed. Yet until recently, the area has been relatively untouched by planning and has seen limited public investment.

This began to change only during the past decade, as confrontational community-based action belatedly commanded the attention of the city's power structure and secured amenities from schools to parks to better air quality. Little Village is a cautionary example of how community power and historical timing matter in the trajectories of Chicago's neighborhoods. Equally important, Little Village shows the importance of population flows to neighborhood health. Immigration may create overcrowding and demands on services, but it has saved Little Village, allowing it to avoid the downward spiral of depopulation, disinvestment, and decline that has battered other Chicago communities.

Immigration Saves South Lawndale
Located on the western edge of the city, Little Village transitioned slowly during the 1960s and 1970s from a first- and second-generation Eastern

European community (called "South Lawndale" by University of Chicago sociologists in the 1930s) into a predominantly Mexican American one. Unlike in Englewood, succession did not involve significant white resistance. Whereas business interests and property owners in Englewood and Uptown sought to use planning tools in the 1950s to defend the class and race status of their communities, South Lawndale whites did not organize in the late 1960s as Mexican Americans from nearby Pilsen moved in seeking better housing. The transition from South Lawndale to Little Village—largely complete by 1980—occurred relatively peacefully, and without it, South Lawndale would have steadily eroded. Between 1930 and 1960, before the arrival of Latinos, the total population dropped 21 percent.[1] The Mexican Americans filled a growing void.

After 1980, accelerating migration from Mexico began to strain the built environment. As the population of Little Village jumped from 63,000 in 1970 to 91,000 in 2000 (a 44 percent increase), the number of housing units rose by only four percent. Not surprisingly, the proportion of overcrowded units nearly tripled to 36 percent, the highest rate in the city. Still, the community did not spin out of control, in part because of the nature of its housing stock. In Little Village, small buildings with four units or fewer accounted for 87.5 percent of all structures; in Uptown the comparable figure was only 12.2 percent, as most apartments were in large, multistory buildings.[2] Little Village's 19th-century bungalows and early 20th-century two- and three-flat buildings allowed owner-occupiers to rent to family members and otherwise police their rental properties. A steady stream of migrants and rental income meant that housing abandonment was rare, unlike in Englewood and Uptown. Even after the collapse of the real estate market in 2007, Little Village had far fewer boarded-up buildings or vacant lots than other low-income communities.

Despite intense overcrowding, the daunting problems of poverty, and the belated development of communitywide organizations, Little Village achieved a community cohesion lacking elsewhere in Chicago. Clear geographic boundaries helped. A welcoming arch marks the eastern edge of the community, while other boundaries to the north (a rail line) and south and west (industrial corridors) create an unusually clear spatial definition. A thriving retail corridor along 26th Street serves as a central market for Latinos across the city and even many suburbs. In 1997, the *Wall Street Journal* vaguely claimed that the street was second only to Michigan Avenue in terms of "business volume" in the

Figure 11.1. Little Village, December 2, 2012

city.[3] A yearly parade fosters civic pride, as do large, colorful murals. With only some exaggeration, community boosters claim that *La Villita* is the "retail, residential and cultural capital of the Mexican Midwest."[4] Sociologist Eric Klinenberg, studying community responses to a debilitating heat wave in 1995, found that Little Village's strong bonds, dense population, and cultural affinities resulted in fewer deaths than in other poor Chicago neighborhoods. By contrast, adjacent North Lawndale's African American residents experienced high mortality rates, as fear of crime and weak social networks meant the vulnerable elderly were far less likely to seek the help of neighbors during the crisis.[5]

Yet planning had little to do with these outcomes. Throughout the transition into Little Village, the area saw scant public investment to ameliorate the effects of growth, in large part because politicians and planners in the late 1960s and early 1970s were focused on the black-white divide; Latino migration received limited attention from planners or City Hall. The 1966 Comprehensive Plan merely recommended "effective code enforcement," "new community facilities," and more parkland, and action on those fronts was slight.[6] At a time when the city was hemorrhaging whites and deindustrialization was decimating black areas, Little Village's relative strengths meant it was mainly left to its own devices.

Figure 11.2. 26th Street, Little Village, December 2, 2012

Latino Politics and Community Action

Municipal inaction in Little Village can also be attributed to its political weakness. Little Village was not the center of Latino politics in the 1980s or 1990s, when prominent leaders emerged from Mexican and Puerto Rican areas of longer standing, including South Chicago, Pilsen, and Humboldt Park.[7] Not until 1986 (following a court-ordered redistricting to reverse a discriminatory ward map) did Little Village's 22nd Ward elect its first Latino, Jesus Garcia, an ally of Harold Washington.[8] But Washington's death a year later led to a fracturing of Latino politics. Independents such as Garcia and his successor Ricardo Munoz split from the United Neighborhood Organization (UNO), the city's largest Latino political coalition, after UNO moved away from its insurgent origins and aligned itself with Mayor Richard M. Daley in 1991.[9]

In 1998, Garcia lost his State Senate seat to a UNO candidate and decided to invigorate the fledgling Little Village Community Development Corporation (LVCDC) as a voice for progressive community planning. A major issue soon emerged over development plans for a large vacant tract, formerly an industrial park, on the western edge of the community. Developers proposed 400,000 square feet of new retail in a shopping area with plenty of parking, presenting a potential threat to 26th Street's 473 small establishments and their 750,000 square feet of commercial and retail space. Consultants to the Department of Planning and Development suggested allowing the new shopping area to go forward "only if reasonable assurances are given that the type of uses to be provided would not adversely impact 26th Street, the cultural, economic, social, and historic heart of Little Village." They suggested "protective covenants" between the city and the developer to allow only "tenants not now found in the community or nearby." The consultants recommended defending 26th Street with a plan for streetscaping, additional parking, and "eliminating incompatible uses" (i.e. single-family homes).[10]

To shape the plan, Garcia's nascent LVCDC and Alderman Munoz launched a community planning process for the site. The resulting 2003 TIF plan proposed a balance of 350,000 square feet of "retail, service, and entertainment uses," new housing (market rate and affordable), and soccer fields. Justifying the new retail, the plan argues that "while day-to-day goods and Mexican-oriented services are readily available, the neighborhood lacks other modern shopping and entertainment amenities, such as major retail outlets, chain department stores, a movie theater, coffee shops, American and other ethnic restaurants and full-service grocery stores." Continued negotiations between LVCDC, the alderman, and the city produced a PD ordinance for the site, a community benefits agreement, and a revised TIF in 2008. Then the housing market crashed, a recession hit, and plans were abandoned. The site remains vacant.[11]

Figure 11.3. Manuel Perez Jr. Plaza along 26th Street, Little Village, May 14, 2012

Figure 11.4. Mural in Little Village Lawndale High School Campus, commemorating the struggle to build the school, 2011

While physical planning stalled, Little Village's greatest capacity gains surfaced from within. Beginning in 2000, Little Village residents organized vigorous public campaigns for community improvement (Figure 11.3). These involved demands for a new high school, a new park, and the closure of two nearby coal-fired electric power plants. In each case, residents took on the city's establishment, conducted community-based planning, and increased their own organizational capacity. These campaigns allowed Little Village to move beyond its social and political isolation and directly influence its built environment.

Overcrowding in the schools proved the trigger to unite Little Village residents in community action. While the school board had expanded five local elementary schools in the 1980s and 1990s, the lack of a new high school was a glaring concern. Little Village's 4,000 high school students were crammed into one overcrowded school on the community's eastern edge, with many other area students scattered by bus to neighboring communities. In 1998, Chicago Public Schools (CPS) announced it would build three new high schools, including one for Little Village, but by 2000 only Little Village High School remained unbuilt. Cost overruns at

the other two schools plus budgetary needs elsewhere had siphoned off the funds. In May 2001, Little Village mothers, supported by the LVCDC, waged an extraordinary 19-day hunger strike, galvanizing the community and generating much publicity (Figure 11.4). Three months after the strike, new CPS superintendent Arne Duncan, sensing the political power of the neighborhood in a city now 26 percent Latino, reallocated money to build the high school.

The dramatic community organizing empowered the female leaders of the strike, and their efforts continued as planning for the school moved forward. New hurdles soon emerged. In 2002, Duncan and Chicago school reformers introduced Renaissance 2010, a plan that required all new schools to open as charter schools, "contract" schools (operated by independent companies or nonprofits), or "performance" schools, with school success tied to specific metrics. Little Village feared "Ren 10" would diminish community input. After numerous meetings, Duncan agreed to exempt the new Little Village High School from Ren 10; it would function under the "small school" reform of the 1990s. The new building would, from the start, be divided into four themed high schools.[12] Little Village residents had an exceptional amount of

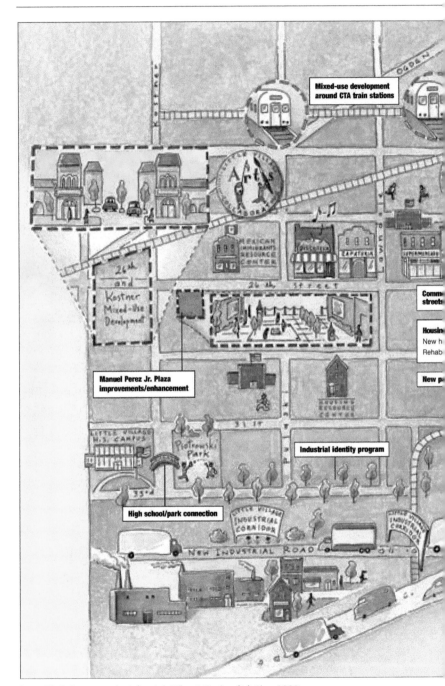

Figure 11.5. Community sketch from Little Village's Quality of Life Plan, 2005

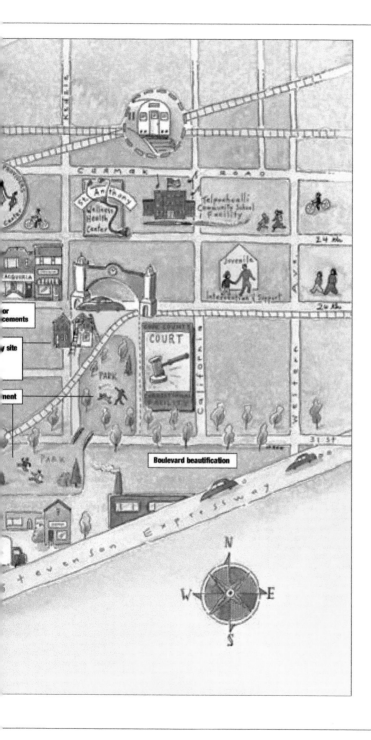

input into not only the educational structure but also the physical design of the school, working closely with the architect in a lengthy process. The resulting $63 million school (costly by CPS standards) opened as a monument to the community's organizing efforts and collaboration.

The struggle over the school had produced a better outcome, not only in physical design but also in terms of capacity building and community engagement. As Jesus Garcia explained, "If the high school had come easily, it would have been just another cookie-cutter Chicago Public School." Instead, the community went through a "journey about public education" and wrestled with curriculum, design, and mission, "ending up with a better result."[13] The community's sense of victory was tempered by policies they could not influence, namely a federal desegregation consent decree. Per the decree, boundaries for the new school included portions of neighboring North Lawndale's African American population to achieve racial balance. Other parts of Little Village were not in the school boundary, and four hunger strikers discovered their children would not be able to attend the new school. Resentment ran high; a state senator placed a nonbinding referendum on the ballot to require redrawing the school boundaries. While race and class tensions remained significant, 55 percent of Little Village voters rejected the referendum and embraced a multicultural school. Still, the episode demonstrates the difficulty of balancing community control with larger social goals.

Little Village's Quality of Life Plan

During the battle over the high school, the LVCDC emerged as a viable community voice, and soon LISC tapped it to be the lead agency in developing a Quality of Life Plan under the NCP. LVCDC helped lead the planning process to produce a realistic set of priorities for the community. The top priority was more park space. Little Village had the second-lowest ratio of open space to residents among Chicago's 77 community areas, with only 61 acres of green space for more than 91,000 residents.[14] The community's largest park offered a mere 23 acres (four square blocks) in the southwest corner of Little Village. Six schoolyards and five other small playlots bore the brunt of community demand for open space. "Most children play on the streets and sidewalks in front of their houses or in parking lots," the Quality of Life Plan explained.[15]

The plan advanced two possibilities for a new park, both in the southeastern corner of the community: a 24-acre Superfund site (a former asphalt factory) and a 26-acre tract in the Little Village Industrial Corridor (Figure

Figure 11.6. Little Village resident Martha Castillon, a supporter of a new park, stands near the capped and now elevated Celotex site, November 24, 2010

11.5). Neither was desirable from a planning standpoint, and both lacked clear connections to residential areas. The Superfund site sat adjacent to the Cook County jail and would require costly U.S. Environmental Protection Agency (EPA) remediation; the industrial corridor area was surrounded by railroad tracks and also offered inhospitable surroundings. But few other options appeared feasible.

Other community voices became decisive in pushing the Superfund site, despite the LVCDC's misgivings. The Little Village Environmental Justice Organization (LVEJO), formed in 1994 by residents concerned about toxicity levels at a neighborhood school, joined the fray. Borrowing tactics from other environmental justice organizations, LVEJO led "toxic tours" of Little Village's Superfund sites, brownfields, chemical plants, freeways, and other hazards.[16]

Practicing a more assertive politics than the LVCDC, the LVEJO pushed the EPA to clean up the site and then demanded the city purchase it for the park (Figure 11.6). The EPA, however, chose to remediate the site by capping it with a layer of clay and gravel rather than removing the contaminated soil, leaving some residents skeptical that the site could ever be safe.[17] Equally important, the cap raised the site six feet, creating an unfortunate pedestal effect with steep boundaries. The EPA finished its work in February 2010, and the city settled an eminent

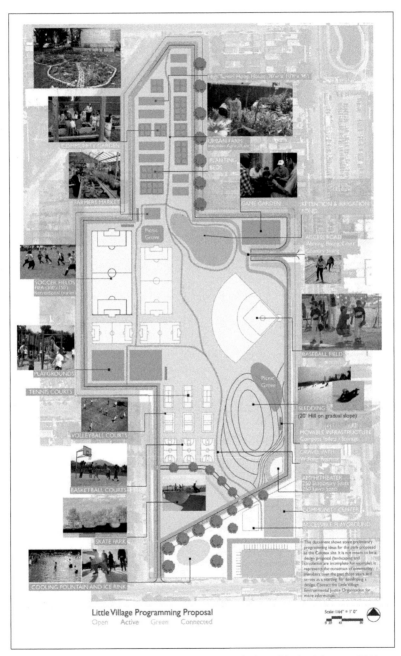

Figure 11.7. Little Village Environmental Justice Organization, plan for park for the Celotex site, 2011

domain suit in 2011, paying $8 million for the site, with the intention of using it for a park.[18]

Despite the numerous drawbacks to the site, the LVEJO proceeded in partnership with the Art Institute of Chicago and the architecture firm Perkins + Will to undertake a six-month community planning process complete with design charrettes to examine options and to help the community visualize a park. The community hoped for not only a community center, soccer fields, and basketball courts but also space for an amphitheater. The LVEJO also suggested selling a northern portion of the site to a neighborhood nonprofit land trust to create an urban farm and community garden. The LVEJO presented its concept plan for the park to the Chicago Park District in 2011, and a year later the mayor announced a scaled-down version of the plan with an $8 million price tag; construction was scheduled to begin in March 2013.[19]

The LVEJO achieved greater success in its campaign against air pollution. The "toxic tours" included stops at the two coal-burning power plants flanking Little Village on its eastern and western edges, by far the area's worst polluters. Protests, activism, and new federal regulations on the issue eventually led to a recent agreement to close both the Fiske and Crawford power plants by 2013.[20] The decade-long campaign represented a remarkable turnaround, and while the LVEJO was not the only organization

Figure 11.8. Little Village arch, 26th Street, decorated for Halloween

calling for reform, its community roots gave the issue greater salience and political force.

By 2012, community activism had emerged as a potent power in shaping Little Village. Still, the recent recession hit the area hard, with many foreclosures and, for the first time in the recent memory of longtime leaders, vacancies have appeared on 26th Street.[21] Even so, the community retains a vibrancy that has been both its strength and a source of its public neglect. The city has not worried about Little Village in the way it has about other neighborhoods. Affordable housing resources have gone elsewhere, and even TIF, a force across the city, has had minimal impact in Little Village. Community organizations like the LVCDC (now called Enlace), and LVEJO have filled a planning void.

Equally important, the Little Village story makes it clear that population flows matter, as they always have in cities. The community's thriving retail sector and neatly maintained (if overcrowded) residences resulted from a steady inflow of newcomers who spurred demand and, in the process, preserved housing from abandonment. Mexican immigrants, in essence, saved South Lawndale by turning it into Little Village and, in the process, helped save Chicago. Like generations of immigrants before them, they occupied houses, paid taxes, and sustained the built environment.

Little Village's long-term health remains an open question. Its status as the gateway for Mexican immigrants is likely to change in the next decades; the pipeline of immigration effectively stopped after 2008 due to a dramatic decline in construction work, and Little Village's total population declined slightly in the 2010 census. This might be beneficial, as the saturated community simply could not absorb more immigrants in its existing housing stock, so a slight shrinking of population will address overcrowding issues. But the longer-run concern of leaders like Jesus Garcia is a "brain drain": "There is a constant outflow of people we've invested in. . . . Can we keep professionals in the community?" In many ways Little Village is facing the flip side of problems confronting Englewood (how do we bring back middle-class families?) or Uptown (how do we avoid complete gentrification and displacement?). As in most communities, the obvious answers involve better housing options, better schools, and expanded community amenities. The Quality of Life Plan offers a road map, but resources both public and private will remain difficult to find.

CHAPTER 12

REMAKING PUBLIC HOUSING: THE CHICAGO HOUSING AUTHORITY'S PLAN FOR TRANSFORMATION

The boldest, most contentious, and perhaps most important community planning exercise undertaken in Chicago in the past decade involves its public housing program. The Chicago Housing Authority's Plan for Transformation, initiated in 1999, combines a massive exercise in physical planning with a broad effort at socializing the poor to middle-class norms. More than $1.5 billion has been spent to demolish high-rise public housing projects containing thousands of the city's poorest residents and, in their places, to construct entirely new "mixed-income" communities, an expenditure of resources not seen since Lyndon Johnson's War on Poverty. The plan has proven controversial, seen by its supporters as a desperately needed and ultimately successful reform of a failed policy and by its detractors as state-sponsored "urban cleansing."

A fairer appraisal lies somewhere in between. The disastrous projects of the past needed to be replaced, presenting an immense challenge to the city. While most public housing residents are better off under the Plan for Transformation than without it, change has been wrenching in part due to inadequate planning. Thousands of public housing families were hastily sent into the private market with housing vouchers, many without adequate support. Buildings came down before redevelopment plans had been carefully negotiated. The lack of consensus on policy and limited patience with resident input led to protracted litigation. Moreover, the mixed income model is still a work in progress, and many of its expected benefits for former public housing residents are not likely to materialize. Officials have been determined not to repeat the mistakes of the past, but the long-term success of the new model remains uncertain.

The CHA Spirals Downward

By the early 1990s, Chicago's largest public housing projects had become some of the worst places in the nation to live. The drug trade dominated the underground economy and wreaked havoc on community life. Violence was endemic, as youths entered gangs for protection and then fell into the criminal justice system. Residents often banded together and formed tight-knit bonds just to survive "project living," as they called it. The Census Bureau found extreme levels of concentrated poverty: 18 of the 100 poorest census tracts in the nation in 1989 were in Chicago public housing developments.[1]

Numerous policy, planning, and political choices created these outcomes. During the 1940s and 1950s, planners in Chicago and Washington, D.C., cleared slums to make way for enormous projects of 2,000

Figure 12.1. The Robert Brooks Homes, mid-renovation, March 2, 1999. The buildings to the left are complete, while once-identical buildings to the right await renovation.

to 3,600 apartments each. Nearly all were located in African American areas, as reformers wanted to rebuild the worst housing conditions while white aldermen insisted on maintaining the city's racial divides. Steep land costs forced high-rise buildings, which, in turn, were programmed for large families with many children (who had the greatest difficulty finding housing in the private market). These parameters housed unprecedented densities of youth in fragile elevator buildings, creating extraordinary social control problems. Working-class families fled in the 1960s, chased out by social disorder, inadequate maintenance, and rents that rose with wage gains—another counterproductive policy.[2]

By 1974, the CHA buildings had become the city's housing of last resort, and a downward spiral ensued. Rental income eroded, energy costs crushed housing authority budgets, and federal subsidies proved insufficient. Housing authorities began abandoning apartments, unable or unwilling to renovate them. Squatters moved in, gangs took over some buildings, and efforts by police to regain control through "sweeps" of entire buildings

frayed community relations. By the 1980s, physically and symbolically, the city's largest projects had become "humanitarian disasters." Public housing residents organized in desperate efforts to gain control of their communities, but the fight was entirely uphill against limited resources, federal policies, and heavy bureaucracy.[3]

Decades of ideas for fixing public housing had made only a small dent in the problem. Until the Plan for Transformation, reform in Chicago centered on issues of race. In 1966, American Civil Liberties Union lawyers initiated what became known as the *Gautreaux* litigation, accusing the CHA of racism in its site selection and rental practices. The resulting judgments gave reformers a partial victory, and to this day *Gautreaux* lawyers play a court-mandated role in public housing policy in Chicago. From the start, they favored racial integration as the primary objective. When new public housing construction in white neighborhoods and suburban areas could not be achieved through the courts, they pushed to use HUD's housing voucher program to move 5,000 carefully selected public housing families to "opportunity areas" mainly in Chicago's suburbs, with modestly positive results.[4]

But moving families out of public housing could not address the dismal conditions that still remained. After nearly two decades of organizational disarray, HUD in 1995 ordered a federal takeover of the CHA. Experienced administrator Joseph Shuldiner arrived from Washington to put the CHA's financial house in order and to begin the difficult task of seeking resident buy-in to redevelopment. Distrust was high, given decades of promises that had failed to materialize. Shuldiner recognized many buildings would have to come down—a Congress-mandated "viability test" in 1996 all but ensured it—but the replacement communities needed careful planning, with tenant input.[5]

The Path to a Mixed-Income Model

Several models existed for public housing revitalization, and the CHA itself had engaged in a range of efforts. Olander Homes, consisting of two 15-story towers built in the 1950s on the South Side, was renovated into Lake Parc Place in 1993 and retenanted with a combination of former residents and working-class families with higher incomes. The results were heralded by planners and residents alike.[6] Similarly, the low-rise Robert Brooks Homes built in 1943 on the Near West Side received a makeover in 1998 with new architectural amenities to disguise the blandness of wartime architecture. Unlike Lake Parc Homes, the renovated Brooks development remained completely low income.

Figure 12.2. Henry Horner Homes undergoing redevelopment into the mixed-income Villages of West Haven, 1998

More significantly, the reconstruction of the Henry Horner Homes on the West Side evolved into a mixed-income model for large projects (Figure 12.2). In 1991, the Henry Horner Mothers Guild sued the CHA, fed up with poor maintenance and the "de facto demolition" of abandoned apartments. A series of consent decrees between 1995 and 1999 agreed to demolish the project but offered residents a range of options: move into newly built town houses on-site, relocate into infill scattered-site units nearby, or accept vouchers to enter the private housing market. Relocation, demolition, and rebuilding were phased over time to minimize displacement.

But as the decrees were being negotiated, federal policy shifted. The federal HOPE VI program, initiated in 1992 to encourage public housing renovation, was overhauled by the Clinton administration to become a flexible incubator for public-private partnerships. Mindy Turbov, a former HUD administrator, explained the new Hope VI's basic rationale: "The idea was to use public housing funds to leverage additional public and private capital, and then employ those greater resources to break up the large public housing sites and build new mixed-income developments that fit into the fabric of the neighborhood." Congress responded positively and made redevelopment easier in 1998 by repealing the requirement that any public housing unit demolished be replaced (known as the "one-for-one" rule).[7]

Both changes undermined resident leaders in negotiations and strengthened the hands of the CHA and *Gautreaux* lawyers who wanted to avoid reconcentrating poverty in rebuilt developments. In phase II of the Horner reconstruction, negotiated in 1998, the proportion of units for public housing families was limited to one-third. While all of the former residents seeking to stay at Horner found a home in the new community, an important precedent had been set for mixing incomes, a choice that would necessarily limit the amount of on-site rebuilding of housing for low-income families in future redevelopments.[8]

The mixed-income model was further hammered out during contentious negotiations at Cabrini-Green from 1996 to 2000. Cabrini, an infamous collection of high rises and some row houses, sat in the middle of gentrifying areas on the near north side and had long been coveted by developers. In 1996, the CHA and city proposed demolishing eight out of 23 high-rise buildings (1,324 apartments) to build a mixed-income community with 30 percent of units for public housing families, 20 percent for working-class families, and 50 percent for market-rate buyers, a mix borrowed from an early Hope VI project in Atlanta (Figures 12.3 and 12.4). An infusion of other city money would build a new school, police station, library, park, and community center.[9]

But Cabrini's resident leadership called the move "the land grab that the residents have been in fear of for years" and filed suit. In 1998 they negotiated a consent decree with the CHA that kept the proposed mix but increased the number of public housing units to 895 (with the additional units off-site) and added protections for existing residents. More important, the decree gave the Cabrini-Green Local Advisory Council, the elected tenant body, a 51 percent stake in the redevelopment partnership—essentially veto power. *Gautreaux* lawyers, however, balked at the deal and intervened in federal court to stop it. They said the deal gave residents too much power, and a judge agreed, forcing residents to back down and accept a revised deal in 2000 that reduced the number of public housing units and removed their veto power. The episode revealed to the city and developers the potential power of tenants and the need to contain it. To residents, it reinforced their ultimate fear that their concerns would be listened to, but not heard.[10]

The Plan for Transformation Takes Shape

In 1999, HUD handed the CHA back to the city, and Mayor Daley appointed new administrators who aggressively accelerated the mixed-income model begun at Horner and refined at Cabrini-Green.

Figure 12.3. Portion of Cabrini-Green, May 5, 1992

Figure 12.4. Portion of Cabrini-Green, July 1, 2010

Homeless in Chicago

After the 1981–1982 recession and economic restructuring hollowed out Chicago's manufacturing sector, few were prepared for the dramatic increase in the number of destitute poor. Panhandlers and street vendors frequented public facilities and street corners, and growing numbers of people slept in parks, on trains, on heating grates, and in other public spaces. The city increased the number of emergency shelters in the 1980s, and the philanthropic community stepped up support for social services. But people entering homelessness too often fell outside the safety net.

Plans have evolved to cope with this reality. The 1987 McKinney Act, which provided federal grants for dealing with the homeless, was reformed in 1994 to require communities to organize a "Continuum of Care" plan for addressing the range of homelessness. Early versions emphasized coordination of services to help the homeless achieve social and economic stability so they could eventually "graduate" to permanent housing.

After a decade of only modest achievement with this formula, however, focus shifted on two fronts. First, prevention of homelessness took center stage, with programs to help at-risk families stay in their current housing. Second, a "housing first" strategy centered on the "chronically" homeless, as research had revealed that about 10 percent of all homeless absorbed about half of expenditures. Placing the chronically homeless in permanent supportive housing with "wraparound" services became a priority.

This new approach was cemented in the nationally recognized *Plan to End Homelessness* (2003). The plan was crafted by the Chicago Continuum of Care (founded in 2001 by funders, advocates, and government agencies), which merged in 2006 with the Partnership to End Homelessness (founded in 1999 by 90 social service providers) to create the Chicago Alliance to End Homelessness, bringing organizational focus to a fractured community. Mayor Daley supported the plan, and the city's Low Income Housing Trust Fund and other grants have increased the number of permanent supportive housing units while decreasing the need for shelters (Figure 12.5).

Research has found that the expansion of permanent supportive housing has been more successful than the previous shelter system.[16] Still, the on-street homeless population was relatively stable from 2005 to 2011 at around 1,700. A revised plan, crafted in an inclusive process and released in August 2012, argues for a 29 percent increase in permanent supportive housing (1,972 units) and an enhanced crisis-response program for at-risk people.

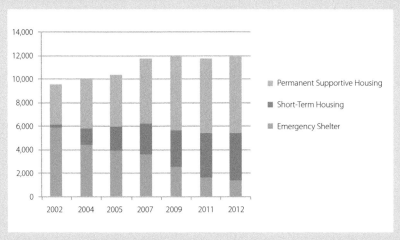

Figure 12.5. Housing to aid the homeless in Chicago, by program type, 2002–2012, from "Chicago's Plan 2.0: A Home for Everyone," August 2012

Homelessness persists, but the ambitious effort to end homelessness in Chicago set important precedents for coping with the complex and shifting dimensions of urban poverty. A collaborative and purposeful effort among public, nonprofit, and for-profit agencies can work in tackling a tough social problem. But the primary safety net for destitute adults remains doubling up. Ending homelessness will require major improvements in inner city neighborhoods, which in turn requires acknowledging the role that persistent racial segregation plays in concentrating low-income households in places with few assets and many problems.

The city also needs to reduce the impediments to building and preserving high-density Single Resident Occupancy (SRO)-type apartments. More than a century ago, Chicago's private sector built hundreds of diverse high-density hotels and apartment buildings to minimally house tens of thousands of very low-income people. Modern SROs—with units that range from 150 square-foot sleeping rooms to 400 square-foot studios—in accessible, nonsegregated, and nonimpoverished locations could ensure safe and secure quarters for the single poor, but this will require amending zoning and building code restrictions that currently outlaw such use. Such units would expand the diversity of dwellings and allow the nonpoor to take advantage of cheap rental units, thereby displacing the stigma now attached to SROs.

—Charles Hoch

In September, the CHA released a draft Plan for Transformation and finalized it three months later, despite the objections of resident leaders. It called for replacing most of the city's elevator buildings (housing more than 8,000 families) with new mixed-income communities. Senior projects, scattered site units, and other family low-rise projects would be renovated. In all, the Plan for Transformation envisioned the CHA overseeing almost 25,000 new and renovated public housing units (15,300 for families, and 9,400 for seniors) by 2010. This figure roughly matched the number of units occupied by public housing leaseholders on October 1, 1999.[11] Critics, however, noted that the CHA at the time owned a total of 38,700 units (29,300 for families, nearly half of which were vacant), meaning the plan contemplated a net loss of well over 13,000 "hard units" from the potential public housing inventory.[12]

But the Plan for Transformation was about more than housing units and, at its heart, represented an effort to bury the failures of its haunted past. In terms of design, the plan embraced new urbanism to make developments indistinguishable from the city's vernacular. Similarly, the mixed-income strategy intended to blend residents into the urban fabric. In operations, the CHA fired its entire maintenance staff and contracted out management to private firms. Finally, the CHA pushed reforming the tenants themselves. A "service connector" program sought to link residents with existing city social services, while strict rules, including drug tests and work requirements, were imposed. The CHA was convinced it needed wholesale reform and a hard line on tenants to avoid returning to the conditions of the past.

In scale and scope, the Plan for Transformation was staggering, and the likelihood of it getting off the ground appeared tenuous at first. But two endorsements saved it. First, the Clinton administration embraced the plan within a month, issuing waivers for numerous federal rules with only minor modifications. More important, HUD agreed to fund the plan with a 10-year commitment worth $1.5 billion, despite uncertain future congressional appropriations. An unorthodox yet viable funding plan was in place.

Second, the city's most important philanthropy, the MacArthur Foundation, did a 180-degree turn on the issue of public housing and backed the plan. Before 2000, MacArthur had funded the resident-led Coalition to Protect Public Housing, the chief critic of the CHA. But MacArthur's new president, Jonathan Fanton, lobbied by Daley officials but also convinced of the plan's necessity, announced that MacArthur would now throw its weight behind the plan and defund the coalition. MacArthur would eventually pour millions into the Plan for Transformation, funding capacity building, research

Figure 12.6. Marketing sign at Oakwood Shores, the mixed-income community that replaced the Ida B. Wells Homes, October 13, 2011

building, and other projects to guide and support its success.[13] The political winds had shifted, and the city's political, business, and philanthropic communities—as well as the *Gautreaux* lawyers—were on board to support a radical restructuring of the CHA. Public housing residents vociferously objected to no avail, and skirmishes moved to a narrow project-by-project negotiation, often waged in federal court.

Implementation

Resident participation was expected by federal officials, and the Plan for Transformation included provision for "working groups" of residents, politicians, and stakeholders to plan for redevelopment. At Cabrini, the consent decree negotiated in 2000 allotted $400,000 for residents to hire planners to assist them in negotiations. As at most projects, the Cabrini Working Group fought for years over proposals to reshape the community, even as demolition proceeded apace. How to accomplish the "mix" became the crucial battleground. Developers wanted town houses reserved only for market-rate buyers to enhance their marketability, leaving proposed mid-rise buildings for working-class families and former public housing residents. The residents, however, demanded that the mix be total, with public housing residents scattered throughout, on every floor of the mid rises and in every row of town houses. Eventually the residents won that fight, a significant concession.[14]

While contentious working groups were often the norm, the more critical relocation did not go smoothly, especially the task of moving roughly 1,200 families per year out of the high rises. Relocation offered a chance for an "opportunity move" to areas with employment possibilities, lower crime, and better schools, as *Gautreaux* lawyers had accomplished in the 1990s. But haste in demolition and limited relocation resources meant the effort quickly became chaotic and badly managed. Most residents were given little counseling and were shunted to poor neighborhoods, triggering slightly higher crime rates than would otherwise have been expected in the "receiving" communities. Others began a game of musical chairs with short stays in projects slated for demolition. A 2003 lawsuit by public interest lawyers, settled in 2005, forced much-needed reforms that improved relocation practices considerably, but by then a great deal of damage had been done.[15]

The service connector program proved equally disappointing. The effort to improve social service delivery put the CHA on the front lines of addressing poverty, a difficult challenge for any organization. But again, haste and inadequate resources led to ineffective planning. Caseloads for counselors were three times higher than in successful models. An investigation by a former U.S. district attorney found the service connector "grossly understaffed and underfunded" and that it did "not come close to accomplishing" its goals. The CHA called in the MacArthur Foundation for help, leading to reforms and finally an overhaul in 2008. Budget resources belatedly grew, rising from $6 million in 2002 to $30 million by 2008, and by 2009 the new "FamilyWorks" program served 10,000 families with reasonable caseloads. A five-year effort helped 5,800 residents find jobs, a remarkable achievement.[17] Still, the long gestation of the service aspect of the plan meant another lost opportunity.

Results

The limited research on the experiences of public housing residents suggests that most are better off than before, a relatively low threshold but an undeniable step in the right direction. Susan Popkin and a team from the Urban Institute (funded by the MacArthur Foundation) have followed a sample of 198 public housing residents from one development over 10 years. Of the sample, only five percent made it into a mixed-income community, while more than half received vouchers and the remainder live in renovated public housing developments. The researchers conclude that "most families in our study are living in considerably better circumstances," reporting higher-quality housing, lower crime rates, and less anxiety. They note this outcome is "far more positive than many observers—including ourselves—would have predicted at the outset."[18]

Popkin is quick to point out that deprivation persists. Most families remain in high poverty in predominantly African American neighborhoods and suffer poor health, with mortality rates that are "shockingly high." Still, she argues that significant gains have been made: "There is no question that, regardless of where they live, CHA relocatees' quality of life has improved dramatically. The CHA's transformation efforts have achieved the goal of making sure that CHA families no longer have to endure deplorable housing conditions and constant fear from living with overwhelming levels of violent crime and disorder. The fact that significant challenges remain does not undermine the magnitude of this achievement."[19]

But proponents of the mixed-income model had hoped for even larger benefits, believing that the values and experiences of middle-class residents would somehow "rub off" on public housing residents. Proximity was expected to result in several gains, including: increased opportunities for jobs ("network effects"), stronger community cohesion ("collective efficacy"), role-modeling of middle-class norms ("behavioral effects"), and better city services due to a more responsive government ("political economy of place").[20]

Careful research on Chicago's mixed-income communities by Mark Joseph and Robert Chaskin has raised doubts about many of these ideas. The benefits of proximity have not materialized, as interactions are weak between relocated public housing residents and market-rate owners, and socialization is limited. Moreover, public housing residents feel stigmatized by their market-rate neighbors, and low-level social conflict is frequent. Tensions arise over community rules and who gets to make them, especially on contentious issues such as the use of public space and drug testing policies. More quotidian concerns also create friction, including noise and the behavior of unsupervised children. Issues of class and at times race simmer beneath the surface. Still, as with Popkin's research, former public housing residents in the new communities are generally happy with their surroundings and have higher aspirations and lower stress. Even if proximity benefits have not materialized, plenty of gains remain.[21]

The housing market crash of 2007 slowed much of the Plan for Transformation to a crawl. Federal funds remained available to build public housing and working-class units, but the CHA and *Gautreaux* parties feared this would skew the mix unless the market-rate units (paid for by developers)

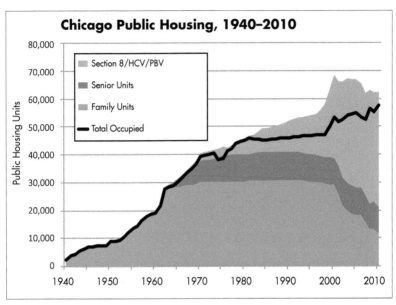

Figure 12.7. Chicago's deeply subsidized public housing stock, 1938–2011. Data from Lawrence J.
Vale and Yonah Freemark

moved forward as well. As a result, the CHA stretched the 10-year plan to 15, and as of 2012, it says it is 85 percent of the way to its goal of producing 25,000 units. Still, the plan has evolved, as the CHA has backed away from earlier commitments to rehabilitate older low-rise developments, despite success with this approach.[22]

Less understood is what has happened to the bulk of residents when the plan started. In October 1999, the plan identified 15,416 occupied family units and promised that all would have a "right of return" to public housing, either on redeveloped sites or through a voucher. But few would actually have the persistence to wait for years, meet stringent admission tests, or live long enough to gain access to the newly built mixed-income properties. As of 2010, only 2,163 of the original 1999 public housing families were living in the new mixed-income properties. Instead, most were in the renovated "traditional" public housing projects and scattered-site buildings (3,592 families) or had taken a voucher (4,060 families). The remainder (5,600 families) either moved out of the area, were evicted, died, or could not be found.[23]

Yet it would be wrong to believe, as many infer from the wide swath of demolition, that the Plan for Transformation has caused an overall reduction in the amount of affordable housing in Chicago. Due to the infusion of a large number of federal housing vouchers to support the plan, the total supply of deeply subsidized housing in all forms has actually held steady. While "hard" public housing units have plunged, the rise in housing vouchers has made up for the loss (Figure 12.7). Of course, waiting lists remain clogged, as there are far more eligible families than affordable housing spaces. But the plan has not devastated the city's total supply of this vital commodity.

While controversy continues to hound the Plan for Transformation, it is evident that the plan—warts and all—has marked a step forward, not backward. Despite early mistakes, learning has taken place and processes improved, though the CHA has also been emboldened by its successes to increasingly resist resident demands. The question of what will come next now confronts the city. In 2012, the CHA announced early exploration into a new strategic plan, an initiative dubbed "Plan for Transformation 2.0." A listening phase that year gave little hint as to whether the CHA intends to continue to develop more of mixed-income projects or whether it will shift even more resources to vouchers, seeking to increase its invisibility.

As a planning exercise, the Plan for Transformation was driven as much by the needs of the city as the needs of residents. The old, disastrous environments had to come down. The CHA and city desperately wanted to erase its failures, but managing its problematic residents was less appealing. Its bureaucratic imperatives involved speed, funding, and a desire for newly built communities to not suffer the same fate as the first. These were not unreasonable concerns, but they led to haste that resulted in tearing down first and planning later. Such impatience might be justified by the dismal conditions of long-neglected projects. But it also cost the CHA precious capital with its residents, who need to be more partners than adversaries in the planning of future low-income communities. Restoring that partnership is vital to the CHA's future.

As in all Rust Belt cities, Chicago's industrial might faltered during the 1970s. A steady outflow of manufacturing firms to the suburbs in the 1970s, coupled with the devastating job losses of the 1981–1982 recession, brought urgency to efforts to keep and lure manufacturers. Through the 1970s, industrial policy in Chicago was ad hoc, with the Chicago Economic Development Commission—a relatively weak body not formed until 1976—marketing the city in general terms to individual corporations. Mayor Michael Bilandic created a Department of Economic Development in 1978, and his successor Jane Byrne devoted some energy to the problem of job retention. But these efforts were reactive, uncoordinated, and largely ineffectual.

Most cities fought a punishing battle against the enormous structural forces—suburbanization, automation, and globalization—that drove job losses. Other cities tried a variety of tactics as early as the 1950s and 1960s. Philadelphia used attractive financing, area planning, and a committee to try to pick "winners" in an unsuccessful attempt to prevent industries from fleeing. St. Louis cleared enormous tracts for industry but failed to land many new firms. Oakland attempted to cooperate with its East Bay suburbs in a regional plan to draw industry to the West Coast, but most firms located directly to the suburbs and not the city.[1] For its part, the federal government, after bailing out Chrysler in 1979, retreated from economic development policy making during the Reagan years. State governments often engaged in "smokestack chasing" on a deal-by-deal basis.[2] This left cities in the 1980s on their own to come up with policies for retaining, let alone expanding, industrial employment in the face of a devastating recession.

Chapters 13 through 16 explore the formation of a planning-centered industrial policy in Chicago, the coordinated effort to retain and expand industry in the city's Calumet district, and a regional effort to invest in rail, freight, and intermodal infrastructure. Beginning with the equity planning ideas of the Harold Washington administration, Chicago developed an assertive industrial policy using planning tools that achieved mixed results against the headwind of structural economic change. If measured solely by the number of manufacturing jobs, industrial policy in Chicago has proved a disappointment. However, an analysis by sector shows the corridors have captured significant nonmanufacturing industrial employment, particularly in logistics and business services sectors. Moreover, the efforts enabled productive victories at times, suggesting a strong role for planning in positioning the city to act on recruitment or expansion opportunities. But the quickly changing employment base of the city and region also suggest that adjustments in the city's industrial policy are needed to focus on those sectors and corridors with the most potential.

CHAPTER 13
DEFENDING THE INDUSTRIAL BASE:
SECTOR AND DISTRICT STRATEGIES

During the Harold Washington administration (1983–1987), planners were desperate for ways to stem the hemorrhaging of employment. Varied ideas emerged from above and below, including "sector" strategies targeted at individual industries and "district" strategies focused on land use, zoning, and infrastructure. Future mayoral administrations refined elements of both strategies to create a city-driven industrial retention and job creation effort, one that evolved into arguably the most ambitious city-based industrial program in the United States.

The Sector Strategy: Industry Task Forces

The sector strategy took shape in 1984 with the creation of several industry task forces comprising business, labor, academic, and planning representatives. The Mayor's Task Force on Steel and Southeast Chicago faced the largest challenges. The 1981–1982 recession triggered the closure of major Chicago steel plants, and even in the mid-1980s steel-related industries continued to shed 4,000 to 5,000 jobs per year, mostly concentrated in the Lake Calumet region of southeast Chicago. In 1984 the Commercial Club of Chicago portrayed the sector as unsalvageable and recommended the city turn instead to nurturing high-tech and service industries.[1]

Not surprisingly, the task force's 1986 report argued that abandoning steel in favor of white-collar employment "would be a serious mistake." Steel-related industries still employed 324,000 people, one-eighth of all jobs and half of the manufacturing ones in the region. While steel firms in the United States were less efficient than those in Europe or Japan, and demand for domestic steel was sluggish, the Chicago-Gary share of total U.S. steel production had made recent gains since the recession of 1981–1982 in relation to Pennsylvania and other eastern locations. The concentration of steel-related industries in the region created positive "network effects" as firms in close proximity conducted business with one another. Further, the task force hoped that just-in-time manufacturing techniques and new steel service centers could attract more related firms to the area. Balancing this optimism, the task force acknowledged that long-term productivity gains would inevitably result in declining employment, but this was no reason to give up on the sector. More broadly, the task force blamed conservative policies for steel's struggles, including a strong dollar that hurt exports, a lack of control on steel imports, and diminished infrastructure spending.[2]

But criticizing the Reagan administration was not a plan, and the task force needed concrete proposals to help save steel. Its report recommended granting public incentives for modernization to steel producers, users, and distributors, though enthusiasm among public officials for the idea soured after the city and state provided $45 million to USX in 1983 for a state-of-the-art rail mill, only to see USX cancel the project, citing a decline in railroad construction. Realizing that more incentives faced an uphill battle, the task force also recommended a technology research program, marketing of a trained workforce to new companies, and alternative forms of ownership (including worker buyouts) to avoid plant closings.[3]

The task force also made recommendations for planning in southeast Chicago, a "district" strategy intended to shape the built environment in ways that would attract and retain employers. It recognized that even successful implementation of its sector-based ideas "will not produce [enough] jobs for all the workers displaced from southeast Chicago factories over the past decade." To attract new, catalytic industries that might fill the voids left by abandoned steel plants, the task force recommended public investment in infrastructure, including upgrades to the Port of Chicago, a consolidated trucking terminal, and a centralized southeast Chicago rail yard.[4] The district strategy recognized the realities of a shrinking steel sector and sought to expand opportunities for new plants from a range of industries.

Other industry task forces added ideas to an emerging city-led industrial policy. The Apparel and Fashion Industry Task Force tackled another sector in steep decline: in 1964, Cook County counted 689 firms employing over 29,000 workers; by 1983 this figure had dropped to 365 firms employing just over 10,000 workers, led by a 100-year old menswear producer, Hartmarx, with 2,000 local jobs. The task force recommended formation of an industry board (organized in July 1987) to undertake shared marketing campaigns and to lobby for more favorable import regulations. But the task force also proposed a Needle Trades District, anchored by an industry incubator space. Here was another version of a district strategy, this time creating proximity for small firms to encourage the networks needed to sustain the sector.[5]

Similarly, the Printing Industry Task Force, in its May 1988 report, recommended greater industry coordination as well as a district strategy to support a network of small printers. The gentrification of Printer's Row in the South Loop in the 1980s had driven out numerous small but struggling printers from their close-in location and accelerated contractions in an industry already under pressure from technological advances and rapid suburbanization. To preserve jobs in the city, a plan for a physical space for the industry was essential. The task force asked for city help in identifying and protecting sites for printing work close to the central business district.[6]

All three task forces offered substantial plans, but the city could implement only a portion of the infrastructure investments, workforce training programs, and other recommendations. Without major funding and execution, the task force reports were more academic exercises than battle plans. The apparel industry continued to see jobs move to the Sunbelt and out of the

Figure 13.1. Abandoned LTV Steel Corporation coke plant, shuttered in 2001, January 12, 2011

country, particularly to Asia and Mexico. The printing industry saw advances in electronic technology completely change business models and make firms less dependent on proximity to the central business district. Steel fared even worse, and by the end of the 1980s all the large integrated steel mills were closed, including Wisconsin Steel, USX, LTV, and Republic Steel (Figure 13.1). Surviving firms invested heavily in automation to increase output and shrink workforces. Labor blamed management incompetence, while management blamed labor contracts, and both pointed to federal trade policies for their woes. These mills and their surrounding railroad yards, coke plants, and support industries remain largely vacant, leaving an enormous swath of blight on the city's Far South Side.

The forces arrayed against these sectors were extensive, and industrial policy was too new and underdeveloped. The industrial sector task forces, even if heeded, could not have mastered all the challenges industry faced. However, as Robert Giloth, deputy commissioner of planning under Rob Mier and a steel task force participant, wrote in 1987, "Perhaps the most promising result of Chicago's industry task forces is the potential role of local government as a catalyst and active participant in industrial policy efforts. This role promises to change the institutional capacity of local government and bring a broader sense of public interest to industry-policy debates."[7] The task forces laid the planning and organizational groundwork for the more ambitious district strategy that followed. The sector strategy never disappeared, and workforce training, industry collaboration, and property-tax incentives remained important planning tools. But physical planning moved front and center as operational and expansion space increasingly mattered in industrial policy in a city with competing land-use pressures.

The District Strategy: Planned Manufacturing Districts and Industrial Corridors

A district strategy gained ground on the North Side in an effort to retain and support existing manufacturers. It emerged among activists applying community organizing techniques to the problems of manufacturers within a defined geography. Place mattered, and a district strategy rightly assumed it would be easier to rally community and political support for a location than for a specific industry.

Kernels of the district strategy sprouted from the Greater North Pulaski Development Corporation, a CDC that in 1982 had begun working with local manufacturers to understand their needs and to advocate infrastructure upgrades along Pulaski Avenue that would benefit employers and potential neighborhood employees alike. That same year, the Local Economic and Employment Development (LEED) Council began organizing manufacturers in industrial areas along the North Branch of the Chicago River, seeking to defend employer interests. Chicago CDCs for years had advocated home-grown economic development and sought to start their own enterprises or fund local entrepreneurs, often without success. But now they turned to support established enterprises. In 1986, the LEED Council published a report on industrial displacement along the North Branch of the river, describing the multiple threats to manufacturers scattered across 27 different industrial sectors but still producing 16,000 jobs, nearly 10 percent of Chicago's industrial employment.

A major threat involved displacement. Moving westward from already gentrifying Lincoln Park, developers were converting abandoned industrial buildings into residential and commercial lofts, while vacant tracts became town homes. Alderman Martin Oberman assumed the obsolescence of manufacturing and used his aldermanic privilege to approve zoning variances for residential use. The ease of variances drove up land speculation within areas ostensibly zoned for manufacturing; property taxes rose along with higher valuations. Existing manufacturers could not afford expansion, and new firms were scared away by high costs and the potential for land-use changes. For their part, encroaching loft residents complained about noise and smells. The report documented job losses from earlier residential conversions in other parts of the city in the 1970s, namely the River North neighborhood near downtown. It predicted future losses along the North Branch of the river without stronger land-use protections.[8]

When zoning laws had been reformed in 1957, planners feared that industry (then in the midst of a postwar boom) would infringe upon residential land. Now the reverse was taking place.[9] The LEED Council organized manufacturers to lobby Oberman, who reversed his position and hammered out an agreement to create new zoning protections for portions of the North Side industrial area. The defended area was called a Protected Industrial District, a term later changed to Planned Manufacturing District (PMD). The *Chicago Tribune* found it "anti-development," but with strong support from Harold Washington holdovers in Mayor Eugene Sawyer's administration, including Rob Mier and Elizabeth Hollander, the PMD ordinance passed in April 1988. The ordinance allowed a supplementary layer of land-use regulation for any area of five acres or more that met the criteria for "industrial viability" in order to provide for "stable and predictable industrial environments." Further, "no residential uses shall be permitted or allowed."[10]

Figure 13.2. Goose Island, looking south, 2011

Improving the District Strategy: Industrial Corridors

The election of Mayor Richard M. Daley in 1989 immediately threatened the city's experiments in industrial policy. During the campaign, Daley had opposed the Clybourn PMD and supported gentrification along the north branch of the Chicago River, telling *Crain's Chicago Business*, "The river is going to be for townhomes, homes, apartments, and offices." But Daley surprisingly reversed his position after the election and embraced the protection and retention of industrial corridors. Not only did he support two additional PMDs along the north branch (the Elston and Goose Island PMDs), he also expanded industrial policy and planning in support of manufacturing in crucial ways.[11]

What prompted this transformation? Several influences were likely in play. Daley's first planning commissioner, David Mosena, a Harold Washington holdover, remained a strong advocate for industrial planning and had participated in the Clybourn PMD fight. Donna Ducharme, who had authored the LEED Council studies that had led to adoption of the PMD ordinance, observed that Daley's change of heart "had required a long effort and taken a long time."[12] She noted the influence of a July 1990 LEED Council study, "Keeping Jobs for Chicago's Future," which estimated that Goose Island, if protected, could add 4,256 more jobs, $326 million in wages, and $40 million more in taxes per year compared to residential/retail development. Ducharme also believed that leading North Side firms, led by A. Finkl and Sons Steel, also pressured the mayor.[13] Finally, Kathleen Nelson, an industrial planner with the city, recalled Daley's eventual enthusiasm for manufacturing as his tenure progressed: "Daley wanted all the corridors to be PMDs, and he was excited by individual projects and individual deals."[14]

Daley's Department of Planning and Development, under Commissioner Valerie B. Jarrett, expanded an effort begun under Mayor Sawyer to create a citywide district strategy to "provide a comprehensive framework for directing future industrial development policies—land use, infrastructure and marketing—in the City of Chicago." The initiative, called Corridors of Industrial Opportunity, produced comprehensive plans for the North, West, and South sides that provided detailed statistics on firms, land use, and employment. Most important, the plans mapped out proposed "industrial corridors," a land-use designation not as strong as a PMD but nonetheless signaling to developers the depth of the city's interest in industrial sites. In many industrial corridors, subsets of land were designated as PMDs for greater protection; as of 2011, 15 PMDs have been established in 24 corridors. For each corridor, the plans offered a profile of industrial uses, infrastructure, and development potentials. Finally, improvements to support existing industries were listed with estimated costs.[15]

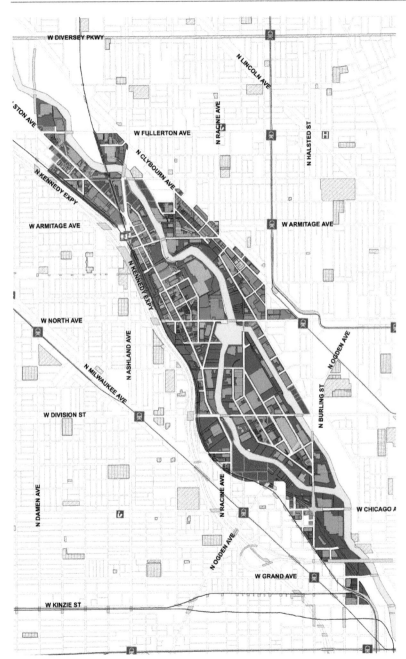

Figure 13.3. Land use in the North Branch Industrial Corridor, from the Chicago Sustainable Industries report, March 2011

The North Side plan mapped out a large area along the river called the North Branch Industrial Corridor, which included the Clybourn PMD (Figure 13.3). It also contained the Goose Island PMD, which included a 32-acre former Milwaukee Road rail yard. The area was subsequently built out with a range of industries and services, many supporting hospitality, restaurant, and office employers in the central area. In May 2005, Goose Island successfully attracted the Wrigley Global Innovation Center, a research and development facility. Many of the new firms locating on Goose Island are not the purely blue-collar employers like the machine tool makers, fabricators, and steel firms originally envisioned by the LEED Council but are suppliers, shippers, and even researchers. (See sidebar, page 180) The space remains protected for employment, much of it working class and reasonably well paying.

Altogether the three Corridors of Industrial Opportunity plans released between 1989 and 1994 mapped 22 industrial corridors (two were added later) covering more than 13,000 acres of land—massive land and development planning unequaled in any other U.S. city. This geographic scope was matched by greater spending on infrastructure improvements, including new viaducts, bridges, and streets to accommodate truck transportation needs, much of it financed in 1992 by $160 million in general obligation bonds. Over time, TIF districts became the preferred financing mechanism, the boundaries of which largely coincided with the industrial corridor boundaries and which also provided redevelopment powers. By 1997, 17 industrial TIFs had been created to support the corridors.

In 1993, Daley hired Donna Ducharme to run the industrial corridor program. Ducharme expanded the city's Local Industrial Retention Initiative (LIRI) to provide funding for new or existing industrial development organizations in the corridors. The LIRI agencies work with employers and the community as advocates for the corridor, ensuring that its interests are looked after even if that means clashing with other agencies over maintenance, infrastructure, or workforce issues. By 2011, there were 15 LIRI agencies covering the 24 industrial corridors and the community areas surrounding them. In addition, two citywide LIRI agencies provided workforce, marketing, and other resources to the industrial program: the Apparel Industry Board and the Jane Addams Resource Corporation. Thus the district strategy stretched beyond mere zoning protection and infrastructure investment to include advocacy and networks for supporting employers and workers.

At the time of the corridors' designation, their combined industrial employment totaled more than 155,000 workers. The largest concentration

Urban Industrial Redevelopment on Goose Island

The Goose Island Planned Manufacturing District (PMD) was established in 1991 along the North Branch of the Chicago River to protect existing industries and provide well-positioned real estate for future industrial developments. In 1996 the area was designated a TIF district. Goose Island has been perhaps the city's most successful PMD, based in part on its location just a mile from downtown but also because of zoning controls, financial incentives, and improved access and infrastructure.

Before the PMD, deindustrialization had shuttered firms, and rising land costs (due to increasing numbers of zoning variances) had led others to move. But since 1991, Goose Island has experienced an infusion of industrial development. FedEx built a new facility, the Chicago Transit Authority improved an existing warehouse, and an Anheuser-Busch subsidiary constructed a distribution center. Republic Doors and Windows built a state-of-the-art manufacturing facility (though the company later declared bankruptcy), and a local developer opened multitenant flex space. An eight-story 19th-century loft building with unobstructed views of the Chicago skyline was renovated as lab space by Sara Lee Corporation and subsequently acquired by Kendall College for its culinary training school (Figure 13.4). A utility substation, parking deck, and boat storage facility filled in other lots.

No longer a district for manufacturing alone, Goose Island now hosts companies that serve the needs of downtown businesses, including a commercial laundry facility for restaurants and hotels, wholesale food distributers, and caterers for large social events. These companies depend on quick and easy access to their downtown customers.

Perhaps the crowning achievement on Goose Island has been the development of the Global Innovation Center (2005) by the Wm. Wrigley Jr. Company. The 7.3-acre site once owned by a metal fabrication firm had been intended in the 1990s to become an Internet *zaibatsu*—a Japanese term referring to large, vertically integrated financial and industrial conglomerates. That project burst with the Internet bubble, but Wrigley, supported by $11.3 million in TIF funds, took over the site and built a 153,000-square-foot facility designed to lead its expansion beyond gum into the broader world of candies. The LEED-certified center features an indoor winter garden, and a 40,000-square-foot pilot plant where new products and manufacturing process can be tested. On-site laboratories allow food scientists, researchers, and marketing staff to collaborate on

Figure 13.4. Kendall College on Goose Island

projects. In 2008, Mars purchased Wrigley, and in 2012 the company moved its global headquarters to Goose Island from the Wrigley Building on Michigan Avenue. There are now approximately 600 Wrigley employees on site.

—William J. Trumbull

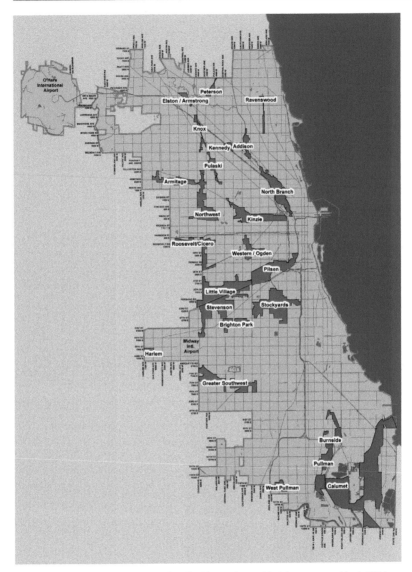

Figure 13.5. Map of industrial corridors, from the Chicago Sustainable Industries report, March 2011

was in the North Chicago River Industrial Corridor, with more than 10,000. The West Side was by far the largest of the three planning areas, with 80,000 employees, including 16,000 alone in the Kinzie Industrial Corridor. The mostly African American South Side followed with more than 50,000 industrial workers, including 17,000 in the 1,348-acre Stockyards Industrial Corridor.[16] Still, the geographic divides of the industrial problem remained stark. The South Side had the most vacant land of the three planning areas: more than 1,500 acres (mostly in the Calumet district) compared to 630 acres on the West Side and fewer than 100 acres on the North Side.

Industrial Parks: A Disappointment

Buoyed by its district strategies, the city next moved in different directions in the mid-1990s. It pursued two urban "business parks" intended to compete with the many suburban planned industrial parks that had enticed so many firms to leave the city. Chicago brownfields would be converted into modern business and warehouse environments, complete with landscaping, signage, fenced perimeters, gateways, truck areas, and ample parking lots. The first, West Pullman Park, on the South Side, offered 160 developable acres, plus the possibility of retaining several existing employers with 500 jobs. A dedicated TIF encompassing only the proposed park, along with a $20 million HUD loan, funded the more than $30 million in total site costs. On the West Side, the Roosevelt/California Business Park offered similar features but also close proximity to an intermodal facility and the Eisenhower Expressway. Again, TIF and HUD loans paid for improvements.

But neither park has developed as planned. The city offered few advantages to greenfield sites, and even significant subsidies could not lure new manufacturers or corporations. West Pullman Park was the more successful of the two, but even with an investment of $30 million from HUD loans and additional TIF funds, it has proved disappointing. The park retained two smaller firms and attracted a commercial plumbing supplies distributor. But the largest firm closed its manufacturing facility, leaving a 21-acre contaminated site. Ed Lewis, a city planner who has worked on this site for more than 15 years, notes: "The uncertainties of environmental cleanup, both the time needed and costs, were discouraging to many companies, and the bottom line is that even more cleanup monies would be needed to sell the sites at usable prices." More recently, West Pullman has seen new interest: much of the site became a solar energy farm and the $160 million Ray and Joan Kroc Corps Community Center.[17] Significant road improvements have been made, but much of the remaining acreage remains in private hands, and much of it is contaminated.

Similarly, the 30-acre Roosevelt/California Business Park has not met expectations. After establishing the 30-acre site as a planned development in 2000, the city first sought a single developer but then hoped to relocate produce and food businesses threatened with displacement at Fulton Market on the Near West Side; to date, the city has found few takers. An armored vehicle firm developed four acres, a private gym facility another acre, and a corner parcel was taken by a social service agency, which also sought to establish a 20-acre hydroponic garden until the remediation costs became prohibitive. One existing manufacturer abandoned an eight-acre site and moved to Wisconsin. As with West Pullman, the uncertainty regarding the cost and time frames associated with remediation were major contributing factors to the disappointing results, despite investment of HUD loan monies and TIF funds.[18]

These poor showings illustrate the limits of industrial policy in Chicago. It takes more than a "build-it-and-they-will-come" or "planned business park" approach, even with significant public subsidies. Chicago will have to produce more targeted and careful planning that combines sector and district strategies to attract fresh activity to its older industrial land.

By 2000, Chicago had developed an extensive, homegrown industrial policy. The completion of the citywide Corridors of Industrial Opportunities plans carefully connected land-use planning and economic development. The LIRI efforts to organize manufacturers and community representatives in each corridor added another dimension to the physical planning, providing a forum for problem solving. And financing from bonds and then TIFs provided essential resources. Economic development planning in the city had moved far beyond the ad hoc efforts of the 1970s and the mostly defensive recommendations of the industry sector task forces to create a sophisticated and comprehensive industrial policy. Yet even so, many firms continued to hemorrhage employment through gains in efficiency or the effects of crushing competition. Planning ultimately could not stop the bleeding of its historic core industrial base, let alone reverse it. But it did position the city for new types of business growth, stabilization in some corridors, and, as will be seen, some impressive victories that would likely not otherwise have occurred.

CHAPTER 14
A CHANGING EMPLOYMENT SCENE

As industrial policy enters its third decade of implementation, Chicago has begun to take a hard look at its industrial corridors. From the start, the city wanted to protect jobs, especially blue-collar manufacturing ones, in the face of plant relocations and relentless economic change. But Chicago firms have not been immune to the persistent downward pressures on manufacturing employment in the United States, as automation and efficiency gains have meant greater output but fewer workers. An evaluation of industrial corridor performance suggests the wide variation among them and that policy should embrace employment sectors that hold the greatest promise of future growth.

Employment in the Industrial Corridors, 2002–2010

By any measure, Chicago's industrial employment figures are sobering. Manufacturing employment continues to contract considerably, even in the industrial corridors. When created between 1989 and 1994, the corridors held 155,858 industrial workers. By 2002, this figure had plunged to 95,164; it slid to 72,874 by 2010, a drop of more than half.[1] The decreases were not limited to the far South Side (57 percent of industrial jobs lost), which had earlier experienced the massive steel layoffs, but also occurred on the North Side (52 percent) and West Side (51 percent).

Chicago's industrial corridor employment has dropped relative to the rest of the city, the county, and the country as a whole, at least in terms of

Table 14.1. Employment Change in the U.S., State, County, City, and City Industrial Corridors, 2002–2010 (%)

	Manufacturing	Nonmanufacturing Industrial	Compatible with Manufacturing	All Other	Total Employment
Chicago Industrial Corridors	−32.2	−12.1	2.5	19.6	−16.3
City of Chicago	−36.6	−6.6	7.3	8.2	1.3
Cook County, excluding City of Chicago	−29.0	−12.1	8.0	−2.4	−5.7
Illinois	−24.9	−5.8	10.5	2.8	−0.6
United States	−24.5	7.6	14.4	−0.5	2.1

Source: U.S. Census Bureau and Center for Governmental Studies, Northern Illinois University

Notes:
Nonmanufacturing Industrial includes utilities; construction; wholesale trade; transportation and wholesale; and waste management and remediation.
Compatible with Manufacturing includes professional, scientific, and technical service; health care and social assistance; arts, entertainment, recreation; and accommodation and food service.
All Other includes retail trade; information; finance and insurance; educational services; and public administration.

manufacturing. Table 14.1 aggregates employment into four broad categories and compares them across various geographies for the period 2002–2010, when strictly comparable data are available. (See also Appendix C.)[2]

Table 14.1 shows that Chicago's industrial corridors lost manufacturing jobs at a faster rate than other areas, though they slightly outperformed the city as a whole, and all jurisdictions saw steep declines. Chicago's overall 1.3 percent gain in total employment occurred largely because postindustrial sectors including hospitality, education, health care, and logistics (captured in the "all other" category) offset industrial job losses. In general, however, we can see that an industrial policy fixated on manufacturing employment misses the significant potentials for growth in related sectors.[3]

In addition, Table 14.1 more directly connects employment categories to potential land uses in broad categories that capture the rapid changes under way in the employment base. The "nonmanufacturing industrial" category includes warehousing and logistics firms that are reflective of Chicago's growing role as an international intermodal center. Indeed, by 2010 more people in the corridors worked in nonmanufacturing industrial jobs than in manufacturing ones. The "compatible with manufacturing" category captures such employers as hospitals that need lab space, catering companies that need large kitchens, and film production companies that need studios. These activities can easily take place in industrial corridors, but the current zoning code offers no encouragement or in some cases actively prohibits them.

More detailed data also indicate the changing nature of the industrial corridors. Table 14.2 presents the three corridors that posted significant employment gains: Kinzie, Little Village, and North Branch. Together they lost 3,378 manufacturing jobs but gained 8,605 nonmanufacturing jobs, for an overall increase of 19.5 percent. Only three other corridors showed any manufacturing gains at all. (See Appendix C.) Clearly, retaining and attracting manufacturing employment in the corridors has been a struggle.

Corridors such as Kinzie, North Branch, and Little Village have become magnets for nonmanufacturing firms that want industrial-type space in proximity to expressways and the Loop. Besides gains in postindustrial sectors, these corridors also show positive growth in transportation and warehousing, wholesale trade, and administrative support sectors. Even retail on the fringes of the industrial corridors—allowable in many tracts under current zoning in the industrial corridor program—has shown considerable employment expansion. As the 2008–2009 recession pounded manufacturing firms, the employment base in some corridors moved into nonmanufacturing sectors. More of this growth could be captured in other corridors with appropriate regulatory, infrastructure, and marketing initiatives.

NAICS CATEGORY	Kinzie		
	2002	**2010**	**Change %**
Construction	852	766	−10
Manufacturing	4,836	2,771	−43
Wholesale Trade	1,961	2,409	23
Retail Trade	535	741	39
Transportation/Warehousing	268	767	186
Information	138	208	51
Finance and Insurance	48	205	327
Real Estate	231	219	−5
Professional, Scientific, and Technical Services	844	967	15
Management of Companies and Enterprises	7	23	229
Administrative, support and waste	1,137	3,323	192
Educational Services	8	125	1,463
Health Care/Social Assistance	163	326	100
Arts, Entertainment/Recreation	48	60	25
Accommodation/Food Service	1,000	915	−9
Other Services [except Public Administration]	322	148	−54
Public Administration	0	1	
All Sectors	12,398	13,985	13
SUBCATEGORIES			
Manufacturing	4,836	2,771	−43
Nonmanufacturing - Industrial	4,218	7,272	72
Compatible with manufacturing	2,055	2,268	10
All Others	1,289	1,674	30

Table 14.2. Employment Change in Selected Chicago Industrial Corrido

	Little Village			North Branch		
2002	**2002**	**2010**	**Change %**	**2002**	**2010**	**Change %**
	258	194	−25	302	205	−32
	1,832	1,137	−38	2,560	1,942	−24
	277	240	−13	2,008	1,452	−28
	8	29	263	1,561	2,619	68
	229	1,605	601	776	1,901	145
	18	17	−6	375	260	−31
	1	2	100	111	1,002	803
	8	1	−88	235	371	58
	27	45	67	614	1,286	109
	0	0	0	359	4	−99
	290	436	50	284	1,072	277
	5	22	340	6	361	5,917
	215	177	−18	766	311	−59
	0	0	0	193	258	34
	0	1		668	649	−3
	92	81	−12	253	282	11
	68	49	−28	0	0	0
	3,349	4,078	22	11,080	13,991	26
	1,832	1,137	−38	2,560	1,942	−24
	1,075	2,517	134	3,377	4,646	38
	242	223	−8	2,241	2,504	12
	200	201	1	2,902	4,899	69

Employment Data in Context

Before concluding that the city's industrial corridors have been detrimental to—or at least not supportive of—blue-collar employment or that industrial policy is an overall failure, we should put this data in context. First, the industrial corridors were already at-risk spaces requiring either defensive measures or major infrastructure upgrades. As such, they were the most difficult cases and could be expected to have losses. Second, several of the industrial corridors are close to the Loop, and over two decades property values had increased considerably, even with the zoning protections and organizing benefits that came with corridor designation. Unless they valued proximity to the Loop, manufacturing firms in these corridors had few reasons to stay. Third, the policy was initially formed in the crisis of several key industries—steel, apparel, printing, and others—already undergoing dramatic structural, technological, and global consolidations and changes. Land-use policy could do only so much to offset the impacts of larger trends in manufacturing employment.

Further, it is important to note that U.S. manufacturing firms have become vastly more efficient, a response to the relentless competition of global capitalism. Significant investment in technology has enabled domestic manufacturing output to increase 600 percent between 1950 and 2007 while employing roughly the same number of workers. Yet due to general population growth, the *share* of manufacturing in the workforce has declined from 31 percent of nonfarm workers in 1950 to 10.1 percent in 2010.[4]

Finally, even with the declines in manufacturing employment, total industrial jobs in Chicago totaled 287,109 in 2010, or 23.2 percent of total employment in the city. Moreover, some 56 percent of the city's manufacturing jobs and 16.5 percent of nonmanufacturing jobs were concentrated in the industrial corridors. These sectors remain vitally important to the Chicago economy, and recent upturns in auto manufacturing and new international investment in U.S. manufacturing—the "reshoring of jobs"—hold promise for further growth. As Ted Wysocki, CEO of the LEED Council explains, "Many manufacturers and businesses now want to be in the city—this is a sea change, and we need to plan more for it. . . . Place-based planning is critical."[5]

A recent successful planning and policy intervention shows the continuing importance of the corridors. For over a century, A. Finkl and Sons has been an important heavy steel firm in the North Branch corridor and was instrumental in convincing Mayor Daley to support industrial policy in the early 1990s. When Finkl announced in 2003 that it had outgrown its 22-

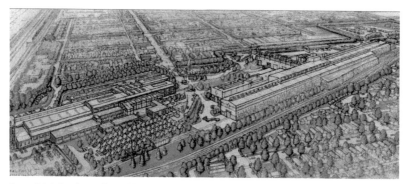

Figure 14.1. Rendering of A. Finkl and Sons industrial campus for the Burnside Industrial Corridor, 2009

acre North Branch space, the firm began working with the Department of Planning and Development to evaluate sites. Stakes were raised when a German company bought Finkl in 2007 and suggested it would relocate operations to a facility in Quebec. To keep Finkl in Chicago, the city in 2009 arranged $20.5 million in TIF funds toward a $160 million renovation and expansion of a former stamping plant on a 53-acre site in the Burnside Industrial Corridor on the far South Side (Figure 14.1). The move doubled Finkl's steel-forging capacity, saved 300 existing jobs, and added 150 more.[6] Previously, large industrial firms often relocated to suburban greenfield sites, out of state, or out of the country. But now planners in the city were able to proactively offer a competitive expansion location and space. Industrial corridors and policy still matter.

Reforming Industrial Corridor Policy

The 24 industrial corridor plans of the 1990s were premised on a "one-size-fits-all" zoning solution that defended manufacturing space against incursions from other uses. But in light of recent trends, the land-use classifications may need to be adjusted to reflect employment growth beyond strictly manufacturing sectors. Cities such as Baltimore and Portland, Oregon, are now moving toward using employment density and employment characteristic measurements instead of traditional Euclidean zoning categories. Flexibility in land-use categories can also abet the changing needs of firms as they adjust to capital and technology movements as well as continuing changes in international shipping and distribution.[7]

In 2011 the city's planners assembled the Chicago Sustainable Industries task force, composed of industry, city, and community representatives and intended to be "a single, comprehensive planning effort . . . to coordinate the economic, social and environmental aspects of Chicago's manufacturing sector." An initial report updated zoning and land-use maps, with acreage and employment information for each of the corridors.[8] Subsequent work found that industrial sectors constituted only two-thirds of all workers in the corridors.[9] In half of the corridors, retail and office employment represented more than 10 percent of the total, helping to offset manufacturing losses. The analysis also concluded that the corridors with less manufacturing were growing more, suggesting the need for further review of the land-use patterns in many of the corridors.[10]

The question for Chicago's industrial policy and the larger economic development policies of the region is how well planning—inclusive of land use, infrastructure investment, and workforce development—can accommodate this changing employment picture. The city will likely need to expand the options for its industrial corridors spaces and offer more nuanced plans to produce employment centers. The wide variety of spaces in the existing corridors, from narrow tracts of densely built loft space to expansive brownfields needing remediation, requires differentiation in policy. Flexibility will likely produce greater job opportunities for the noncollege-educated workforce as well as the groups of new technology workers and service economy employees, which are growing most substantially in the city. The current recession and the long-term declines in manufacturing suggest that major adjustments are needed in Chicago's industrial program—changes that a long-term planning perspective should guide.

CHAPTER 15
THE CALUMET DISTRICT:
PLANNING FOR BROWNFIELDS

Chicago's district-centered policy originated on the North Side in response to displacement pressures. But the city's South and West sides—where African Americans and Latinos predominate—have had different sets of problems and opportunities. Here, the city faced the more conventional challenge of finding new industries for vast brownfields. Attracting new firms proved difficult, but one remarkable sector-based planning effort achieved a significant victory. The city not only saved a Ford automotive plant but developed an auto supplier park around it, solidifying an important job base. Concurrently, the city produced a plan for the Calumet district that blended industry with open space preservation. This success shows the extensive need for both sector and district planning to retain and expand industrial employment.

A decade into its industrial policy, the city asked consultants at Arthur Andersen for a study on the city's overall industrial status and potential. The resulting report, completed in March 1998, noted that the Midwest and Chicago had done well in the national economic expansion of the 1990s, but it predicted—correctly—that manufacturing employment would drop after 2000. However, it identified new growth opportunities in various sectors where firms needed "flex" building types that could accommodate a range of services, offices, warehouses, labs, and testing facilities. Not quite industrial but not pure office, the report saw a demand for 1.2 million to 1.8 million square feet per year, with much of it potentially located in the ostensibly industrial corridors. Manufacturing, meanwhile, remained the smallest of the space demand categories.[1]

On the supply side, the study identified more than 2,200 acres of land available for industrial development in the city. The report emphasized that more than half of this land was concentrated in the Calumet district on the city's far South Side. The analysis also noted the strong resistance in the development and brokerage community to South Side sites. Race and class fears undoubtedly played a role in these market perceptions; the South Side was severely strained by high unemployment, distressed property values, and deteriorating social conditions, in part because of the departure of the large integrated steel mills and their associated businesses. Crime problems and security concerns were magnified in evaluating sites. The report posited "a mismatch between industrial demand and land supply. . . . The Calumet area has less than 20 percent of the overall demand but almost 60 percent of industrial land in Chicago."[2]

The city commissioned a follow-up Calumet Area Implementation/ Action Plan, issued in May 1999, which identified 13 key opportunity redevelopment sites on 1,300 acres surrounding Lake Calumet. These included all of the large former steel mill tracts—U.S. Steel, Republic Steel, Wisconsin Steel—and several smaller sites. The inventory documented sizes, ownership, access, and development characteristics. It also identified several "demand" potentials for the area, especially in the auto sector. Five auto or truck plants in the broader Chicago region had begun adopting just-in-time production methods whereby third-party suppliers delivered parts shortly before they were needed on assembly lines. The suppliers, in turn, needed ready access to manufacturing plants, creating demand for "supplier parks"—warehouses for storing parts within easy connectivity to assembly lines. The action plan listed the Ford Motor Company's aging Chicago Assembly Plant in the Calumet district as having "the best potential of generating spin-off supplier demand." The report noted nearby brownfield sites as possible locations for a supplier park. Another potential demand came from intermodal and logistics firms who might benefit from the complex web of railroads, roadways, and waterways, though connections would require substantial investment. The plan recommended collaboration with Norfolk Southern Railroad, the dominant carrier in the Calumet district, to expand intermodal service at strategic points.[3]

Perhaps the most significant recommendation of the Implementation/ Action Plan was to create a TIF district for the entire Calumet study area. Unlike most TIFs, extensive planning backed the proposal, including a

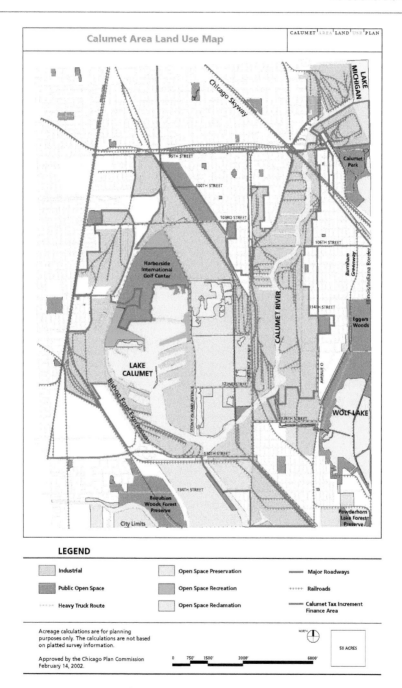

Figure 15.1. Land-use map, from the Calumet Area Land Use Plan, December 2001

Department of Planning and Development feasibility study; the city council adopted the Calumet Industrial TIF in December 2000. It covered roughly 12,000 acres, by far the largest TIF district in Chicago, and would enable a wide range of predevelopment activities, including acquisition of land, environmental remediation related to both development and restoration, and the construction of public infrastructure and new open spaces. In particular, the plan noted the "importance of implementing previous proposals that will improve routes for truck traffic," particularly reducing conflicts between road and rail traffic, increasing weight limits on bridges, and building a crucial industrial road to address an east-west bottleneck.

The economic planning in the Calumet district created momentum for a broader effort that produced the Calumet Area Land Use Plan in 2001 (Figure 15.1). The EPA funded the $200,000 effort, recognizing the critical need for environmental remediation of abandoned industrial sites while protecting "the most significant wetland and natural area within the city." The Department of Planning and Development partnered with the city's Department of the Environment and several private groups on a comprehensive open space plan and accompanying design guidelines. Their plan noted the "enormous opportunities . . . for protection of important open space . . . where Chicagoans will regain access to wild lands and restored landscapes that were unavailable for public use for half a century." Of the Calumet region's 12,000 acres, approximately 4,600 were devoted to public rights-of-way and waterways, 1,500 were for improved industrial uses, and 1,300 were for future industrial uses. This left more than 4,000 acres for a Calumet Open Space Reserve.[4] Norfolk Southern and Ford subsequently made land contributions to expand and protect valuable marsh and open areas, while the city has undertaken an acquisition program to add acres under public control. An extended trail system around Wolf Lake is now providing the basis for an expanded use of the area by both citizens and ecotourists. (See sidebar, page 198.)

The sustained commitment to planning—including a market study, action plan, TIF study, land-use plan, and open space strategy—gave the city a strong base on which to guide investment for public benefit and job creation. Doris Holleb, a member of the Chicago Plan Commission who reviewed much of this work, maintained that planning in the Calumet district "was the most significant new planning undertaken in the City in several decades."[5]

The Ford Supplier Park and Chicago Plant Renewal

The comprehensive planning effort for the Calumet area laid the groundwork for a dramatic success for the city industrial policy. In mid-1999, Ford Motor Company announced that it wanted to build its first automobile supplier park in North America and asked Atlanta and Chicago to submit proposals.

The competition appeared lopsided. The Atlanta Assembly Plant, built in 1947, sat near an international airport with direct expressway access and nearby site availability. Labor costs in Georgia were lower, as were utility costs—two competitive advantages that had been luring manufacturing plants south since World War II.

Chicago, by contrast, started with huge disadvantages. The Chicago Assembly Plant—at the epicenter of the Calumet district at 130th Street and Torrence Avenue—was one of Ford's oldest, finished in 1926. The plant was also landlocked: trucks could not access the whole east side of the plant because it butted up against Torrence Avenue and an abandoned railroad yard; 130th Street was blocked for hours every day by railroad freight operations; the Calumet River and adjoining uses to the west precluded any meaningful expansion. The local United Auto Workers (UAW) chapter had a long history of aggressive negotiations and would need to be involved in decisions about expansion. Utility costs were relatively high, and Commonwealth Edison (Com Ed) had not shown flexibility with large users in the area. Vacant sites available to the east were brownfields that needed a variety of remediation measures. Moreover a crucial truck route (126th Street) was substandard. As Tony Reinhart, manager of governmental affairs for Ford, said, "The project wasn't supposed to go to Chicago—it was going to Atlanta, which was considered the crown jewel of the Ford plants in the U.S."[6]

Nevertheless, Reinhart encouraged Ford Motor "to at least take a look at Chicago," and he shared this possibility with Mary Culler, the city deputy commissioner working on industrial retention. The city's Department of Planning and Development, the Illinois Department of Commerce and Community Affairs, and consultants spent a frantic three months producing a proposal, aided by the extensive prior planning in the Calumet district.

Yet a successful bid required vigorous private party participation as well as public incentives and action. Center Pointe Properties, a prominent industrial real estate investment trust, stepped up as a developer and optioned a nearby site that had been identified as a potential supplier park in the 1998 Implementation/Action Plan. Arthur Andersen managed

Calumet: Industry and Nature Working Together

The purpose of the Calumet Area Land Use Plan (2002) is to create a "landscape where industry and open space are intermingled, interconnected and to the greatest extent possible, co-existing harmoniously." Goals include improving the quality of life in the Calumet area, enhancing existing industries and attracting new ones, and protecting wetland and natural areas while improving habitat for rare and endangered species.

A related document, the Calumet Open Space Reserve Plan (2002), details a network of 4,000 acres of natural areas and wetlands. More than 200 species of birds are known to visit or stay in the Calumet area every year. In addition, aquatic life is surprisingly abundant, considering that many of the bodies of water are degraded, dredged, or filled. The plan outlines specific areas for wetland and natural area preservation, rehabilitation, recreation, and trail connections for the local governmental bodies to pursue. Since 2002, the city has acquired 700 acres of wetland and natural areas, over half of which were once intended to be private landfills; most of this land is now owned by the Chicago Park District and will be managed for ecorecreation and habitat.

Further, the Calumet Design Guidelines (2004) are directed at the private property in the area that is to be redeveloped for industry and detail the city's site design requirements. The Chicago Manufacturing Campus (2004), also known as the Ford Supplier Park, was the first development to adopt the principles of the guidelines. The 88-acre development houses Ford's only North American just-in-time delivery system of supplier companies to serve its nearby assembly plant. The site features shared stormwater management, restored wetlands, multipurpose paths, and a waiver for ornamental fencing, all of which are recommended in the guidelines.

In 2011, federal, state, and local officials announced the Millennium Reserve, a major partnership and conservation initiative to create the largest urban open-space project in the country, eventually encompassing 140,000 acres of land in the Calumet region. The initial Calumet Core phase will restore 15,000 acres of open space and construct a regional trail connecting Chicago with the south suburbs. It will also renovate historic buildings, improve public access, and restore habitats.

Similarly, the Hammond Lakes Area Project on the Illinois-Indiana border is spending $54.2 million on infrastructure and open space projects that will connect with the Calumet Core. Finally, Ford has donated $6 mil-

Figures 15.2a–b. Renderings of Ford Calumet Environmental Center, designed by Studio Gang Architects, 2009

lion toward a $20 million public education and visitation center designed by Studio Gang Architects (Figures 15.2a–b).

The area that once was the core of the steel industry is becoming a national model for recycling sites into new recreational and educational uses alongside major industry.

—Kathleen E. Dickhut

Figure 15.3. *Chicago Manufacturing Campus, known as the Ford Supplier Park, 2012. The park is bounded by the Calumet River to the left and Wolf Lake on the right, with the Hegewisch neighborhood in the foreground.*

a large team of consultants, which assembled an incentives package, preliminary design drawings, timetable, workforce training, and development cost analysis. To create a competitive proposal, the developer's partner, FCL Builders, modeled the cost of space construction and operating costs in the proposed 155-acre supplier park compared to those in Atlanta. The analysis found savings in energy efficiency for the new supplier park could close some of the cost gap and could be paid for in part by a fund created by a recent settlement between Com Ed and the city. Those funds could also be used to make Ford's existing plant more energy efficient, resulting in meaningful long-term savings. More conventionally, the analysis argued for the locational superiority of Chicago in terms of product transportation costs, quality of workforce, and access to population centers.

On October 12, 1999, Mayor Richard M. Daley and Governor George H. Ryan hand-delivered their proposal to Ford's CEO and president. Ford officials later confessed that the Chicago package "blew them away" and was far more developed than the Atlanta proposal. Chicago won the bid. Culler later reflected on the work involved: "The thing that won the day was leveraging the existing city planning with the ideas of Arthur Andersen and Center Pointe to create a robust proposal. . . . No other city was thinking this way."[7]

Final painstaking negotiations with Ford continued for several months.[8] In discussions with the UAW and the city, Ford agreed to employment levels

Figure 15.4. Ford Motor Company, Chicago Assembly Plant, December 1, 2010

at the existing plant and to cooperate with the union at the supplier park. Ford, the city, the state, and the UAW also agreed to collaborate on a new workforce training center to be developed adjacent to the assembly plant. The city promptly began work on the infrastructure, including rail grade separations and both relocated and new roads built to heavy truck standards, which benefited not only Ford but the Calumet district overall.[9] The supplier park, named the Chicago Manufacturing Campus, opened in 2003 directly east of the Ford plant on 126th Street with an initial nine auto-parts manufacturing tenants occupying 1.6 million square feet (Figure 15.3). The Mayor's Office of Workforce Development trained some 600 new employees for the campus and Ford expansion. Overall, employment at the Chicago assembly plant and its related stamping plant in nearby Chicago Heights has increased from 2,788 in 2001 to 3,870 in 2011 (Figure 15.4).[10] Ford's plant has become its most flexible and energy efficient, allowing three separate models to roll off the line at once, using just-in-time parts from the supplier park. In the brutally competitive world of plant retention and global auto production, Chicago had won a remarkable victory.

The Ford Motor story and the earlier A. Finkl expansion (chapter 14) illustrate successful combinations of the industry sector approach and the district/corridor approach. The focus on enhancing the economic efficiency, productivity, and continued viability of a single facility and its related suppliers (sector strategy) resulted in a package of incentives and strategies that improved plant competitiveness—thereby extending the useful life of the Ford and Finkl sites for years. The city had also garnered extensive experience in providing the types of site remediation, roadway infrastructure, utility upgrades, and other site and area improvements (district strategy) to retain and enhance industrial operations. In both cases, the combination proved successful. Equally important, as a case study for redevelopment of troubled industrial areas, the Calumet Area Land Use Plan demonstrated the benefits of careful planning that is sensitive to both industrial and environmental concerns. This was a more balanced paradigm for industrial policy, and a model for planners to adopt and adapt in the future.

CHAPTER 16
PLANNING FOR GLOBAL FREIGHT
IN THE CHICAGO REGION

Industrial policy has typically focused on job retention in high-profile sectors like auto and steel. But heavy-rail planning is another key element in Chicago's industrial competitiveness. Although this effort is beyond the realm of traditional city planning, it has brought together transportation planners and private railroads to spur large-scale private and public investment in ways that directly affect economic growth in Chicago. In the past decade, the Chicago region has seen an enormous investment in its rail capacity, which should secure its place as a transportation node for the next century.

Since the mid-19th century, railroads have dominated Chicago's economic landscape and directly shaped its built environment, as seen in Part 1. During the 20th century, railroads moved most of their freight operations out of the central area to yards on the edge of the city and eventually farther out. Declining passenger ridership and growing truck traffic led to bankruptcy, reorganization, and general neglect of the heavy-rail network. But globalization sparked demand, and advances such as containerization and double-stacked trains improved efficiency. Coupled with investments in port facilities to handle larger container vessels, these innovations dramatically reduced shipping costs worldwide and accelerated rising volumes of trade.

Twenty-five percent of all U.S. rail traffic passes through Chicago, while 46 percent of all intermodal units—mostly containers—are processed in its intermodal yards, making it the key node in the nation's rail network (Figure 16.1, page 204). Even as traditional manufacturing

Tonnage of Trailer-on-Flatcar and Container-on-Flatcar Rail Intermodal Moves: 2009

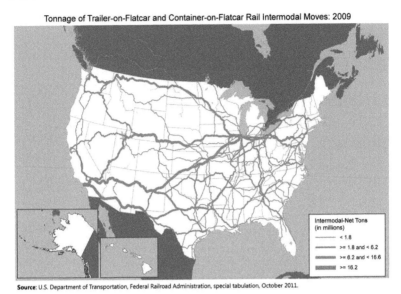

Source: U.S. Department of Transportation, Federal Railroad Administration, special tabulation, October 2011.

Figure 16.1. Map of intermodal traffic across the United States, from the U.S. Department of Transportation, 2009

has declined, logistics, warehousing, and wholesale trade have meant a boom in warehousing space throughout the region, representing two-thirds of new "industrial" space development.[1] The warehouses function as transshipment, storage, and packaging facilities for container freight and also function as assembly points for food and manufactured products exported to international markets.

Planning for Intermodal Growth in Chicago

Freight has been a component of regional transportation planning since the 1950s, focusing primarily on grade separation—reducing road-rail conflicts with viaducts and bridges.[2] But it became a more central element of metropolitan growth strategies in 1991 with the passage of the Intermodal Surface Transportation Efficiency Act (ISTEA). This landmark legislation recognized that the Interstate Highway System was nearly complete and that serious constraints existed on further highway expansion in metropolitan areas. The law sought to link metropolitan transportation planning to federal and state air-quality plans, promote investment in intermodal connections, and emphasize the need for input from all transportation providers, including rail-freight operators.

In response, the regional transportation planning agency for greater Chicago, the Chicago Area Transportation Study (CATS), convened the Intermodal Advisory Task Force (IATF), which included the major freight railroads, state and city transportation planners, and others.[3] The IATF documented an "infrastructure improvement needs list" of more than 60 city and regional projects and estimated a need for 7,400 acres for warehousing and intermodal facilities. One study by transportation planner F. Gerald Rawling calculated that the region's 19 intermodal yards performed 6.3 million "lifts" (movements of trailers and containers) in 1995, making the area "the third largest port in the world." (See Figure 16.2, page 206.) This headline galvanized attention to freight planning, helping break down previous barriers to collaborative planning. Rawling later observed, "The IATF was something of a cultural phenomenon—a network where everybody had a sense of what everybody else was doing and why, and the movement was towards a consensus of action. By 1999, there was a culture and a library of research. Does that qualify as planning?"[4]

Not all planners, however, bought into the overriding importance of intermodal. The city of Chicago balked in 1996 when CSX proposed reusing an abandoned 132-acre railroad yard in Englewood as an intermodal terminal linking the primary East Coast railroads (CSX and Norfolk Southern) and the primary western ones (BNSF and Union Pacific). The city, in its Corridors of Industrial Opportunities plan, had targeted this site for new manufacturing. It believed the intermodal facility would "produce fewer job opportunities or other tangible benefits in the Redevelopment Area and surrounding communities" compared to other kinds of development, though none was in the works. Further, under state tax law, the city would receive less revenue from an intermodal facility than from an industrial one.[5]

CSX was eager to move forward with the yard, so it negotiated a Neighborhood Investment Fund administered by the city to "further economic development" in surrounding communities, including Englewood. CSX made an initial $1 million donation and then paid one dollar for every truck that entered or exited the facility. With that, the project moved forward; since 1998, the fund has generated an estimated $4.5 million and will have generated up to $7 million upon its expiration in 2018. It has funded job training, land acquisition for commercial development, housing renovation, industrial facilities rehabilitation, new street lighting, and other economic development on the South Side.

Collaboration in freight planning increased further after a January 1999 snowstorm paralyzed railroad operations in and through Chicago. "Trains

Figure 16.2. Burlington Northern Santa Fe Railroad, Chicago (Corwith) intermodal facility, 2012

were backed up all the way to Omaha and the East Coast," recalled Rawling. "The railroads and Mayor Daley got the message that we were out of capacity." Officials realized the importance of investing in the regional railroad system, while the railroads, which had traditionally seen one another as competition and had kept the public sector at a distance, also understood that greater cooperation was needed. They formed a Chicago Planning Group to coordinate operations and plans. Chicago's Metropolitan Planning Council, which had taken little interest in freight in the past, also joined the table. Gradually but convincingly, freight had arrived at center stage in planning.[6]

The Chicago Region Environmental and Transportation Efficiency Program (CREATE)

Attention to freight planning issues in the 1990s culminated in the Chicago Region Environmental and Transportation Efficiency Program (CREATE), which was endorsed in 2003 by a "joint statement of understanding" signed by the six major railroads, Metra (the Northeast Illinois commuter rail system), and the state and city departments of transportation. CREATE undertook to "restructure, modernize and expand the freight and passenger rail facilities and highway grade separations in the Chicago metropolitan area . . . while reducing the environmental and social impacts of rail operations on the general public." These goals addressed both the environmental and the transportation objectives of ISTEA. CREATE proposed $3.2 billion in 70 railroad corridor improvement projects—funded mostly by the state, the federal government, and the freight railroads—to ease congestion of rail traffic through Chicago and to reduce conflicts with passenger-rail traffic.[7] The plan also sought to reduce fuel consumption and emissions, limit the growth of traffic congestion on the region's highways, provide additional acreage for open space and other land uses, and foster the flow of goods and people, including international traffic.

The program is initially focusing on congestion points with regional rpassenger trains and key junctions with multiple freight lines. Major components of the effort include 25 new roadway overpasses or underpasses, six new rail overpasses or underpasses, 37 freight rail projects including upgrades of tracks, switches and signals, viaduct improvement projects, and grade crossing safety enhancements. Further, CREATE has produced new information systems, including the Common Operational Picture, which integrates dispatch systems of the major railroads into a single display.

As of 2012, CREATE has received or committed $1.24 billion in investment from the railroads (25 percent), the state (42 percent), and the federal

Department of Transportation (34 percent).[8] To date, 14 projects are complete, 12 are under construction, 19 are in final design or environmental review, and 25 remain. The results so far include a 28 percent reduction in freight rail delays, along with a 33 percent reduction in passenger delays. Some of these projects are enormous, including a $130 million rail flyover at the aptly named Grand Crossing on the South Side that will end conflicts among 78 commuter trains and 60 freight and Amtrak trains each day.[9]

CREATE in turn has spurred further investments in Chicago by railroads seeking stronger connections there. The Norfolk Southern recently upgraded rails through Ohio to reduce travel times from Norfolk, Virginia, to Chicago in anticipation of greater container traffic through Norfolk via a widened Panama Canal. Norfolk Southern further desires to build a new intermodal facility in a proposed Dan Ryan Industrial Corridor on the South Side to handle the load. Similarly, several major new logistics parks, which combine intermodal yards and associated business/distribution parks, have since been developed on large sites surrounding Chicago—most notably at the former Joliet Arsenal. And in 2012, the railroad locomotive division of General Electric announced it was moving its international headquarters to downtown Chicago. Already GATX and TTX, the two largest railroad-car fleets in the world, are headquartered in Chicago. Global trade and freight thus have local and regional implications.

The freight sector and its intermodal yards are no longer seen as a problem by the city and region; rather, they are seen as one of the area's strongest growth engines. There is some irony here, in that this engine is powered in large measure by the globalization of trade, which had previously devastated traditional manufacturing sectors in Chicago and across the country. While the city and region had little say in global trade policy or in the rise of automated manufacturing processes, they could and did pursue the railroad, logistics, shipping, wholesale, trucking, and warehouse jobs found in the transportation sector. These jobs are neither high tech nor necessarily high paying, but they are a vital part of the Chicago area economy.

More generally, freight transportation planning has facilitated a whole new level of regional collaboration. Private railroads and public actors at all levels had come together to rationalize and update an aging infrastructure. The work of the IATF continues and informs the "freight cluster" research and advocacy work of CMAP, the regional planning organization. Clearly, freight and intermodal sectors have become central to the region's future.

ENT ERA

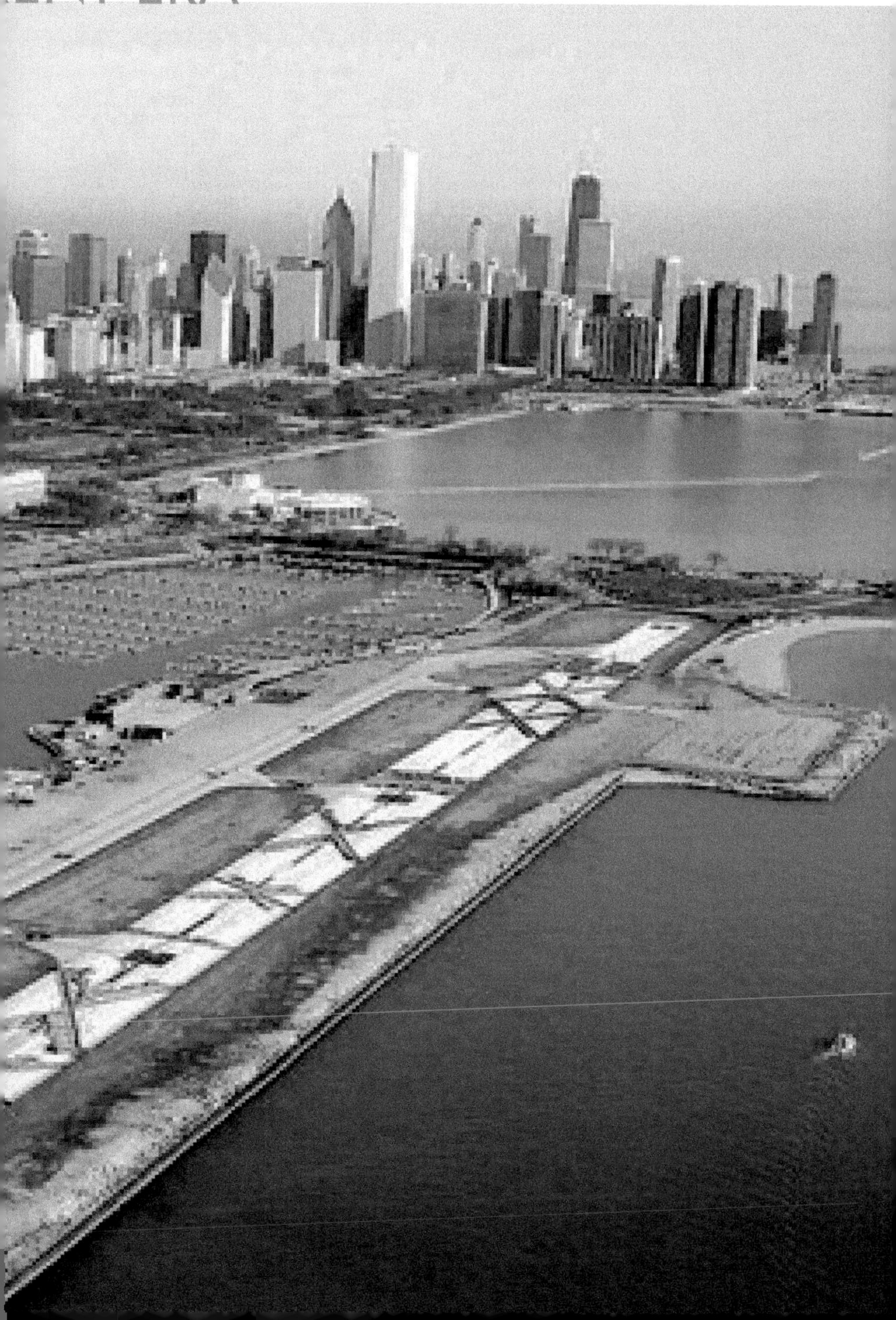

In 2009, the Burnham Plan Centennial offered a yearlong series of programs dedicated to the anniversary of the 1909 Plan of Chicago, ranging from symposiums to a traveling exhibit for elementary school students. While the Centennial celebrated the "Bold Plans and Big Dreams that shaped metropolitan Chicago," it also challenged "our region's communities, leaders and institutions to build on the success of the Burnham Plan and act boldly together to shape our future." The Centennial's rhetoric held that "Chicago is set apart by a robust tradition of action, and we have proven that bold, creative regional plans can work; we must do it again!"[1] Implicit in the call to action is the argument that Chicago has not been venturing "bold" or "big" ideas and instead has been reactive, even complacent.

This section makes the case that the issue before the city is not so much the size or audacity of its plans but their systemic quality and comprehensiveness. Planning need not be "bold" to be realistic, data driven, inclusive, and unifying. The success of individual projects like Millennium Park masks a decline in the hard work of organizing, analyzing, and presenting the city's problems and then finding a consensus for addressing them. As a result, elements of the city's growth may be successful as stand-alone ventures but not as an interconnected system. Popular tourist sites like Navy Pier and McCormick Place, profiled in chapter 17, are still difficult to access because of long-unaddressed transit needs in the central area. Similarly, the city's TIF program, described in chapter 19, has funded impressive projects but nevertheless has distorted the city's capital budgeting process, leaving priorities unclear. In chapters 18 and 20, we will see analytic planning on a broad scale, but the largest efforts—the 2003 Central Area Plan and 2009 Central Area Action Plan—have not received the support needed to make them guiding forces for the city. Residents barely know of their existence.

Most visitors perceive a city renaissance, yet the city as a whole has lost population and struggled in terms of economic growth according to the most recent census, a decline profiled in chapter 21. In response, Mayor Rahm Emanuel has focused on attracting jobs, but long-range physical planning has been demoted. Instead, the city remains stuck in deal-making and regulatory modes, focused on individual zoning decisions with little or no reference to the well-crafted plans on its shelves. Day-to-day city actions have become technocratic rather than proactive or future-oriented. The city needs to foster a more public stance on planning to build the momentum required to meet its substantial challenges.

CHAPTER 17
THE TOURIST CITY: NAVY PIER, MCCORMICK PLACE, AND MILLENNIUM PARK

Chicago came belatedly to the idea of planning for a tourist-friendly city. Tourism as a possible economic growth sector was not envisioned by the 1966 Comprehensive Plan or Chicago 21 in 1973. Instead, growth coalitions in other cities, including Boston and Baltimore, led the nation in the 1970s in creatively planning tourist-friendly attractions. Chicago sought to copy these ideas in the 1980s, but political delays and the failure of transit plans left major attractions difficult to reach. Over time, Chicago built several successful, even spectacular, tourist attractions, but these were produced in the Chicago way—deal by deal and largely disconnected from broader planning. Only in the past 15 years have hospitality and tourism been major growth sectors in the economy, yet they have evolved more in spite of careful planning than because of it. Still, Chicago has stumbled upon a winning formula that attracts large numbers—46 million visitors per year at the peak in 2007—to both its middlebrow amusement-centered playground spaces and its highbrow cultural spaces.[1]

Navy Pier
The major innovation in urban tourism in the 1970s was the pedestrian-friendly "festival marketplace," inaugurated by Boston's Faneuil Hall (1976) and Baltimore's Inner Harbor (1980). Both were conceived by developer James Rouse, though financed by quasi-public development corporations or public subsidies, and both created urban destinations out of decaying

spaces. Many other cities—including New York (South Street Seaport), St. Louis (Union Station), Miami (Bayside Marketplace), and New Orleans (Riverwalk Marketplace)—followed suit.[2]

Chicago had an obvious amenity ripe for redevelopment, Navy Pier. In its prime, the pier served not only as a shipping facility but also as a port for excursion vessels, while a large auditorium hosted concerts and dances through the 1920s, with throngs arriving by a streetcar that traveled to the end of the pier. But in the 1930s, shipping functions shifted to the Port of Chicago, and the pier became a wartime training facility, then a University of Illinois campus, and then, in the 1970s, a popular summer music festival venue. By that time, deteriorating infrastructure and periods of dormancy made the facility a costly burden.[3]

Competing visions for the pier emerged in the late 1970s. City architect Jerry Butler advanced a modest plan including a "passive" children's park, expanded concert facilities, a marina, and an exhibition hall, along with "small stores featuring ethnic and specialty goods that don't compete with Michigan Avenue." The ebullient architect Harry Weese promoted a more ambitious privatization of the pier, suggesting a huge Ferris wheel, large marina, a hotel, and extensive commercialization. "The city doesn't know how to lie down with the private sector," Weese told the *Chicago Tribune*. "A private developer should do the entire pier . . . a top guy." He proposed James Rouse as the ideal candidate. After a trip to Baltimore, Mayor Jane Byrne agreed. A 1980 Rouse proposal went beyond Weese's ideas to include a performance stage and movie theaters. To handle traffic, Rouse added a massive parking garage just southwest of the pier and a new trolley line connecting the pier to North Michigan Avenue and a CTA station.[4]

The Rouse scheme, however, bogged down on two fronts. First, the city and Rouse could not agree on the details of the public-private partnership, which had too many unknowns given the riskiness of the commercial venture and potentially explosive costs of infrastructure (everything from shoring up pylons under the pier to building new off-ramps from Lake Shore Drive). Rouse and the city, under Mayor Harold Washington, negotiated a "linkage" agreement to ensure "targeted purchasing, local business development, and local hiring." But then Navy Pier became embroiled in the city's racial politics, as Washington's enemies did not want him to get credit for a big redevelopment project. Alderman Ed Vrdolyak, leader of the anti-Washington majority bloc in the council, had supported Rouse's redevelopment under Byrne, but he now callously led it to defeat. The *Chicago Sun-Times* called Navy Pier a "headstone in the Council Wars."[5]

By 1990, at least nine planning studies of Navy Pier had been completed—including a Washington administration proposal heavily influenced by local arts groups—yet the project remained in limbo. Costs for infrastructure had ballooned from $60 million to $150 million, according to the last plan by the Urban Land Institute. The deadlock was finally broken by Governor Jim Thompson, who offered state funds in return for folding Navy Pier into the state authority that controlled McCormick Place, the city's convention center. (The new authority became known as "McPier.") "The people of Illinois are investing $150 million," Thompson told the *Chicago Tribune*. "This underpins the infrastructure of what will be, by the end of the century, the state's largest industry: tourism."[6]

The governor's vision—closer to Rouse's commercialism than Washington's cultural park—set the tone for the design competition, with 10 submissions from prominent national firms. The winning design was labeled a "safe" choice: the pier's storage sheds would be replaced with an arcade, a winter garden, performance spaces, a museum, a theater, and a small exhibition hall, along with a parking garage on the pier, all centered on creating a mall-like experience (Figure 17.1). *Tribune* architecture critic Paul Gapp was aghast, calling the design "another tragic event in the continuing degradation of Chicago's lakefront." The design is "flashy and

Figure 17.1. Navy Pier, 2004

bulbous," he contended, and the placement of parking on the pier "again gives primacy to highway engineers."[7]

While the decade of political and planning haggling had made little improvement over Rouse's original vision in 1980, Gapp's criticism misses the goal of Thompson and Daley: they wanted a tried-and-true tourist attraction, a place for suburbanites and conventioneers to have a controlled if artificial city experience. Much of the pier is everything Gapp says: gaudy, commercialized, and, at times, tacky. But it offers spectacular views, middlebrow entertainment, and excursions. Moreover, the pier includes the Chicago Children's Museum and Chicago Shakespeare Theater, which coexist with carnival rides and IMAX theaters. The final product struck a balance between commercialization and public space, between culture and middlebrow entertainment. By 2000, Navy Pier had become a surprising success, drawing seven million visitors a year.

The planning failure lay not in Navy Pier's mix of amenities but in the inability to connect it to the rest of the city. Most of those seven million visitors do not have an easy time getting to the pier. Bus connections exist, but they are challenging for tourists and out-of-towners to navigate. The city established a free tourist trolley on weekends to transport visitors to suburban rail stations, but service is spotty and riders often cram onto inadequate vehicles. Those who drive either pay a major premium (currently $23 per day) to park on Navy Pier or troll for street parking blocks away. The pedestrian experience is not inviting either, with a poorly planned and overbuilt Lake Shore Drive precluding an easy path to the pier. Navy Pier succeeds as an element of the "tourist city" envisioned by Thompson and Daley, but only in spite of its dismal access.

The Circulator

The city did produce a plan to address the transit isolation of both Navy Pier and McCormick Place, a light-rail effort known as the Central Area Circulator. Planners made a strong case for the nearly $600 million capital investment, but the ad hoc nature of the planning and the lack of strong backing from Mayor Richard M. Daley ultimately helped sink it. Despite the investment in tourist city attractions like Navy Pier, McCormick Place, and Millennium Park, Chicago still lacks a downtown area transit system that is friendly to commuters, let alone tourists.

The Circulator idea emerged from the Metropolitan Planning Council in 1989 as the successor to the Distributor subway, a cross-Loop subway proposed in the 1970s. Both sought to solve the long-standing problem of

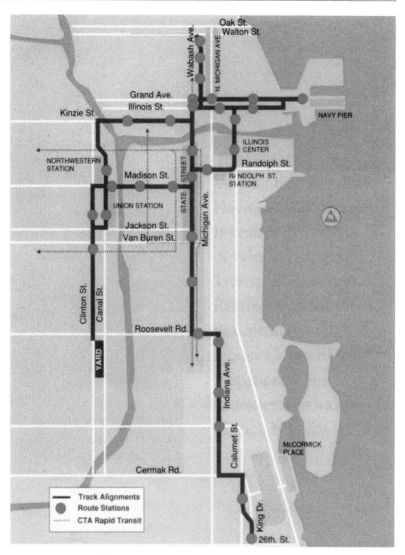

Figure 17.2. Route map, from "Chicago's Central Area Circulator: Transit for the City's Future," 1994

transit connections between commuter rail stations and major portions of the central area, as well as the lack of easy transit options for major destinations serving workers and tourists alike, including Illinois Center, North Michigan Avenue, Navy Pier, and McCormick Place (Figure 17.2). Anecdotally, downtown drivers were willing to drive from the suburbs rather than use commuter rail if it also entailed cross-Loop trips on slow buses, as

Chicago Sun-Times columnist Dennis Byrne related: "What finally pushed me into my car was the fact that getting from Union Station to the office took as long as the 20-mile train trip between home and the station. Whether I walked or took the bus, the cross-Loop trip took 25 minutes." The case for additional transit capacity in the central area appeared obvious. With an office boom, an expanding Loop, and attractions drawing millions, Chicago needed better ways to move people around the central area.[8]

Light rail emerged as the transport choice for the Circulator for cost and amenity reasons. It operated on existing streets, making it less costly than a heavy-rail subway, and offered a version of mass transit that planners believed could attract large numbers of middle-class riders who disdained or feared buses and subways. Circulator planners explained that light-rail passengers would board bright, modern European rail cars from attractive curbside stations, with only a one-step climb. Circulator trains would also operate independently of the CTA. As one commentator put it, "It is hard to look at the Circulator and not conclude that it is intended as a middle-class alternative to the CTA."[9] Still, light rail amounted to an imperfect solution to the Loop's transportation capacity issues. As an on-street platform, it lacked capacity and speed compared to a grade-separated solution.

A combination of NIMBYism and other parochial interests forced numerous route changes, often more for political than planning reasons.[10] In one response to neighborhood pressures, Circulator officials reluctantly moved a route from east of Michigan Avenue to west of it. The move made little planning sense, as the ill-served areas lay east of Michigan, including Northwestern University's Chicago campus and hospital. Circulator planners projected a drop of 5,000 daily riders from the shift. The university, for its part, offered no support for what would have been a major benefit for its students and employees; instead, its expansion plans called for more parking garages.[11] Similarly, dubious criticisms about traffic from a powerful community group in the Streeterville neighborhood also dampened enthusiasm for the Circulator.[12]

NIMBY concerns were to be expected, but the attitude of both the CTA and Metra toward the Circulator was equally unhelpful. The CTA resented scarce federal funds going to a new system beyond its control and feared potential Circulator operating losses might absorb its own scarce operating subsidies. Metra's opposition was even more baffling, as its largest stations would be more directly connected to important destinations, potentially increasing ridership. But Metra's chairman Jeffrey Ladd told Chicago Public Radio, "Our people are not going to use it [the Circulator]. The figures I've seen are clearly exaggerated. Our people just walk [to work]."[13] Metra's leadership instead wanted funds to extend its lines further into the exurbs of the Chicago region.

Despite institutional indifference, the Circulator had strong support from downtown business interests as well as city and federal officials. Capital costs were to be split equally among the city, the state, and the federal government. With surprisingly little difficulty, downtown associations lined up behind a tax increase on commercial properties within the central area to fund the Circulator; neither taxpayers in the neighborhoods nor residents downtown would be funding construction. Plans submitted to Washington received high marks from the Federal Transportation Administration, which guaranteed the federal share.

Only the state of Illinois was in doubt, as its contribution was dependent on annual appropriations. In November 1994, Republicans captured both state houses, and the Circulator quickly became caught up in a complicated political battle between state Republican leaders and Mayor Daley. When the mayor moved to preserve his control over Chicago airports—a power long coveted by the legislature—Republicans retaliated by denying him Circulator funding. Neither the governor nor Metra was willing to expend political capital on behalf of a downtown transit project, and so the Circulator lost one-third of its funding. Five years of planning and engineering studies (at a cost of roughly $30 million) fell apart only months before construction would have begun.

Circulator executive director Steve Schlickman later reflected on the plan's demise, saying, "Perhaps we bit off more than we could chew. If we could have built a starter line, then everyone would see that it would work, and political support would materialize." Sufficient funding was in hand to build much of the Riverbank line stretching from the Metra stations to North Michigan Avenue—the most important part of the system—but political will had evaporated, and even Daley in frustration called the Circulator "dead."[14]

The Circulator plan had done nearly everything right within the narrow confines that defined transit planning in the 1990s. Planners had been responsive to community and political input. The funding plan had been reasonably apportioned between those who stood to benefit. But the lack of political support from Metra, narrow-minded politics, and the compromises inherent in light rail left the Circulator with too few friends and just enough powerful enemies to sink it. The problem of moving people around the Loop remained a planning headache, one that persists to this day.

McCormick Place and the Tourist City

Like Navy Pier, McCormick Place has been a crucial piece of Chicago's tourist city, yet the massive convention facility is its own fiefdom, largely disconnected from broader city planning. The sprawling exhibition halls—the largest in North America—are a major economic engine for the city; in 2006, McCormick Place estimated its economic impact at $3.4 billion.[15] Throughout the past two decades, the state- and city-appointed "McPier" authority has been determined to keep McCormick the largest venue, building multiple expansions. But the authority has neglected redevelopment opportunities around its property and has failed to lead on the creation of better transit connections to it. Planning for the larger neighborhood has not been its strong suit, yet it is essential to its future.

McCormick Place has exploded in size from its initial lakefront building. In a convention arms race with Las Vegas and Orlando, McPier has added several large halls, including McCormick Place North (1986: 510,000 square feet of exhibition space), McCormick Place South (1996: 840,000 square feet), and McCormick Place West (2007: 460,000 square feet plus 250,000 square feet of meeting space). This construction binge was funded largely by city and county excise taxes on rental cars, hotels, and restaurants. McCormick has remained the nation's largest convention center, but the trade show business has diminished as a growth sector in the past decade. Attendance at McCormick Place shows fell 37 percent between 2001 and 2011, from 1.3 million attendees to 828,000. The McPier operating budget plunged into the red during the recent recession, requiring a $20 million annual state operating subsidy, set to expire in 2014. Fierce competition means McCormick will continue to need to find new ways to attract trade shows.[16]

Part of McCormick Place's difficulty centers on its location, one that presents both problems and, more recently, opportunities. The convention center complex is physically isolated from the central area, cut off by railroad tracks, highways, and warehouses—a problem even greater than at Navy Pier. The location two miles south of the Loop dates to 1956, when Colonel Robert McCormick, publisher of the *Chicago Tribune*, demanded the lakefront site, and newly elected Mayor Richard J. Daley went along over the vociferous objections of the CPC and other civic groups. Paul Gapp later called the decision one of the city's "biggest planning mistakes."[17] When the original hall burned down in 1969, Daley missed an opportunity to rectify the mistake and instead rebuilt it in the same place.

Figure 17.3. Motor Row, along the 2200 block of S. Michigan Avenue, steps from McCormick Place, 2010

McCormick Place has only one hotel in the vicinity, no direct CTA rail connections, and no restaurants within walking distance. Walkability outside is poor, and even a Metra station within the complex—highly underused—is an unfriendly space. Instead convention goers are dependent upon fleets of shuttle buses to drive them to convention hotels in the Loop, on North Michigan Avenue, and—during peak conventions—out at O'Hare Airport. In 2001, McPier paid for an extravagant two-mile, $100 million dedicated roadway that passes underneath Millennium Park for the exclusive use of shuttle buses so they can quickly reach downtown hotels.

Yet McPier has resisted other investments that might spur development of attractions and transit within walking distance. Just across the street from McCormick Place West lies the Motor Row historic district, a compact area of former auto showrooms with impressive facades dating from the 1920s (Figure 17.3). These spaces lie vacant, begging for restoration and investment. The untapped potential for Motor Row is obvious: it could easily be transformed into a highly walkable entertainment district full of restaurants and music venues, all a stone's throw from McCormick Place.

Motor Row may eventually become such a district, but for over a decade McPier has been reluctant to lead in its own backyard. The reasons for this shortsightedness are unclear, but several factors are likely at work. First, McPier leadership has long had an inward, "campus" orientation (Figure 17.4, page 224), focusing on creating a tightly sealed experience for out-of-towners who barely need to touch the street as they are whisked

Figure 17.4. McCormick Place complex and Motor Row district (center), October 10, 2012

from their hotels to the convention center by motor coach. Undoubtedly, the excuse for this bubble around conventioneers involves fears of crime and race: for decades, two large, problematic public housing projects lay to the west of Motor Row. But one was carefully renovated in 2004 and is now an asset to the area, while the other was demolished in 2009 and 2010. Further, Chinatown has thrived for decades just beyond the public housing developments and attracted tourists, suggesting that race and class fears are overblown.[18]

But despite changes in the surrounding neighborhood and vast tracts of available land, McPier has balked at creating a master plan to redevelop Motor Row and expand the area into a walkable entertainment district stretching all the way to Chinatown. In the void, mistakes have been made. McPier assembled land adjacent to Motor Row for a much-needed convention hotel that would have anchored new development, but then abandoned the effort and decided to expand the on-site Hyatt Hotel, which it owns. Similarly, the city failed to protect a crucial Motor Row parcel—directly across from the convention center—against rezoning for an anonymous data center. In 2011, the city did, however, take the lead on transit improvements, designating TIF funds to build a new $50 million CTA Green Line station to serve Motor Row and McCormick Place, with completion expected in 2014.[19] It could be a valuable driver of development, but McPier officials have shown little interest in promoting the station to its conventioneers or employees. The city has taken other steps to assist Motor Row, including a new streetscape on Michigan Avenue and assistance to individual deals, most recently a brewpub. However without a plan and with halting leadership from McCormick Place, Chicago has missed opportunities to establish a potentially thriving convention district. Trade show business could suffer: convention planners have commented that the empty environment surrounding McCormick Place is a perceived negative, and convention goers have expressed a preference for the Orlando convention center's relative walkability.[20]

Millennium Park

While Navy Pier is a deliberately middlebrow experience, and McCormick Place corrals deep-pocketed convention goers, Millennium Park aspires to bring high culture to the masses. The 24.5-acre park, completed in 2004, is packed with whimsical yet thought-provoking art. It offers visitors a range of experiences, from commercial to introspective, and its programming varies considerably, from ice skating to classical concerts. Philanthropists, architects, and engineers designed and built Millennium Park, producing a unique and inviting public space that has driven tourism and accelerated development. More than any other addition, the park symbolizes the arrival of Chicago on the world stage and the perception of its renaissance. But in many respects, Millennium Park's chaotic gestation suggests how far removed planning has become from influencing the city's major projects.

Like Illinois Center and Dearborn Park, Millennium Park's site was reclaimed from railroads after a protracted effort. By the 1970s, Illinois Central Railroad freight operations had shriveled, and much of the space served as an ugly parking lot for Loop commuters. The underuse of such prime land on Michigan Avenue had long been a civic disappointment. The 1983 Central Area Plan included a "Lakefront Gardens" proposal, which called for formal park spaces along with an unassuming band shell, designed by Bruce Graham at SOM. Despite enthusiasm from numerous civic organizations, Lakefront Gardens withered on the vine, as Chicago Park District ambivalence, lack of mayoral leadership, and daunting land acquisition costs doomed the effort.[21]

As historian Timothy Gilfoyle expertly relates, a fortuitous set of circumstances beginning in 1997 soon made a new park possible. A Chicago Park District lawyer discovered that the city's 1848 lease-in-perpetuity to the Illinois Central required that the site be used for railroad purposes; its use as a parking lot appeared to violate the lease. This fact alone would not have been enough to pry the site from the Illinois Central, but a year later "fortune shone on Chicago," as Gilfoyle tells it. The railroad entered into merger talks, giving executives an incentive to boost the company's after-tax profits, and a donation of valuable land to the city would entail a big write-off. By maximizing the potential value of the land, the Illinois Central received federal and state tax deductions, and the city gained site control at no cost and without a punishing legal fight.

The city asked SOM to plan a new park funded by revenue from a parking garage beneath it. (This was unrealistic, and eventually $95 million in downtown TIF money helped pay for infrastructure, including decking over the remaining Illinois Central tracks.)[22] SOM's Adrian Smith proposed a variation of the earlier Lakefront Gardens idea with a music pavilion and an extension of the Beaux-Arts styles that defined the rest of neighboring Grant Park. The SOM design would, within reason, faithfully complete the 1909 Plan of Chicago. Mayor Richard M. Daley, sensitive to the politics of building a new downtown park when neighborhoods also needed investment, insisted that the visible part of the park be paid for by private donations, with estimated costs at a modest $30 million. In a critical move, Daley asked John Bryan, chairman of the Sara Lee Corporation and past chairman of the Art Institute of Chicago, to lead the fund-raising effort.

As Gilfoyle persuasively argues, Bryan's fund-raising prowess and vision ultimately transformed Lakefront Gardens into Millennium Park, a vastly different undertaking. Instead of a Beaux-Arts extension of Grant Park, Bryan maintained that Chicago needed a bolder vision that would engage multiple audiences and include art. He pitched this vision to the philanthropic community as a spectacular gift to the city and proved exceptionally adept at bringing Chicago's "modern-day Medicis" to the table, raising an astonishing $173.5 million from the city's wealthiest families. They embraced Bryan's vision, and soon the park became filled with massive sculptures. Philanthropist Cindy Pritzker brought in Frank Gehry to give the music pavilion a showpiece headdress in his signature style. Pieces of the park came together as donors surfaced, with a dance theater, an elaborate garden, a bike pavilion, and a serpentine bridge added on the fly. An Anish Kapoor sculpture and a Jaume Plensa fountain were so enormous that the parking garage—already under way as the frenzied planning continued above—had to be reengineered and retrofitted to accommodate the weight of the new structures.[23]

The park had been taken out of the hands of the SOM planners and handed to Bryan and the major donors who pieced together a chaotic but playful cultural playground (Figure 17.5). Planning purists like Adrian

Figure 17.5. *Millennium Park, July 13, 2011*

Smith—who had deftly designed Museum Campus and who objected to the diversion from his Beaux-Arts scheme—saw a disjointed outcome. Gehry's gaudy music pavilion clashed with the gardens, and ice rinks lay adjacent to what Smith called a "sculpture gallery extravaganza."[24]

But the public adores the park and its over-the-top nature. When diverse crowds play in Plensa's fountain, marvel at their reflections in Kapoor's *Cloud Gate* sculpture, or cross the whimsical Gehry bridge, they explore new built environments and experience a version of art and architecture that delights more than the order of grand Beaux-Arts parks. Great cities need great spaces, and surely Millennium Park, despite being crammed with so many uses, is one of the most impressive in the country for its audacity and playfulness.

Despite its unusual gestation and the lack of integrated planning, the park has been a boon to the city. Not only has it become a tourist magnet, it has sparked major investments in the East Loop, including conversion of older Class B buildings into residential use. A study in 2005 attributed $1.4 billion in nearby residential investment to the "Millennium Park effect," and a further 2,600 hotel rooms were added to the Loop between 2001 and 2011.[25]

Of deeper concern is the extent to which the public has taken itself out of the conversation of planning for spaces such as Millennium Park. In its unwillingness or inability to raise public funds to build the park, the city ceded control to philanthropists. Their gift was substantial and ultimately successful, but the space speaks to the vision and values of its donors. Planning, including systematic thinking about the use of public space, has taken a back seat. Measured by the crowds that visit its creative cultural playground and by the boom in nearby real estate, the park is an impressive achievement. But the irony is that Millennium Park was not part of a larger planning effort, and its success seems to only reinforce the perception that broader planning is not even needed. Why plan systematically when wildly successful individual deals like Millennium Park can produce such accolades? Yet as we will see, a lack of planning has its costs.

CHAPTER 18
THE ERA OF BIG PLANS IS OVER

By 2003, Chicago's central area had a strength and vitality unimaginable 30 years earlier. The city had avoided the tailspin predicted by the *Chicago Tribune*'s 1982 series "City on the Brink" and risen as a global city, attracting tourists, convention goers, and affluent residents to its downtown core. Yet much of this revival happened piecemeal, on an ad hoc, deal-by-deal basis. As Reuben Hedlund, the CPC chairman through much of the 1990s, explains, "There was a growing opposition to big plans in the 1990s—a combination of aldermanic privilege coupled with the mayor's office wanting control."[1] Comprehensive plans had given way to incremental efforts, one planned development at a time. The lack of a master plan for downtown, let alone a comprehensive plan for the city, meant Chicago had neither a systematic examination of its needs nor a vision for the future at the start of the 21st century. With a wave of residential growth and a downtown office boom under way, planning needed to get ahead of the curve, to help guide development rather than react to it.

The 2003 Central Area Plan
The lack of a plan for the central area between 1983 and 2003 was emblematic of the declining interest in systematic planning in the city and the declining resources to do so. City Hall never asked for a downtown master plan, as Mayor Richard M. Daley's distrust of comprehensive planning was well understood by those around him, nor were aldermen eager

for plans that might subordinate their prerogatives.[2] The CAC, the driver of most previous plans, had become quiescent in the 1990s, seemingly without an organizing principle once the city had rebounded from its depths in the 1970s and early 1980s. Moreover, earlier central area plans had clearly stated purposes: protecting the city's core (1958); addressing social change and positioning the city for federal aid (1966); building a new town on the edge of the Loop (1973); and attracting a world's fair (1983). Together, these plans by experts and business interests wanted to "save" downtown from threats perceived and real. But by the turn of the 21st century downtown appeared to be thriving. Why plan at all?

Indeed, a three-year process of research, discussion papers, and roundtable discussions initiated by the Department of Planning between 1988 and 1991 produced few arguments for urgency. The resulting draft report, its authors noted, "does not propose major changes or grand new visions, nor does it address specific economic development concerns" and instead focused on marginal regulations to shape development on the fringes of the central business district. The principles were in tune with planning thinking in the early 1990s, emphasizing zoning reforms to enhance a "walkable environment," directing "high density office development to where transit exists," and encouraging developers to "build great spaces."[3] But the principles were tinkering rather than thinking systematically about future needs.

The need for a data-driven analysis became clearer in 1998 after a change in zoning policy prompted a major debate about land use in the central area. Due to weak office demand at the time, the Department of Planning and Development responded to developer requests to repurpose older Class C office buildings, often built in the 1920s, into residential spaces. The change divided the Chicago Development Council, which represented both commercial and residential developers. The council allowed that conversion might be acceptable in the eastern portion of the Loop closest to Grant Park, but sites in the central and West Loop—closest to suburban rail stations—should be banned for residential use. The commercial developers, especially council cochair Robert Wislow, believed that Loop sites could attract up to four million square feet of office development per year through 2030, an output requiring at least 100 acres of land over the next 30 years—but only 45 acres were available. Wislow's estimates were back-of-the-envelope calculations, but without solid data or a master plan, developers reasonably feared that excessive amounts of land might be gobbled up by the housing boom then under way.

Wislow's argument suggested that Chicago's land-use situation had changed radically. Since 1958, planning and zoning had sought to defend a tightly compact office core by encouraging residential and institutional development on the Loop's fringes to serve as buffers against office dispersion. That strategy had worked, as plenty of land for new office development remained within the Loop. But now the Loop was potentially running out of prime land, in part due to residential construction within it. Further, the West Loop, which contained most of the underused land and which made the most sense for office expansion, remained zoned at relatively low densities. A central area master plan, then, was essential to managing downtown land use.

These arguments set off a flurry of empirical studies to project land-use needs, but their conclusions conflicted. The Chicago Development Council funded a study in May 1999 that backed down considerably from Wislow's estimates, suggesting demand of around two million square feet of office space and 1,500 to 2,000 apartments per year through 2030.[4] A month later, the Department of Planning and Development issued a detailed inventory of 215 million square feet of available and "soft" sites, assuming the maximum densities allowed under the existing zoning code. The department reasoned these sites could accommodate both commercial and residential needs, providing "enough development potential for the next 35 years." Still, the department recommended that zoning in the West Loop be revised to allow for high-density "office only" development.

Neither of the new estimates was a plan that considered the complete range of density, land-use, infrastructure, transit, and traffic issues. The business community, unsatisfied, asked the city to produce a new central area plan.[5] In June 2000, the Department of Planning and Development announced an elaborate planning process to develop "a bold plan for Chicago's Central Areas." The 24-member steering committee, comprising "leaders from the business, government, and civic sectors," would preside over seven task forces that totaled "over 120 experts and opinion leaders," representing a much broader collection of individuals than any previous plan. Further impetus for action came from an unflattering October 2000 *Business Week* cover story entitled "Chicago Blues" that portrayed a city slipping as a business capital.[6] Pressure had finally intensified for serious planning.

The 2003 Central Area Plan was data driven and structured around specific goals for economic growth. Consultants produced comprehensive estimates for office, residential, and institutional development between 2000 and 2020, as well as acreage needed to accommodate this growth. A data-

The Retail Revival in and Around the Loop

In the 1980s, downtown Chicago's retail sector reached its nadir, with State Street losing six of its seven department stores. The opening of Water Tower Place in 1975 led to an increase in sales on North Michigan Avenue, but retail continued its decline elsewhere in the central area. But by 2012, State Street had revived, central area neighborhoods had sprouted numerous new community centers, and North Michigan Avenue attracted international stores. What role did planning play in creating this retail growth?

The retail transformation followed a housing boom that took almost two decades to mature but resulted from the creation of residential areas recommended by city plans between 1958 and 1983, including Dearborn Park, Illinois Center, Dock and Canal, Central Station, and the West Loop. Downtown housing units surged from 48,000 in 1991 to an estimated 110,000 in 2013 (Figure 18.1). In the last decade alone, the census reports 48,000 new residents within two miles of city hall.

These new residents have brought major grocery stores to the central area for the first time. In 1998 with city assistance, the Near South finally attracted a full-service grocer—Dominick's—which then proceeded to ring the Loop with new stores in Greektown, Cabrini-Green, and Streeterville. Between 2000 and 2007, eight new grocery anchors opened in the central area. Since then the number has more than doubled. Spaces are also getting larger. In 2012, Mariano's Fresh Market, a recent entrant to the Chicago market, announced an 80,000-square-foot flagship store just a block from an 80,000-square-foot flagship of Whole Foods. Further, Target in 2012 opened a branch in the former Carson Pirie Scott department store on State Street designed by Louis Sullivan.

Alongside the new residents, new public attractions and spaces like Millennium Park and Navy Pier attracted a new clientele of suburban families and Midwestern tourists to the central area, particularly for the South Michigan Avenue and State Street corridors, which saw significant new restaurant and retail development.

The 2003 Central Area Plan concentrated on channeling retail growth to new areas. When the plan's Retail Task Force first met in July 2000, chair Norm Elkin argued that the city needed to consider the potential of the whole central area for retail district rather than concentrate just on State Street. The plan commissioned a survey of more than 4,700 shoppers and

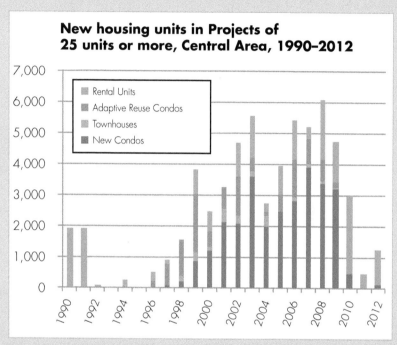

Figure 18.1. Downtown housing production, 1990–2013. Data from Appraisal Research Counselors

found that residents and tourists spent over twice as much per visit as the traditional core client, the downtown worker. The most compelling findings, however, were that the new Near South Dominick's was pulling shoppers from the entire South Side, while the North Side's relatively unplanned Clybourn corridor, with its big box retailers, was attracting South Side shoppers who would bypass the Loop to reach those stores. Both of these shopping patterns indicated that the South Side was badly underserved for retail and that if properly planned could be another source of retail demand in the central area.

As a result, the 2003 Central Area Plan recommended the creation of a major new retail corridor in the Near South along Roosevelt Road by encouraging big box retailers of all types to locate on former warehouse and railroad sites there. By 2012, four new retail centers, a Target, new grocery stores, and a theater have entered the corridor, bringing more than two million square feet of new shopping to city residents.

—Larry E. Lund

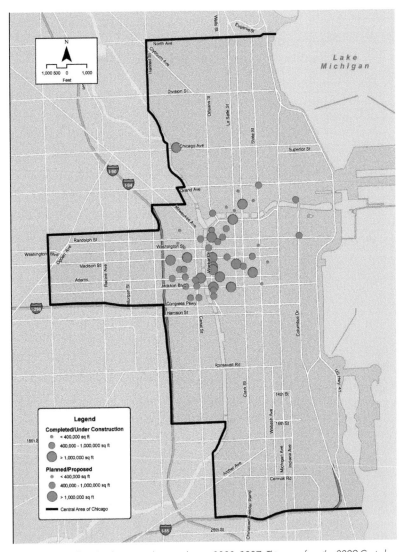

Figure 18.2a. Office development in the central area, 2000–2007. This map, from the 2009 Central Area Action Plan, shows that the economic analysis for the 2003 Central Area Plan proved prescient; office growth migrated to the West Loop, clustering around Wacker Drive and the train stations just west of the Chicago River.

base projected the year-by-year shifting of demand among central area submarkets. A survey of 300 Chicago companies profiled space needs, future growth plans, employment characteristics, and location factors. And a survey

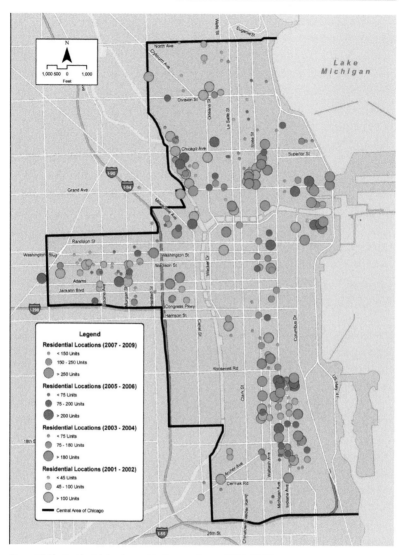

Figure 18.2b. Residential development in the central area, 2001–2007

documented the behavior of more than 4,600 shoppers. The range and breadth of data far exceeded earlier plans, part of a larger national trend to bring economic development issues front and center in the planning process.[7]

The economic analysis anticipated office development at 1.6 million square feet per year, less than in the previous 20 years. Other space needs, however, were projected to grow at higher than historical rates: retail (250,000 square feet per year), institutional (150,000 square feet per year), residential (1,800 units per year), and hotel rooms (600 per year), trends justified by the rise in downtown living since 1990. If the plan's transit, zoning, and urban design recommendations were adopted, demand for the central area space would rise another 20 to 40 percent. Land-use estimates suggested a 35- to 40-year supply of building sites in the central area, but submarket analysis indicated a shift in demand to the West Loop (Figures 18.2a–b). And the survey showed a strong preference for letting the market decide land use rather than creating office-only zones. Overall, the economic analysis quashed the idea that there was a shortage of development sites in the central area.[8]

Other fears of the office developers, however, were justified. While Chicago had one of the highest concentrations of metro office space in the downtown of any U.S. city—55 percent, second only to New York City—the central area had lost office market share to the suburbs in the 1990s, capturing only 40 percent of new demand in the region. In other words, the suburbs were winning. Still, the company survey and rent/occupancy data showed a continuing strong preference for downtown locations for employee recruitment and business synergies. A strategic goal of the plan, then, was to increase the central area share of regional office demand to at least 50 percent, with the hope of increasing further if other elements of the plan were implemented.[9]

To do so, however, required more transit capacity, a crucial long-term problem. A majority of central area workers utilized transit (52.1 percent), with additional workers walking (5.8 percent) or carpooling (9.3 percent); only about one-third were driving alone. But the CTA and Metra were near capacity on several lines and stations. The CTA Red and Brown lines were already at capacity, as were the major Metra stations. The bridges over the Chicago River connecting the Loop to the stations were at their pedestrian and vehicular limits during rush hours, and pedestrians often spilled onto streets. If the city was to add more office space and residential space over the next 20 years and still sustain a high share of commuting trips—or reach even higher, more desirable levels—then transit capacity had to expand.[10]

The Chicago Department of Transportation (CDOT) thus became deeply engaged in the central area planning process for the first time. The 2003

Central Area Plan included numerous transit projects to update the city's long underfunded core with expanded stations, modern signalization, a passenger information system, and new train-to-bus transfer facilities. But the plan's most ambitious recommendation was the West Loop Transportation Center (WLTC), intended to address multiple planning goals: to better connect the two Metra stations and the CTA via a new Clinton Street subway tunnel, to incorporate two new cross-Loop bus transitways, and to develop a high-speed-rail station (Figure 18.3, page 238). Further, the WLTC would support the continued migration of high-density office development west of the river, where the most space for expansion existed. It was an elegant but potentially costly solution: digging new tunnels and building a massive rail station were sure to have hefty price tags.

Beyond the transit centerpiece, the 2003 Central Area Plan included numerous smaller recommendations, many of which built on previous work. Ideas for improved walkability, greater access to waterfronts, expanded open space, and bike lanes found support. Various central area neighborhoods had specific improvement plans. Finally, Mayor Daley's effort to label Chicago as a "green and sustainable" city meant that the Department of the Environment was also invested in the plan. Its recommendations included green roofs, starting with City Hall itself, electrical grid improvements, and expedited approvals and density bonuses for LEED (Leadership in Energy and Environmental Design)-certified green buildings.[11]

Distracted Implementation and the Decline of Planning

On June 12, 2003, the CPC adopted the Central Area Plan, noting that it "lays out an ambitious twenty-year program. . . . An equally ambitious implementation strategy will be required to bring it to fruition."[12] But little action ensued, and the inattention to implementation revealed the continued decline of planning as a valuable exercise in the minds of city officials.

Several factors explain the city's lack of urgency. First, Daley sent signals that he wanted to distance himself from the plan, fearing it as an intrusion on his own power. Taking a cue from Daley, the rest of City Hall did not regard the plan as a guiding document. At that time, the mayor's political stature was nearly at its peak. He was in full command of the city council and not yet sullied by scandals that would blemish his last term. The city's downtown vibrancy appeared assured, and Millennium Park's completion was near. The mayor didn't need a plan for the future—that future had already arrived. While Daley liked the drawings for the massive West Loop Transportation Center, he made little effort to find the funds for it.[13]

Figure 18.3. West Loop Transportation Center, showing multiple levels including (from bottom to top) high-speed rail station, CTA station, Transitway station, and ticketing and shopping concourse, 2003

Second and more important, the plan dropped by the wayside as the mayor became enamored of hosting the 2016 Summer Olympics. After 20 years of waiting for a new central area plan, city attention was diverted into another global beauty contest. Daley wanted the games badly, and City Hall, the business community, and philanthropists turned their energies and funds toward that goal. In a major fund-raising effort, Aon CEO Patrick Ryan announced plans to find $25 million of private money just to fund the costs of a bid. In September 2006, the Chicago Olympic committee released a plan encompassing 33 venues stretching from Lincoln Park to Hyde Park and west to the United Center, with an estimated price tag of $2 billion; others quickly suggested the cost could be much greater.[14] The planning, public relations, and fund-raising continued at a fever level, yet in 2009 the International Olympic Committee soundly rejected Chicago, dealing a major blow to the city's ego.

A further embarrassment also reflected the distracted nature of implementation in this period, producing a fiasco at Block 37, the North Loop
site that had lain vacant for two decades. The 2003 Central Area Plan
included the CTA's idea of express train service to Chicago's two airports
and recommended identifying a site for a central downtown terminal.
The idea had emerged two years earlier as a pet project of both Mayor
Richard M. Daley and CTA chairman Frank Kreusi, and Block 37 was
an obvious place for the station. But at the time of the plan's writing, CTA
and CDOT were conducting separate studies and could not agree where
the station should be located. Meanwhile, the Department of Planning
and Development, under pressure to find a use for Block 37, had already
signed an agreement in late 2003 to sell the site to the Mills Corporation
to build a mixed use development that included an urban retail mall but
no station.[15]

CTA Intermodal Transit Center at Block 37

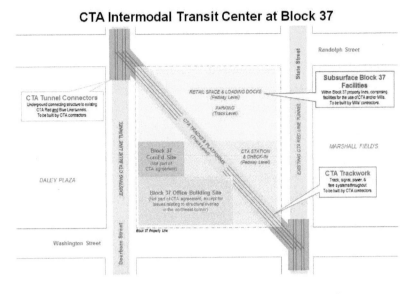

Figure 18.4. Schematic of tunnels, track, and airport express train terminal beneath Block 37, 2003

Then, belatedly, the CTA and CDOT reentered the picture in May 2004 and decided that they wanted Block 37 for the airport express terminal (Figure 18.4). A painstaking and costly renegotiation with Mills was required to revise the sale, redesign its building, and reschedule construction in order to shoehorn a train station underneath the site. (The delays contributed to Mills's bankruptcy, and it left the project in 2008; Joseph Freed and Associates took over.) The CTA planned to spend $130 million and the city an additional $42 million in TIF funds on the station, yet the feasibility of express service to O'Hare was never fully planned out.[16] Cost overruns propelled the price tag for the station to $250 million in public funds, but, without a plan in place for service, the partially finished space was mothballed in 2008. As Terri Haymaker, a city planner involved at the time, explained, "The problem with Block 37 was not some kind of curse, but rather that everybody tried to put so many goals on one piece of ground."[17] The city had spent an enormous sum but gained only a placeholder for an idea whose merits had not been fully assessed. Moreover, Block 37 had been the signature project of the North Loop since the 1980s, but poor planning 30 years later had inflicted needless damage and delayed its still promising role in a revitalized State Street.

The Central Area Action Plan

Even as the Olympics dominated, then deflated, Chicago's scene, the Department of Development and Planning tried to move forward with efforts to implement the 2003 plan, an effort designated the Central Area Action Plan (CAAP). Commissioner Lori T. Healey initiated work on this in 2006 but was subsequently tapped by Daley to run the Olympic bid. SOM declined to join the effort, citing its Olympics work and frustration with costs and delays in finishing the 2003 plan. A planning department reorganization in 2008 into the Department of Zoning and Land Use Planning did not improve focus.

While it was theoretically possible to coordinate infrastructure investment for the proposed games with future city needs—such as the major waterfront, transit, and park improvements identified in the 2003 plan—actual synergy did not develop, and city planners were marginalized in the effort. Instead, consultants were needed to complete the CAAP in 2009, using reconstituted task forces from the earlier 2003 plan and additional neighborhood representation. A full six years elapsed between the 2003 plan and its implementation blueprint, a costly delay given the radical change in the city's economic circumstances in that time.

The Central Area Action Plan, for the first time, offered concrete, engineering-based cost estimates for infrastructure projects along with an implementation schedule. It focused not only on large projects like the WLTC but also on upgrades to existing systems, ranking signal, track, station, and equipment improvements for existing CTA lines as top priorities. Using updated forecasts, the CAAP, working with the city Department of Transportation and Metra, determined a need for more peak-hour trains on virtually every CTA and Metra line by 2020, while Union Station and the surrounding bus and pedestrian areas would need significant upgrades.[18]

Two projects suggested in the 2003 plan received greater detail and estimates. The first was a slimmed-down variation of the Circulator: three dedicated, off-street, grade-separated transitways for light rail or bus rapid transit (Figure 18.6, page 244). The Carroll Avenue transitway connected the Metra stations with Michigan Avenue and Navy Pier using an abandoned railroad right-of-way that ran under several buildings, including the Merchandise Mart and the new Trump Tower. A second east-west transitway would run under Monroe Street using an existing right-of-way as well, while a third would connect McCormick Place with Streeterville, north of the river. Because the transitways would not operate on the street grid, the issues that dogged the Circulator could be avoided, and the use of a small vehicle system (light rail or bus) could keep costs relatively low. The com-

Union Station Master Plan

Union Station, the third-busiest railroad terminal in the country, is served by more than 300 trains per day carrying about 120,000 passengers, a level that would rank it among the 10 busiest *airports* in the country. Ridership on both commuter and intercity trains has more than doubled since the 1980s. These gains have strained the station, which is now at capacity. In 2010, the city Department of Transportation (CDOT) initiated the Chicago Union Station Master Plan Study, in collaboration with Amtrak (the station's owner), Metra (its primary tenant), and other stakeholder organizations.

Union Station was built in 1925 with a head house containing a Great Hall for waiting and ticketing and, a block to the east, a low-rise concourse. In 1968, the Penn Central railroad sold the air rights over the concourse (as it had done earlier with New York's Penn Station) and by 1970 an office tower had been erected along with a new but smaller passenger concourse in the basement, designed under the assumption that rail travel would continue to decline.

The new concourse quickly proved inadequate. Even after extensive renovations in 1992, its passageways remain too narrow, with low ceilings, multiple levels to navigate, a forest of columns, no natural light, and poor wayfinding. During peak rush-hour periods, the entire facility is overcrowded with dense flows of commuters. Further, station activity is constrained by street-level conflicts among taxis, buses, automobiles, shuttles, pedestrians, and bicycles. Equally important, track capacity is constrained by the river to the east and air rights above.

The Union Station Master Plan, completed in May 2012, offers a range of projects to address capacity issues, most significantly the creation of a modern off-street bus terminal adjacent to the station. This facility will significantly improve traffic flow around the station and also integrate with the proposed central area bus rapid transit (BRT) route connecting Union Station, Ogilvie Transportation Center, City Hall, State Street, and Millennium Park. The BRT project will improve bus operations and customer amenities along one of downtown's most heavily traveled bus transit corridors. Both projects are currently being designed by CDOT and are planned for construction in 2014.

In the medium term (five to 10 years), the plan calls for converting baggage and mail platforms to widen the station's narrow commuter-train platforms and to accommodate intercity passenger trains. A second goal

Figure 18.5. Conceptual drawing of rebuilt Union Station terminal beneath 300 S. Riverside Plaza, from Union Station Master Plan, 2012. This concept would require replacing an existing office building with the new station and new tower above it.

is to more effectively use space and improve pedestrian flow in both the concourse and head house buildings.

Longer term, the Master Plan considers completely replacing the existing facilities. One option is to develop a new train station one block to the south, which would require purchasing an existing office tower. Another would be to rebuild the entire concourse site, replacing the office towers above (Figure 18.5). Less dramatically, the plan defines concepts for creating additional track and platform capacity in a new alignment adjacent to the existing station.

This last proposal was a central feature of the West Loop Transportation Center plan, which the Union Station plan builds upon. The current regional plan, GO TO 2040, also recognizes that the transportation center plan would be necessary to meet significant regional needs.

Finally, the Master Plan Study also promotes placemaking principles for any redesign to create a vibrant public space that has the potential to transform an imposing historic structure into one that invites interaction with its users and the surrounding city. The station will be expected to not only evolve into an efficient hub, with easy connections to other transit modes, but also become a truly great place that attracts travelers and nontravelers alike. Barring that, Chicago will continue to offer a poor experience for intercity travel as well as daily suburban commutes that remain uninviting and inadequate.

—Jeffrey J. Sriver

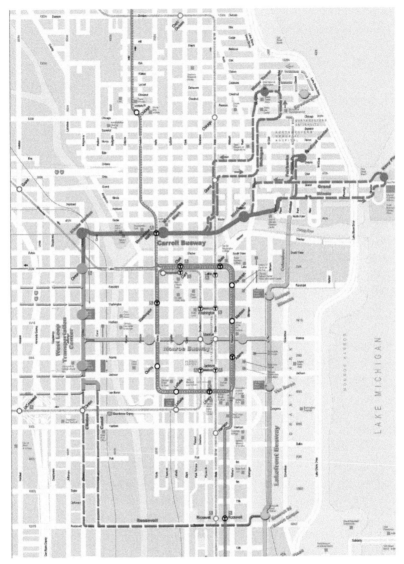

Figure 18.6. Map of proposed transitway system, the Chicago Central Area Plan, 2003

plete transitway system was projected to cost $670 million, roughly the cost of the Circulator more than a decade earlier.[19]

The West Loop Transportation Center, the centerpiece of the 2003 plan, would prove costly, however. Scaled back from a four-story to a three-story underground structure, the station alone would cost $2 billion. The crucial mile-long Clinton Street subway tunnel that would tie the train stations to the CTA and also expand transit capacity in the West Loop would cost another $3 billion. These are prohibitive sums without a major federal commitment.

The CAAP ranked projects according to transportation, growth, and sustainability goals and then proposed a logical phasing plan over the 2008–2020 period. The total costs came to $15.5 billion, of which transportation accounted for $14.2 billion. This heavy allocation reflected the capital-intensive nature of the projects, the long deferment of transit investment, and the central rationale of the plan to maintain and attract a majority of regional white collar / office employment in the central area.

Could Chicago undertake such massive transportation investments? The city capital budget at the time was averaging about $2 billion per year, but directing most of this investment to the central area was politically unpalatable. The city's share of the proposed projects would have been roughly half of the total, assuming some federal, state, and public/private funding as well. The massive expansions at O'Hare and Midway, though paid for by user fees, have often taken sums within these ranges, and most consider these wise long-term regional investments. The estimated impact of the CAAP investments would have been 11,000 direct new jobs per year and growth in the office, hospitality, education, and medical fields.

Yet despite adoption of the CAAP by the Chicago Plan Commission in August 2009, there has been little new commitment to central area and regional transit. With the city in a recession-induced fiscal crisis, large capital expenditures appear out of the question. Even the plan's "proposal-ready" and "shovel-ready" items did not get much support from federal stimulus money, most of which went to road repair projects. To date, the CAAP is another casualty of the city's unwillingness to embrace systematic and comprehensive planning for its future.

Instead, CDOT and the CTA are betting on low-cost bus rapid transit (BRT). BRT can be implemented quickly, a political advantage, yet the latest plans call for rolling it out in stages, with only limited deployment of its four key elements: dedicated bus lanes, signal priority at stoplights, level boarding of buses, and prepaid boarding. As a result, BRT in Chicago represents only a planned upgrade to the bus experience and not a commitment to extensive new capacity. And unless the BRT is coupled with transit-oriented development efforts, it will not increase transit mode share—the proportion of riders using transit. BRT is not a bad idea, but used as a substitute for real transit investment, it risks becoming another lost opportunity.[20] It is unclear how it would address the congestion issues in the central area, where planning dreams have decayed from a heavy-rail subway solution (The Distributor, 1974–1982), to light rail (The Circulator, 1991–1995), to a grade-separated transitway (The Central Area Plan, 2003–2009), and now to BRT, an enhanced bus lane at its core. This gradual diminishment of aspirations reflects not only the high costs of transit infrastructure but also the city's declining capacity to promote a vision for its future, even as other cities such as Los Angeles and Denver compete successfully for scarce federal funding to pay for essential new transit lines.

When the Olympics Committee did not choose Chicago in 2009, the city and the mayor became demoralized. When Lee Bey asked Daley in December of that year, "What's next?" the mayor responded, "Basically nothing — no money from the feds, no money from the state." Many in the planning community expected the CAAP to become "Plan B." That did not happen.

Ironically, the city celebrated the Burnham Plan the same year the CAAP was released. In a yearlong series of events, the city recognized the historical legacy of Burnham, reminding citizens that city planners were expected to think big. But in reality, even carefully constructed, reasonable plans became more planning exercise than political reality. Complacent after Millennium Park and a surprising downtown residential boom, the city lacked direction. Once a recession punctured the housing bubble and city revenues tanked, Chicago had to face the implications of a decade of debt-fueled development rather than pushing ahead to invent its future.

CHAPTER 19
THE DISCONNECT BETWEEN FINANCING AND PLANNING

Much of the spending on Chicago's "global city" as well as numerous improvements across city neighborhoods has been funded by debt—a veritable mountain of it. By itself, debt can be a helpful tool for investing today and repaying costs over time, and the relatively low interest rates of the past decade made it a good time to invest. But such investment needs to be prioritized, assessed, and planned. Instead, financing sources have driven choices and decisions. This has long been the nature of infrastructure development in U.S. cities. In the 1950s, categorical federal grants on generous terms led to binges of highway building, urban renewal, and public housing. As seen earlier, state bonding authority targeted investments in the tourist city at Navy Pier, Museum Campus, and McCormick Place. More recently, TIF, often leveraged through additional debt, has come to dominate Chicago's capital budget.

But when financing drives planning, rather than the other way around, decisions are made on a deal-by-deal basis that serves the needs of political actors more than the general public. Lack of prioritization, coordination, or consideration of trade-offs end up distorting investment choices and even lead to significant blunders. Moreover, leverage and debt have put Chicago dangerously close to living beyond its means.

Debt

Chicago's overall debt levels have skyrocketed since the early 1990s. Much of this borrowing has been in the form of general obligation bonds

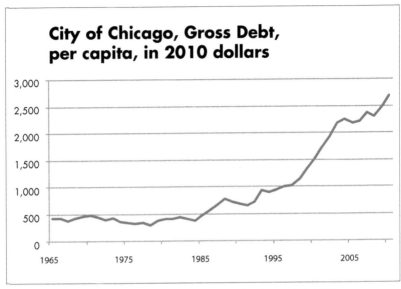

City of Chicago, Gross Debt, per capita, in 2010 dollars

Figure 19.1. City of Chicago, gross debt per capita, adjusted for inflation, 1965–2009

and TIF-related notes. Figure 19.1 shows Chicago's debt per capita in unadjusted dollars from 1965 to 2009.

Servicing this debt has grown burdensome. In 2011, Chicago's debt service costs were 21 percent of the city's general budget, a figure considered high and sufficient to result in a significant downgrade in the city's bond rating that year.[1] Trend lines are clearly unsustainable, and the city in 2009 entered a period of budget austerity that will affect its ability to further plan and invest in the future.

Asset Sales

In response to its higher debt levels, the city turned to new tools for raising capital, especially asset sales. In two deals—one a surprising success and the other an embarrassing failure—Chicago raised enormous sums. Yet the hasty nature of both meant decisions were not well thought out. In one instance, the city was relatively lucky, but the second deal revealed its shortsightedness.

The winning deal was the sale of the Chicago Skyway, a toll road built by the city in 1955, the year before federal grants made user-fee roads unnecessary.[2] Traffic volumes on the Skyway did not meet initial expectations, especially when other freeways were constructed as part of the regional network—a failure of regional coordination. The city defaulted on its Skyway bonds in 1963, but increases in traffic volume eventually allowed the Skyway to run a modest cash surplus—$17 million in 1996—which the city leveraged into additional borrowing with proceeds dedicated mostly to neighborhood road improvements. The Skyway had become a cash cow and, lured by international investors, the city called for bids on a 99-year lease on it. Australia's Macquarie Bank offered a stunning $1.83 billion, nearly double the competition, and the city council quickly agreed in 2005, though the deal allowed substantial toll increases over time. Mayor Richard M. Daley said he would use the enormous windfall to draw down debt, establish a "rainy-day fund," and pay for neighborhood needs and social programs.[3]

The success of the Skyway deal made the city eager for more, and in 2008 Mayor Daley rushed through the city council a deal to privatize the city's parking meters. The city received $1.16 billion in cash in return for a 75-year agreement with a consortium led by Morgan Stanley. Critics soon charged that the city had undervalued its asset by as much as $1 billion, though this estimate assumed the city would significantly raise future parking meter rates, something aldermen had been loath to do. The consortium had no such qualms. It promptly quadrupled parking rates across much of the city and lengthened enforcement periods, triggering outcries from city residents but no real pain at the polls for aldermen. Raising parking fees was actually a good idea, as street parking had been widely undervalued, but the one-sided agreement also made the city pay hefty fees for removal of any parking spot—even temporarily—restricting the city's freedom to manage and plan its own streets. Finger-pointing on the deal left a black eye on Daley's last term in office.[4]

The Skyway, the parking meter lease, and an additional $562 million deal for a 99-year lease on the Millennium Park parking garages had been deal-driven opportunities, with little debate about the merits of privatization. Worse, few limits had been placed on the rainy-day fund. Within two years, $973 million of the parking meter money had been spent, 94 percent of it on operating costs to fill budget holes in the wake of the recession. In 2010, only 27 percent of the Skyway funds remained.[5] Still desperate for cash, Mayor Daley unsuccessfully pursued privatization of Midway Airport until the end of his administration. The mayor had sold future streams of revenue and spent the proceeds immediately, yet he defended his actions in generational terms: "The people own the asset to be used today for this generation of people and not for 2050. . . . Our responsibility is to help the generation right now."[6]

Tax Increment Financing

Asset sales have gone into remission, but the city remains heavily reliant upon TIF as the primary tool for economic development. The strategy took on a life of its own during the Richard M. Daley years, as a coalition of developers, consultants, corporations, and aldermen realized that the most flexible and often the quickest way to accomplish a major development was to take advantage of the generous TIF laws in Illinois. Before TIFs, the city's capital improvements budget offered only limited discretionary funds for aldermen to shape their communities. In a city where politicians

Tax Increment Financing in Illinois

Tax increment financing (TIF) is used by municipalities and counties across the country to foster desired development and economic activity, though not without controversy. The TIF process begins by drawing a boundary around an area—called the TIF district—deemed to meet specific criteria in the law. In most states, those criteria center on "blight" or economic development goals. An assessor calculates the current property-tax assessments within the district, and then local taxing agencies (the municipality itself, school district, library district, etc.) agree to freeze the amount they will receive in property taxes for a specific period, usually several years. The tax bills of property owners in the district are not frozen, only the amounts directed to various governmental coffers. If property values in the district rise over time (as they tend to), any increase in property tax collections above the base amount—the "increment"—is deposited in a separate TIF fund. These monies are then directed toward projects allowed by TIF law; these projects are usually guided by a redevelopment plan that is intended to spur growth and thereby further increase the value of property in the district. Cities often borrow funds in the first year of a TIF for upfront improvements, using expected TIF gains as collateral. When used strategically, TIF can generate the resources to catalyze affordable housing, economic development, infrastructure, and other local improvements that would not otherwise occur, benefitting the city and its residents. This last element, known as the "but for" test, is critical: it must be apparent that the desired redevelopment would not occur without the creation of the TIF district.

TIF laws vary considerably from state and state; Illinois law is generous to municipalities. The definition of "blight" is flexible, and TIFs can last up to 23 years, among the longest in the nation. Further, Illinois's are rewarded for specific projects—street improvements, new schools, new manufacturing plants—TIF offered aldermen the chance to fund large-scale projects with considerable control, as seen in Uptown's Wilson Yards project (chapter 10). In fairness, TIF emerged as the "only game in town" for funding many projects, as state and federal funds have receded over the past two decades.

Chicago has embraced TIFs more than any other city in America. As of 2011, Chicago has 163 active TIF districts covering 30 percent of the area of the city and encompassing roughly 10 percent of its prop-

"but for" test is weak, and the TIF funds can be spent on a wide range of subsidies, including corporate relocation incentives. Further, Illinois law allows transfer of TIF funds to adjacent districts. Finally, redevelopment plans can be thin and vague, allowing great flexibility in future projects. In other states, TIFs are more tightly regulated and narrowly contained.

Controversy arises on several fronts. First, assessing the "but for" test can be difficult, as predicting what might or might not happen without the TIF requires careful and unbiased judgment. If a company was planning to expand its activities, then the TIF was unnecessary; still, other taxing bodies must forgo increased revenue until it expires. For this reason, many argue that TIF robs from school districts and other agencies.* Second, the TIF fund often lacks the transparency of other governmental activities, as it is a pot of money segregated from the scrutiny and prioritization inherent in normal capital budgeting. Still, when used thoughtfully, TIF offers local planners a targeted way to fund complicated redevelopment, rather than requiring governmental grants or general obligation bonds that are often subject to the whim of voter referendums.

---

* School districts do not directly lose funds under TIFs, though they are forced to raise their levies to meet needs. Even TIF supporters concede that TIFs generally lead to higher taxes in a municipality: "Schools, parks and other overlapping taxing districts may collect the same amount of revenue as they would without TIF districts—and in fact benefit from the public projects that TIF helps to fund—but the existence of TIF districts increases the individual tax burden on property owners both inside and outside of TIF districts." From "Findings and Recommendations for Reforming the Use of Tax Increment Financing in Chicago: Creating Greater Efficiency, Transparency, and Accountability," report of the TIF Reform Panel, August 23, 2011, 24.

erty tax base (Figure 19.2). The districts generate nearly $500 million a year, which is directed into TIF coffers. Since 1983, more than $3.7 billion has been spent on TIF projects, ranging from neighborhood sidewalks to subsidies to major corporations. Roughly half of these dollars have gone to private development and half to public works. Unlike other cities, which tend to define TIF boundaries narrowly to cover an individual project, a greater proportion of Chicago TIFs cover areas large and small, giving flexibility to accomplish numerous initiatives across an entire community over the 23-year life of the TIF. Where TIF boundaries are adjacent, the city has the authority in state law to "port" funds between TIFs. Further, districts drawn to encompass most of the Loop—the LaSalle Street TIF followed by the Central Area TIF—have given the downtown its own separate (and large) capital budget, independent of citywide capital budgeting priorities.[7]

The projects funded by TIFs are often reasonable and beneficial, but the fracturing of capital planning into individual districts has precluded a citywide discussion of priorities. Capital budgeting in Chicago has long had poor transparency, and TIFs have added to the problem. The redevelopment plans in nearly all TIFs are exceptionally thin documents, often merely vague categories of spending rather than specific lists of proposals or options. Even annual reports offer only the most limited descriptions of where TIF funds have gone. This lack of transparency is deliberate, as Les Pollock explains: "TIF planning is weak, designed to create maximum flexibility for city officials, and it rarely includes any graphics or anything to hem them in."[8] TIF spending is approved by a community development commission, whose 15 members are appointed by the mayor and confirmed by the city council, but they have rarely confronted the city over its choices or priorities. TIFs now amount to an "off-budget" pool of funds, resulting in a perception of corruption and widespread cynicism about the tool.[9] This outcome is unfortunate because in the right circumstances and with careful planning TIF can be a powerful tool.

In 2011, Mayor Rahm Emanuel appointed a Tax Increment Financing Reform Task Force, which issued a report highlighting the weak connections of TIF to planning. The task force's first recommendation is to "establish the city's TIF goals" by developing a "multi-year Economic Development Plan," submitted to the city council in order to "guide all future TIF designations and project allocations." The second recommendation is to incorporate TIF spending into the city's capital budget to "ensure that TIF investment is

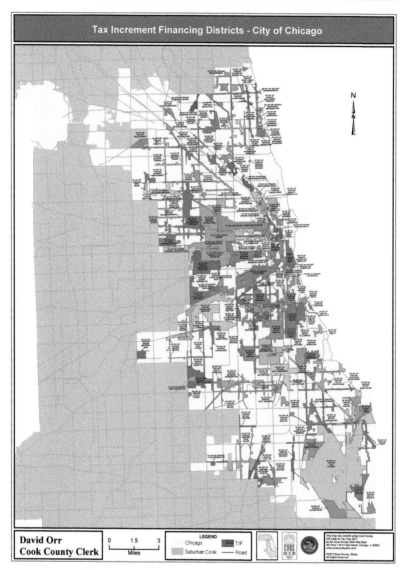

Figure 19.2. Map of TIF districts in Chicago, from Cook County Clerk's Office, 2011

coordinated with other funding sources available to the city" and that TIF is "the appropriate funding source for proposed projects." This would make TIF spending "less reactive" and "better optimize the allocation of scarce resources." Other recommendations include tracking, assessment, accountability, and transparency.[10] In other words, the reform task force said TIF needs greater connection to planning and to be part of a real budget. Whether these reforms will occur is uncertain.

Financially, Chicago is nearly tapped out. Recently, as one way around the debt problem, Mayor Emanuel announced a new Infrastructure Trust Fund intended to attract private capital for public investment. Specifically, Emanuel proposes to "Retrofit Chicago," letting private firms spend their capital to retrofit public buildings for energy efficiency and then capture a portion of those savings as revenue. The projects would be overseen by a nonprofit with a five-person board appointed by the mayor. Aldermen feared the new idea would lead to further privatization of public assets and demanded greater transparency; after minor reforms, the Infrastructure Trust Fund passed the city council, though it has yet to produce a deal. It remains to be seen whether the fund will be an effective tool for planning or a desperate and potentially costly way to pay for infrastructure. The city could, if it had the borrowing authority, finance energy efficiency retrofits on its own and reap the rewards in lower operating costs.[11]

Debt has always been an important tool for planners and for cities to grow, and by itself it is not a bad thing. But with Chicago approaching limits, resources for needed investments may be scarce. Had those resources been better managed and planned for in a comprehensive planning and budget process over the past few decades, the city might be in better fiscal shape. The explosion in TIFs in the past 10 years, the rise in general obligation bonds, and the shift to asset sales all suggest a city desperate to leverage itself in order to afford an ambitious agenda that has become divorced from comprehensive, sustainable planning.

CHAPTER 20
POSITIVE MIDDLE-RANGE PLANNING

Chicago's planning apparatus has been diminished by the lack of a comprehensive plan, the overreliance on TIFs, and the failure to aggressively implement major efforts such as the 2003 Central Area Plan. Despite these weaknesses, however, Chicago in the past decade has produced several "middle range" plans with more modest goals that regulated the built environment, organized specific areas, and rebuilt spaces. This chapter examines four such plans that show areas of leadership and innovation. Chicago *can* plan, quite effectively at times, and it can even find ways to implement its good ideas. The city needs to bring similar energy to prioritizing, funding, and coordinating its major plans.

Updating Zoning Codes
In 2004, Chicago reformed its zoning code, a signficant political as well as planning achievement. For over three decades, Chicago had been unable to produce an update. Repeated zoning reform committees from the 1960s through the 1980s lacked political capacity or failed to find common ground. Neighborhoods clamored against high rises and other undesired building types, while downtown the city's density bonus system for skyscrapers grew excessively generous under pressure from developers yet failed to produce positive public amenities. Reform was much needed, though only piecemeal changes had been possible, which in turn created even more complexity and unpredictability. The

issue appeared a potential hornets' nest to aldermen content with a system that required their constant intervention to untangle deverlopers' zoning problems.[1]

Yet in the period 2001–2004, a carefully structured process resulted in a clear and comprehensive set of much-needed zoning reforms. Several factors influenced the success. First, key pieces of the zoning code considered too sensitive to include in the overall udpate were negotiated separately or excluded from consideration. The city in 2001 separately hammered out a much improved density bonus ordinance to govern design of downtown high rises with the help of expert groups including the American Institute of Architects and the Metropolitan Planning Council. Two other delicate areas of zoning policy were taken off the table: the Lakefront Protection Ordinance of 1973 (chapter 5) and the Landmark Preservation Ordinance (chapter 7).[2] Tampering with either had the potential to bog down the overall rewrite in contentious but relatively needless battles with powerful constituencies.

Second, Mayor Richard M. Daley threw his weight behind a zoning rewrite during the height of his power, and leadership on his Zoning Reform Commission mattered. Daley appointed a commission, supported by high-level staff from within his administration, that balanced multiple interests. Experienced consultants provided critical advice, and the Metropolitan Planning Council convened neighborhood focus groups to understand public sentiment in advance of community meetings. For their part, the aldermen came to see zoning reform as a way to lower thresholds for Planned Development reviews and thereby "get themselves back into negotiations with developers," according to Dennis Harder.[3]

Third, the Zoning Reform Commission skillfully educated interested citizenry and solicited community input. In June 2002, the commission distributed a glossy report, "Principles for Chicago's New Zoning Ordinance," which, with clear language and illustrations, made a strong case for new zoning codes to manage contemporary development. The report led off with a section catering to neighborhood concerns, explaining how existing zoning regulations abetted out-of-character building forms in residential areas. It continued with graphics illustrating how new codes including limits on setbacks, building heights, and design features would offer stronger protection than traditional FAR limitations (Figure 20.1). In a nod to developers, a later section explained the need to "simplify and streamline" the zoning ordinance to declutter its verbiage, make it more predictable, and acclerate approvals. Accompanied by an organized education effort, the report

Figure 20.1. Illustration from "Principles for Chicago's New Zoning Ordinance," explaining that Chicago's old zoning code did not regulate building heights, only floor area ratios, resulting in incongruous development, 2002

elicited a wave of publicity in advance of a favorably received public meetings. Minor modifications resulted from stakeholder input, and the new zoning code was adopted with suprising ease in May 2004.[4] The reform process had been managed fairly and without high levels of rancor, though developers remained disastisfied with portions of the proposal.

In substance, the new code had a clear "bent towards conservation" of existing neighborhood character.[5] Height limits, setbacks, and other restrictions sought to ensure new construction was deferential to neighborhood characteristics. Pedestrian-friendly elements included restrictions on curb cuts, reductions in parking requirements, and creation of new pedestrian-friendly commercial zones, thereby "correcting the overly deferential treatment of the automobile in the 1957 code," as Lawrence Okrent argues.[6] In the central area, the city created new definitions for downtown districts, which received separate zoning treatment. The downtown bonus system was expanded to include affordable housing as an option on the bonus "menu." Finally, PDs received new regulations and lower triggers for entering the PD process, pleasing aldermen, though the rewrite and subsequent remapping reduced the need for rezonings, an aldermanic mainstay.

Of course, not everyone was happy. Longtime zoning and development lawyer Jack Guthman sees the 2004 zoning update as "basically
quite good, but it still needs to become more predictable and self-enforcing,
and it has far too much process." In particular, new regulations for planned
developments "mistakenly changed the criteria for approval from 'substantial compliance' with the underlying code to 'strict compliance,' which has
slowed the approval process." For their part, housing activists clamored
unsuccessfully for "inclusionary zoning" to require affordable housing in all
new large developments.[7] Still, on the whole, the 2004 zoning update
carefully constructed a reform process, educated members of the public,
and responded to their concerns, demonstrating the city's capacity to undertake positive planning reform when the political will exists.

Bringing the Riverfront to the 21st Century

Positive planning has also taken place along the Chicago River through
modest, incremental plans that have slowly transformed it into an urban
amenity. Leadership, however, came from citizen groups that prodded the
city into belatedly protecting and embracing one of its most important natural assets.

The 1974 Riveredge Plan and the 1982 Riverfront ordinance (chapter
4) gave limited guidance to planners when reviewing PDs along the river.
Friends of the Chicago River, the citizens group founded in 1979, insisted
on a stronger set of design guidelines to direct any review of development
proposals. In 1987, Friends collaborated with the Department of Planning
to produce the "Chicago River Urban Guidelines," a far more detailed set
of proscriptions that signaled what river edge construction in the central area
should look like. Specific directives covered building orientation, massing,
setbacks, walkways, and landscaping. The guidelines were intended to
ensure that any PD respected broader goals for the river as a pedestrian,
recreational, and, at times, commercial amenity. Beyond design issues, the
Friends-inspired guidelines advocated for "a continuous riverside walkway
throughout the downtown corridor" along with "oases of quiet green space
easily accessible to central area workers and visitors" so that the river would
become a "high-profile tourist attraction and recreational amenity, thereby
enhancing Chicago's image as a desirable place to live, work, and visit."
In 1990, with widespread support including a *Chicago Tribune* endorsement, the CPC approved the guidelines.[8]

In the 1990s, environmental cleanup began to show results, and the Chicago River turned a corner. Friends of the River organized annual cleanups

that made progress, and, as pollution levels decreased, nature returned. For decades, river pollution and trash along its banks scared off paddlers and anglers; the handful of people who plied the river or fished it were thought to be somewhat crazy. But now the river no longer resembled a dump. While bacteria levels remained dangerously high, cleanup efforts and the 85 percent reduction in sewage overflows meant the river shed the intense stigma of earlier decades. News articles regularly expressed astonishment at the revival of nature and recreation in the central area: smells became less pronounced, beavers were visible, and access to the river improved.[9]

The improvements snowballed into greater awareness of the river as a natural asset to be thoughtfully managed. In 1995, the Chicago Tribune editorialized in favor of a "Riverfront Protection Ordinance" on the same level as the Lakefront Protection Ordinance. Two years later, Friends of the Chicago River again partnered with the Department of Planning and Development to engage other stakeholders in a process to produce a Chicago River Corridor Development Plan to "enhance the river's attractiveness as a natural and recreational resource, while respecting the needs of residential and business developments." The newest vision for the river stretched its entire length, recognizing its importance to the neighborhoods as well as to industry and downtown. Goals had expanded since 1990: instead of mere pedestrian access in the Loop, the new plan called for "a connected greenway along the river, with continuous multiuse paths along at least one side" of its entire length, without disturbing industrial access. Riverbank restoration and environmental remediation became priorities, including controlling erosion, removing debris, and clearing invasive species. Expanded public access in the form of docks, fishing piers, and parks were envisioned. Finally, the plan included a proposed setback ordinance of at least 30 feet from all riverbanks throughout Chicago. These reforms were approved by various bodies in 1998, and the river finally had a plan comparable to the lakefront ordinance.[10]

A major goal of the Chicago River Corridor Development Plan is a continuous Riverwalk in the central area. Using Central Loop TIF funds, the city spent roughly $22 million in 2009 on a two-block stretch between Michigan Avenue and State Street to build calming outdoor spaces and new walkways underneath the previously obstructive bascule bridges. The new passageways include canopies that shelter pedestrians beneath the otherwise ominous bridges.[11] That same year, the city contracted with SOM to write the Chicago Riverwalk Main Branch Framework Plan to guide extension of the walkway west from State Street. The SOM plan includes

Figure 20.2. Rendering by SOM of proposed Riverwalk along south bank of Chicago River, from Chicago Riverwalk Main Branch Framework Plan, 2009

restaurants and landscape, along with proposed landfill to expand the riverbank 50 feet at the junction of the north and south branches of the river, near Lake and Orleans streets. This fill would become a riverfront park at a dramatic corner of the city, with room for commercial activity (Figure 20.2). The Riverwalk Framework Plan would create "placemaking" in an area of the city that lacks public space.

In October 2012, Mayor Emanuel called the river "our second shoreline" and said he is "committed to finishing the final phases of the riverwalk." Costs are estimated at $100 million, and the mayor acknowledged that his Department of Transportation will need to "find creative ways to finance" its construction.[12] Still, over three decades, Friends of the River has convinced the city to give its second shoreline the planning attention it deserves. A collaborative process between stakeholders and the city has produced targeted plans focused on reasonable goals, solid regulatory structures, and a long-term vision.

Converting Northerly Island

Another rediscovered asset is Northerly Island, which is actually a peninsula south of Grant Park (Figure 20.3). Conceived as a natural promenade in the 1909 Plan of Chicago, the man-made space has been contentious ground, and only recently has careful planning taken place there, much of it promising.

Daniel Burnham thought of Northerly Island as the start of a much longer man-made formation stretching south to create lagoons and protected spaces along the lakefront. But the business community saw the half-completed "island" and proposed a downtown airport, succeeding in 1948 over the objections of the CPC. For the next 56 years, Meigs Field served primarily private planes and a commuter route to the state capital in Springfield. The small airport never sat well with many in the city. In 1974, Mayor Richard J. Daley proposed returning Northerly Island to its original intended use as public open space, as did the Central Area Plan of 1983. In 1996, the Chicago Park District proposed a reuse plan that included playgrounds, an expanded beach, a botanic garden, wetlands, and other natural features. Soon after, the city refused to renew the airport's $1 lease and closed it for five months before backing down under pressure from Springfield. Intense political wrangling continued for several more years. In December 2001, Mayor Richard M. Daley and Governor George Ryan reached an agreement to keep the airport open for 25 years, contingent upon state operating subsidies and the state's support for O'Hare airport expansion.[13]

The deal collapsed, however, over funding for O'Hare, leading Daley to make one of the more breathtaking power grabs of any mayor in U.S. history. At midnight, under the mayor's orders, park district bulldozers carved up Meigs's runway with large "X" marks, making the airfield unusable and stranding 16 small planes. In one stroke, Daley had ended the debate about the future of Meigs Field. The lack of a public process appalled many, including federal officials, who demanded repayment of improvement grants. The *Chicago Tribune* editorialized: "The issue is Daley's increasingly authoritarian style that brooks no disagreements, legal challenges, negotiations, compromise or any of that messy give-and-take normally associated with democratic government." *Tribune* architecture columnist Blair Kamin noted that he "had eagerly awaited the day when Meigs's dismantlement would begin. But it was supposed to happen in the daylight of an open public process—not, literally and figuratively, in the dead of night." The episode was an extreme example of the way Chicago planned, Kamin argued. Unlike other cities, which debated major public initiatives at length, Chicago "winks. It nods. It holds public hearings that are play-acting exercises in democratic city design, not the real thing."[14]

Daley's unilateral closing of the field cast a pall over what should have been the positive reclamation of lakefront land. Worse, the bulldozing took

Figure 20.3. Conceptual images from the Northerly Island Framework Plan by Studio Gang Architects, SmithGroupJJR, and Studio V Design, 2010

place without much planning thought. When asked what would come next, park district officials said they would "look at" the 1996 plan but would affirm only that they would turn Meigs into a "natural" space. Within two years, the earlier plan gave way to competing interests. In 2005, the city allowed a sizeable semipermanent 7,500-seat concert venue to be erected, something not conceived of in previous plans.[15]

The park district, however, did hire experienced firms to produce the 2010 Northerly Island Framework Plan, written by the landscape architecture firm SmithGroupJJR and Studio Gang Architects (Figure 20.3). Building on the 1996 plan, the Framework Plan lays out concepts for an ambitious range of built-environment and natural habitats intended to lure visitors. Jeanne Gang, an influential Chicago architect, explained the Framework Plan's concept as "a Millennium Park of Nature," implying a desire to draw large crowds to an eclectic yet stimulating set of experiences. An outdoor concert amphitheater would remain on the north end of the park—a concession to the park district, which needed a revenue source to sustain park activities—along with other commercial enterprises, including a restaurant and kayak rentals. To the south end, natural habitats would take over. By adding barrier islands to the existing island and creating a reef, the framework plan envisions a whole new set of natural experiences in the city: "Imagine canoeing through calm lake water to quiet off-shore islands, hiking an island oasis under shade provided by a thriving woodland canopy, or discovering a remote rocky beach with breathtaking views. Imagine all of this within walking distance of Chicago's bustling urban center." Landscape work would reintroduce natural habitats including a "woodland-prairie continuum," and a new pond on the island would offer wetland environments for aquatic life.[16]

The strong vision of the framework plan is intended to guide the park district in its development of Northerly Island over a 20- to 25-year period. Promisingly, the U.S. Army Corps of Engineers has already agreed to fund the pond and major elements of the woodland-prairie environment for $7 to $10 million, marking an important first step.[17] After a decade of political conflict and an egregious power grab, Northerly Island is finally on a path to becoming a park for the whole city. It has a coherent concept for its future, one that could complement Millennium Park: natural rather than cultural, calmer rather than frenzied, recreational rather than spectacular.

Bike Planning

With its flat terrain, Chicago is an ideal biking environment, and the city was an early innovator in bike planning in the United States. Like the Chicago River, incremental, citizen-based activism pushed the Department of Transportation to engage in citywide planning around the issue. In 1991, the Chicagoland Bicycle Federation encouraged Richard M. Daley (a recreational bike rider) to appoint a Mayor's Bicycle Advisory Committee and create a plan. A year later, the resulting Bike 2000 Plan won accolades for its call "to make Chicago bicycle-friendly by the year 2000." The plan premised its work on improving air quality and sought as a primary goal to "attain 10 percent of all short (five miles and fewer) individual vehicle (single-occupancy) trips by bicycle in the year 2000" and to "develop bicycling as a serious alternative transportation mode." A "minimum of 300 miles of bikeways" were requested, including on-street bike lanes. Bike parking and parking safety measures were also stressed.[18]

Implementation required cooperation with several departments, most prominently CDOT. With prodding from the mayor, CDOT did embrace bike planning, eventually producing 100 miles of on-street lanes and 50 miles of off-street routes by 2006, well short of the goal but nonetheless significant. The city's bike parking program, with 10,000 racks ("more than any other city in the U.S.," according to CDOT), also overcame resistance. Roughly half the racks were funded by the Federal Highway Administration's

Congestion Mitigation and Air Quality (CMAQ) Improvement Program, authorized under ISTEA in 1991. Locations were chosen by the Chicagoland Bicycle Federation then sent to aldermen, most of whom initially responded "negatively, but only a handful of racks were actually relocated," according to CDOT planners. Moreover, once racks were in place, "several of those who asked that racks be removed asked to keep them; and businesses that didn't get racks wanted to know why they were overlooked."[19]

Chicago rested on its laurels until 2006 when, in cooperation with the Chicagoland Bicycling Federation, it produced an updated version of the 1992 plan. The far more comprehensive 2006 plan now called for a 500-mile bikeway network by 2015, including a nearly 50 percent increase in on-street lanes, plus new types of bike routes, including raised bike lanes (five miles) and "rush hour bikeways" (five miles). In other ways, the plan scaled down its ambitions: now the goal was to get five percent of all trips five miles or fewer to be by bicycle. Still, the plan offered a detailed set of 150 recommendations based on best practices to bring Chicago in line with other cities that had moved bike planning in fresh directions. The largest section of the report deals with education, safety, and law enforcement. The latter elements are aimed at changing the culture of Chicago riders and drivers. Between 2005 and 2010, the number of bicycle injury crashes has risen in the city, from 1,236 to 1,566, though the number of riders seems to have increased as well.[20] Safety improvements and culture changes will be essential to keep political support for additional bike amenities.

Bicycle planning received a boost with Mayor Emanuel's appointment of Gabe Klein as head of CDOT in 2011. Klein had helped change the bike culture and environment of Washington, D.C., in a relatively short period of time. With the support of the Chicagoland Bicycle Federation (renamed the Active Transportation Alliance and with the added mission of encouraging safe pedestrian streets), Klein launched a sophisticated $40 million effort in planning, design, and implementation of a new bike plan, called the Streets for Cycling Plan, 2020, with funding from a federal CMAQ grant.

The planning process includes a more involved effort to collect perspectives from riders, who were encouraged to submit information on routes, destinations, barriers, and gaps in the system. Four public meetings in 2011 and 2012 were attended by 300 citizens, and social media logged numerous rider suggestions. To facilitate fine-grained analysis, the city was divided into nine subareas, each with an assigned lead planner. The subareas formed a Community Advisory Group, led by two volunteers

Figure 20.4. *Protected bike lane along Kinzie Street, 2012*

who ran monthly meetings to gather additional knowledge. Drafts by CDOT were returned to the Community Advisory Groups for reaction and input.[21]

In the latest draft of the 2020 plan, the bike network has been refined into three levels of routes: "Bicycle Superhighways," heavily traveled, longer routes into and out of the Loop, intended as "red carpets" for riders; "Crosstown Bike Routes," with similar levels of protection but intended to suit interneighborhood destinations, as opposed to Loop ones; and "Neighborhood Bike Routes," on streets with lower bike traffic and suitable for connecting to the first two categories, schools, parks, and other institutions.

Overall, Chicago bike ridership remains low but is growing. According to the League of American Bicyclists analysis of American Community Survey data, only 1.3 percent of Chicagoans commuted to work by bike in 2010, though this is a 159 percent increase since 2000, a figure that ranks favorably among the nation's 70 largest cities. The league gives Chicago a "silver" ranking for bike-commuting friendliness, short of the "gold" standard attained by Seattle, San Francisco, Minneapolis, and Tucson, Arizona, as well as the "platinum" ranking attained only by Portland, Oregon.[22]

Still, the city has returned to a leadership role in the field of bike planning, and its new efforts should accelerate ridership growth. The potential concern is political. A backlash against bike lanes such as the one in New York City in 2011 could derail plans. In public forums, Klein and CDOT present a cautious stance, noting that excessive use of bike lanes could trigger a revolt among drivers in Chicago. The biking community remains small and therefore politically weak, even if its members are passionate. City and federal support exists for continued expansion of the bike lane network, but the broader electorate also needs to buy into the idea that biking is not a niche program but an integral use of the streets. In this aspect, the city still has a long journey ahead.

The four examples in this chapter suggest that planning on a broad scale is eminently possible. The work on zoning, the river, and biking extend across ward boundaries and beyond physical planning to improve entire systems in the city. The Northerly Island Framework Plan, while focused on one large site, is nonetheless sensitive to the broader context of the city's park offerings. This planning, however, is not well understood by Chicagoans unless they are actively engaged in interest groups like Friends of the Chicago River or the Active Transportation Alliance. By contrast, the 1909 Plan of Chicago received wide attention, including promotional campaigns and elementary school curriculums. To a far greater extent than today, residents understood that large-scale planning served a broader purpose.[23] Of course, not everyone agreed with Burnham's plans or the taxes to pay for them, but a relative consensus existed that planning could produce a better city. This optimism is difficult to see in today's public culture, even at the level of individual projects. In a different world, a comprehensive plan—collaboratively produced with strong citizen input—would advance policies that in turn would be elaborated in framework plans and then presented in specific projects. This approach could build the understanding and momentum needed to advance planning not as a disjointed project-by-project, TIF-by-TIF incrementalism but as an organized, systematic conversation about the future.

CHAPTER 21
THE LOST DECADE

Just as Chicago was emerging triumphantly on the global stage in the first decade of the 21st century, it was underperforming on numerous counts. The 2010 census offered only sobering news. The city had lost nearly 200,000 people, or seven percent of its population, and the region as a whole gained only four percent during the decade, mostly on the exurban fringe. Other figures on productivity, employment, and real GDP pointed to erosion either in absolute terms or relative to other cities.[1] A decade earlier, the 2000 census had been cause for optimism, showing gains across the board, banishing the declension narrative of the 1970s and 1980s. But the 2010 census suggested stagnation, and even Mayor Emanuel noted that the "city and region lost economic might. . . . [W]ithout wanting to cast judgment about why and how, it was a lost decade."[2] Of course, understanding the "why and how" of Chicago's slowdown is a central task for planners.

Among the most notable findings of the 2010 census was the net loss of 181,000 African Americans in a decade, a steep 17 percent drop. Black communities that had stabilized during the 1990s were now shrinking. Even the region as a whole saw a five percent decline in African Americans, indicating an outmigration, possibly to southern cities.[3] Several factors combined in this exodus. Easy credit allowed many African Americans to chase home ownership, and suburbanization exerted a steady pull on blacks as it had on whites for decades. Further, the Plan for Transformation scattered tens of thousands of low-income African American households

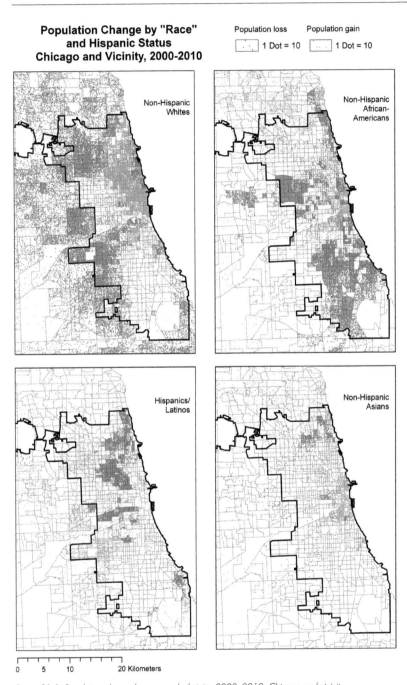

Figure 21.1. Population change by race and ethnicity, 2000–2010, Chicago and vicinity

into other African American communities, destabilizing some, as shifting gang turfs triggered violence. Longtime residents in these working-class "receiving" communities, such as Englewood, deeply resented a plan that disproportionately sent public housing newcomers their way.[4]

The city lost 52,000 whites as well. Much has been made in the media of people "returning" to the city, but gains in the central area (35,000 net whites) and gentrifying north side neighborhoods (29,000) did not offset the substantial outmigration from older bungalow belt areas on the Northwest and Southwest sides. Many of these neighborhoods transitioned from white to Latino, but the overall increase in the Latino population was only three percent in the decade, a drastic slowdown from the 38 percent gain in the 1990s.[5] Hit hard by the recession and immigration policy, many Latino immigrants left the city and region, some for their homelands. Moreover, Chicago is no longer the primary entry point for either Latino or Asian immigrants since most are heading directly to the suburbs. The only bright spot in the census data was a significant rise in the city's Asian population (16 percent), though from a relatively small base.

The 2010 census also showed salient trends in the spatial distribution of the city's racial, ethnic, and class mix. Throughout the 20th century, U.S. cities tended to have lower-income populations clustered around the central area in decaying buildings, surrounded in turn by a ring of working-class housing, followed by an outer ring of middle-class neighborhoods. But the 2010 data show a steady inversion of these patterns in Chicago. Affluent families—generally white and Asian—now dominate the central area, while working-class Latinos and African Americans have been pushed outward to previously middle-class areas.[6] Despite all this movement, Chicago remains the most segregated large city in the nation, though steady improvement has taken place in the past two decades.[7] Both of these class and racial patterns are hardly rigid; Figures 21.1 and 21.2 (page 270) show the clear flux in the last 10 years alone.

Population decline was only one element of the lost decade. Overall private-sector employment dropped as well, a reversal from the 1990s. Not only did manufacturing continued to slide, but even central area employment fell five percent, as the city's main economic engine began to sputter. Table 21.1 (page 271) shows percentage declines across several geographies.

Data on employment by sector help explain the central area's weakness (Table 21.2, page 272). Declines in information, finance and insurance, real estate, and professional employment indicate that white-collar employment

Change in Real Per Capita Income by Census Tract
1999 to 2005-2009 Average, Chicago and Vicinity

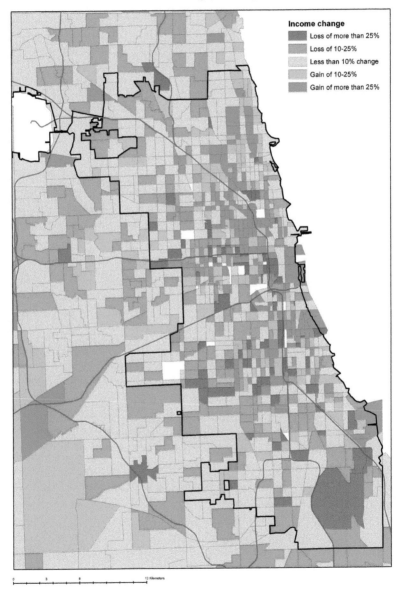

Income change

- Loss of more than 25%
- Loss of 10-25%
- Less than 10% change
- Gain of 10-25%
- Gain of more than 25%

Figure 21.2. Change in real per capita income, 1999–2009, Chicago and vicinity. The 2009 data are from the American Community Survey and are five-year estimates covering 2005–2009.

Table 21.1. Change in Private-Sector Employment in Chicago, 1992–2010

	1992–2002 (%)	2002–2010 (%)
Metro Area	13	–7
City of Chicago	1	–8
Central Area	5	–5

Source: Illinois Department of Employment Security, "Where Workers Work," 1992–2011

Note: Metro Area includes six counties: Cook, DuPage, Kane, Lake, McHenry, and Will

in Chicago might no longer be driving growth. Gains in health care, hospitality, arts, and education fields—almost 25 percent of employment in 2010—did not offset these losses. Meanwhile, construction, manufacturing, wholesale trade, and transportation continue to fall precipitously.

Many of these trends are also true for other cities, but Chicago's employment loss was the worst among the nation's 10 largest metro areas during the decade. Similarly, real GDP per capita and personal income per capita in the region nudged up only three percent, ranking seventh among the 10 largest areas.[8] Finally, the rupture of the housing bubble in 2007–2008 hit Chicago and its suburbs hard. While the region was not nearly as ravaged as Florida, Nevada, or California, an estimated 17 percent of white borrowers and a crushing 40 percent of black and Latino borrowers are believed to be "underwater," with negative equity in their homes.[9]

Mayor Emanuel's administration responded to the "lost decade" by focusing on attracting corporations to downtown. An October 2012 press release highlighted "the more than 60 companies that have announced nearly 25,000 jobs coming to Chicago," including most prominently United Airlines, Motorola Mobility, and a division of Nokia. Emanuel used his extensive connections from the Clinton and Obama administrations to engineer some of these moves, and he also chairs World Business Chicago (WBC), a nonprofit, economic development organization led by a board of corporate leaders and tasked as the economic development arm of the city. This organization represents a new version of the growth coalition, one centered primarily on corporate relocation. It has had some singular successes, most notably attracting Boeing's world headquarters.[10]

Table 21.2. Private-Sector Employment in the City of Chicago and the Metro Area, March 2002–March 2010

Industry	Percentage of Chicago Employment 2010	City of Chicago Change 2002–2010 (%)	Percentage of Total Metro Area Employment 2010 (%)	Metro Area Change 2002–2010 (%)
All Private-Sector Employment	100.0	−8.2	100.0	−6.7
Major Private-Sector Industries				
Construction	1.9	−31.0	3.5	−34.9
Manufacturing	6.4	−40.5	11.1	−28.6
Wholesale Trade	3.4	−20.0	6.1	−11.2
Retail Trade	8.5	−2.0	11.9	−6.7
Transportation & Warehousing	5.5	−19.2	4.6	−6.9
Information	3.1	−27.4	2.4	−27.7
Finance and Insurance	10.5	−14.7	6.7	−10.1
Real Estate and Rental and Leasing	2.5	−17.1	1.8	−13.2
Professional, Scientific, and Technical Services	12.5	−4.3	8.6	−5.9
Management of Companies and Enterprises	1.5	8.5	2.4	16.3
Administration, Support, Waste Management and Remediation	8.0	−3.9	7.9	−1.5
Educational Services	5.2	22.2	3.6	29.7
Health Care & Social Assistance	14.0	8.3	14.1	16.6
Arts, Entertainment, and Recreation	1.7	7.0	1.6	−3.9
Accommodations & Food Services	9.6	12.1	9.0	10.3
Other Services (except Public Administration)	5.2	−1.3	4.3	−3.2

Source: Illinois Department of Employment Security, "Where Workers Work," 2002, 2010

Yet beyond the corporate recruitment effort, actionable strategies for addressing the city's competiveness remain in short supply. Two reports from 2012 highlight the lack of a concrete agenda coupled with a robust implementation effort. In March 2012, WBC released "A Plan for Economic Growth and Jobs," which recommends 10 unobjectionable strategies, including supporting advanced manufacturing, developing workforce skills, supporting entrepreneurship, and investing in infrastructure. But how to execute these strategies is unclear. The plan vaguely calls for "new institutional capacity to carry this work forward," without much elaboration. Ownership of the plan falls on WBC, but ideas for engaging other city agencies, reforming public programs, or creating local partners to carry out its ideas are left unexpressed. As Ted Wysocki, a local economic development leader, explains: "WBC is a privatization of planning—where are land use and infrastructure in the WBC vision for growth?"[11]

Similarly, an Organisation for Economic Co-operation and Development (OECD) Territorial Review of Chicago released in September 2012 highlights the region's anemic economic growth in the past decade and offers five strategies that mirror WBC proposals. But neither report's strategies connect with the existing institutions, capital budgets, or political systems that define year-to-year governmental action. Observer Aaron Renn summarized the problem for Chicago: "This [OECD] report got it half right in giving [Chicagoans] a very good look at the current conditions, strengths, challenges, and international comparisons. Where it lagged was in fully articulating the structural landscape driving [the region's economic] underperformance and developing compelling strategies for turning the ship around."[12] The "structural landscape" includes, among other features, an inability to effectively capital budget or to conduct comprehensive planning. The challenge now is to integrate the high-level strategies of WBC and OECD plans into existing systems and plans ranging from the Central Area Action Plan to the region's GO TO 2040 comprehensive plan, issued in 2010. Otherwise, the separation of economic and physical planning will only hamper both efforts.

The gloomy data from the past decade imply that Chicago's renaissance is incomplete and that the city's population and job bases will continue to shift dramatically, as they have for the past 30 years. Was the global city built on sand? No, but the likelihood remains high that a strong central area will eventually be surrounded by declining neighborhoods on the city's fringes, creating a new set of planning problems. Since 1958, the city has sought

Boeing Comes to Chicago

The economic development sprint of a generation began on March 21, 2001, when Boeing chairman and CEO Philip Condit announced that the company was relocating its world headquarters from Seattle to Chicago, Dallas, or Denver. It was seeking an existing Class A building of 225,000 contiguous square feet, available immediately for fitting out in time for September occupancy. There were 14 such sites in northeastern Illinois, most of them in the suburbs. More generally, it was in search of "a culturally diverse community; a business friendly environment; good connections to Boeing operations; and convenient access for Boeing customers."

Mayor Richard M. Daley named the World Business Chicago (WBC) group as the city's lead in developing a bid. In its first 18 months of existence, the WBC had created a database, covering 14 jurisdictions, that detailed the drivers of the metropolitan economy and analyzed the nature of the workforce. The WBC used this data to demonstrate the region's assets, including schools, culture, and lifestyles. This research proved critical to the bid, since Boeing demanded 80-plus datasets that could articulate the region's qualities.

The Boeing evaluators were engineers: they wanted to work the numbers, see the possibilities, and otherwise be left alone to decide. They toured the three competing cities in alphabetical order. In Chicago, one team checked out the suburban and city buildings that had made the cut, while another assessed the suburban and city neighborhoods' residential and educational qualities of life. At a dinner that night, the teams were pitched by Tribune Company chairman John Madigan, who was also chairman of the Commercial Club of Chicago, surrounded by a who's who in Chicago business, culture, education, and government, including the Republican governor and the Democratic mayor.

A second team of Boeing executives then came to town for meetings on the 67th floor of the Sears Tower to hear local incentive offers from Bannockburn, Schaumburg, and Chicago. Mayoral chief of staff Sheila O'Grady assembled 15 city cabinet heads behind Planning and Development commissioner Alicia Berg, who offered a $2 million cash grant for energy-efficiency office retrofitting. The city's chief financial officer, Walter Knorr, and others figured out a way to offer just under $1 million a year for 20 years without using TIF funds, because Boeing insisted that local school funds not be affected. Pam McDonough, representing the state of Illinois, of-

Figure 21.3. Mayor Richard M. Daley, Boeing chairman Phil Condit, and Alderman Walter Burnett (foreground) at announcement of Boeing's move to Chicago, September 5, 2001

fered an annual corporate income-tax credit based on the personal income tax for each new hire for 15 years.

McDonough commissioned Arthur Andersen to model the incentives against Boeing's likely fiscal contribution to Illinois, and it worked out to about $43 million to the positive. Nevertheless, with Boeing revenues running north of $60 billion, incentives were never the key issue. The decision makers later said that the educational, financial, cultural, and governmental resources they saw in Chicago's central area were the real benefits—not the incentives.

The night before the decision, a tenant in the stack of floors in 100 N. Riverside Plaza that Boeing wanted for its offices rejected Boeing's offer. The bad news came by phone to Alicia Berg well after midnight. She had no authority to do so, but she offered the tenant $1 million in cash. Philip Condit then announced from a plane that had left Seattle (with flight plans filed for three cities) that Boeing had chosen Chicago.

—Paul O'Connor

to defend and rebuild its central area, with some success. But the lost decade shows the need for continued investment and greater planning to sustain those gains, while at the same time attention and investment are also needed in the city's neighborhoods to improve schools, strengthen communities, reduce crime, and improve livability. This is a tall order, yet the city has engaged in no comprehensive, systemic planning to tackle these issues. Reasonable strategies as presented by the WBC and OECD need coherent implementation and coordination. Without greater attention to the city's structural weaknesses, and with large fiscal deficits making new investment difficult, Chicago could easily experience another decade of stagnation.

CHAPTER 22
CONCLUSION: RESTORE PLANNING TO CHICAGO

Chicago's run of good news into the first years of the 21st century, ranging from the opening of Millennium Park to the euphoria of the housing boom, transformed the city's personality. The central area finally looked "finished," with blank railroad spaces reclaimed, warehouses converted, and housing rehabbed. The city had "arrived," both on the world stage and at the destination prophesized back in 1958. The doom-and-gloom of a declining Rust Belt metropolis with rough edges had given way to a cosmopolitan city that attracted corporations such as Boeing and Ford as well as hipster artists, immigrants, and tourists from around the globe.

Of course, this perception of impressive success required compartmentalizing the deep poverty and insecurity in large swaths of the city touched neither by gentrification nor the information-age economy. Here, planning ideas struggled to take hold for decades, only recently finding tenuous footing through LISC's New Communities Program and its carefully structured planning. Sweeping aside the problems in neighborhoods like Little Village, Englewood, and Uptown means neglecting the city's greatest challenges. Race and class divides and disinvestment still exact a fierce toll on the city.

To many, the contrast between downtown and the city's struggling impoverished neighborhoods is the heart of the problem. But a simplistic "downtown versus the neighborhoods" narrative understates the complexity of Chicago's urban revival, missing the shared connections between the two. The neighborhoods need a vibrant downtown to generate employment and tax revenue to fund neighborhood services, while the downtown needs healthy, affordable communities to attract a workforce. Further, despite perceptions of neglect, much public investment *has* gone into Chicago's poor communities. New schools, police stations, and libraries dot this landscape, and the Plan for Transformation has completely reconfigured entire poor communities, albeit displacing many. In addition, aggressive industrial planning developed by Harold Washington and implemented under Richard M. Daley has meant the city hardly stood still on the issue of jobs and employment. The "downtown versus the neighborhoods" formulation implies a simple trade-off, but the city's ecosystems are more complex.

Instead, focusing attention on the extent of planning explains, in part, why downtown thrived while poor neighborhoods could not turn city investments into revival. The central area had a powerful growth coalition behind it to support repeated and substantial planning. Central area plans were paid for or driven by the growth coalition in 1973, 1983, and 2003/2009 to create a vision, an identity, and a set of priorities for downtown. TIF districts and other resources supported implementation of individual projects recommended by these coherent and comprehensive plans, although implementing the latest plans has decidedly lagged.

By contrast, for decades neighborhoods such as Englewood, Uptown, and Little Village relied upon the city to produce plans and a fickle federal government to pay for them. These neighborhoods underwent several iterations of planning, including conservation in the 1950s and comprehensive planning in the 1960s. But expected federal funds materialized either too late or insufficiently, and few projects were realized. From the 1970s until recently, efforts in these neighborhoods have been limited, with struggling CDCs building housing while scattered other programs worked in separate silos. No comprehensive plan emerged to attract broad-based investment. When Mayor Richard M. Daley began using TIFs across the city, the choices were largely ad hoc, with the thinnest of redevelopment plans and no overarching policy or plan to guide the creation of these districts. Still, flush with TIF dollars, the city went on a building spree, constructing new schools, police stations, and—as in Englewood—institutions like a new community college. The city built 32 full-service neighborhood libraries between 1995 and 2010, a remarkable accomplishment.[1]

But mayoral instinct and aldermanic power, more than citizen input, guided these choices. New schools, libraries, and police stations have undoubtedly been positive additions, yet they were not derived from a careful plan based on a set of criteria, priorities, or targeted needs. Most proposed capital projects in Chicago are individually evaluated by departments and added to a Capital Improvement Plan each year. If funding becomes available from a variety of sources (federal, state, TIF, bonds, special purpose funds) and political stars are aligned, then they are built. But we cannot evaluate progress toward a larger goal or plan, because one rarely exists. The Neighborhood Capital Budget Group, an activist watchdog organization, spent a decade trying to piece together an overall picture of the city's capital priorities but could not nail down hard numbers on actual spending. The city simply never assessed its Capital Improvement Plans. Instead, projects are decided on the basis of influence and arbitrary criteria. As Laurence Msall of the Civic Federation puts it, "Planning should be an anticorruption tool, making sure that public spending is done wisely, rather than politically."[2]

As Chicago looks to its future, we see several crucial challenges. Addressing these in a comprehensive way will require reform and a renewed assertion that planning matters, as it has in the past:

Increasing transit capacity, especially in the central area, is essential for retaining regional job growth within the city, with implications for the city's tax base. The new economy is largely office-based, and it still values face-to-face networking and clustering effects. Only by biting the bullet on expensive transit systems can the city's Loop continue to be an attractive location for employers. This means not only maintaining the city's rapid transit systems but also expanding capacity at Metra stations, building some version of the West Loop Transportation Center, and offering new routes to the east Loop and North Michigan Avenue. These problems have been around since Burnham and concrete plans to address them have existed for 40 years, yet we continue to be immobilized.

Expanding and refining LISC's New Communities Program offers the best chance to bring coherent and comprehensive planning to Chicago's struggling neighborhoods. As a model of structured yet inclusive planning, the NCP builds capacity, empowers local actors, and balances vision with readily attainable goals. The program needs continual evaluation and support, and the city could offer greater coordination between its agencies and NCP without trampling on its community-based approach. Still, NCP communities need to implement policies not only to retain existing populations but to attract new ones.

Adapting industrial policy to the city's rapidly changing employment base is essential to capture new job growth. Industrial policy cannot be wedded to the idea that the best jobs are inherently in heavy manufacturing. Many nonmanufacturing employers and firms compatible with manufacturing need industrial space for their enterprises and should be encouraged to use the industrial corridors. A hard-nosed reevaluation of existing corridors and policies is needed to measure their effectiveness so that scarce resources can be directed strategically to those corridors that show the most potential for job growth.

Implementing rather than ignoring existing plans could reverse a decade of scattershot capital budgeting, TIF-based inefficiencies, and project-by-project thinking. Even without a comprehensive plan, Chicago can still use the area plans produced over the past decade and organize its priorities coherently around them. The mayor should put these plans before the city council so they can be enacted into law, which in turn will mean that zoning applications will be judged not merely by the underlying zoning code but also by consistency with carefully crafted plans. Adoption of plans will help restrain if not entirely reform the current structure where aldermanic privilege and mindless NIMBYism distorts and paralyzes debate over development.

Finally, planners need to assert themselves. Lacking a city department with the name "planning," Chicago has fragmented its planning apparatus and left it at the mercy of mayors, aldermen, and constituent city agencies. Economic development, as practiced by World Business Chicago, should not be seen as the primary planning effort and should instead be integrated with physical planning. A city that once prided itself on visionary planning needs to recapture that confidence through the prominent restoration of a fully funded city planning department.

This book posits that not having a strong city planning department vigorously planning in a comprehensive way for the city's future is risky. Is the city going to continue designating one TIF after another with rudimentary goals, maximum flexibility, and little serious planning? Will it continue to delegate planning repsonsibilities to semiprivate organizations and corporate volunteerism? Or will the city do the hard work of laying out a vision, creating policy to set direction, and prioritizing its resources? Planners in Chicago are perfectly capable of producing these kinds of plans. The Central Area Plan and the Central Area Action Plan of the past decade are comprehensive, well-documented, and achievable. The Northerly Island Framework Plan, the Riverwalk Framework Plan, and recent bike plans attest to the wealth of planning experience in the city. The New Communities Program and other innovative work of nonprofits are models of community-based process that offer realistic guidance to struggling neighborhoods. And there have been successful examples of economic development efforts to retain and attract firms to both the central area and many of the industrial corridors.

We can build a comprehensive plan that examines all aspects of the city, creates a shared purpose, raises consciousness about important challenges, and then summon the resources so they can be allocated effectively for our future needs. We just need the political will to do so.

Figure 22.1. View from the CTA's Morgan station looking east toward the Loop, May 23, 2012

APPENDIX A

	Mayor	Planning Department Name	Planning Commissioner	Chicago Plan Commission Chair
1955	Richard J. Daley			William M. Spencer
1956				
1957		Department of City Planning	Ira J. Bach	Clair M. Roddewig
1958				
1959				
1960				
1961				
1962				John L. McCaffrey
1963				
1964				Edward C. Logelin
1965				
1966		Department of Development and Planning	John G. Duda	
1967				
1968				
1969				
1970			Lewis W. Hill	Patrick L. O'Malley
1971				
1972				
1973				
1974				Julian H. Levi
1975				
1976				
1977				
1978	Michael A. Bilandic	Department of Planning, City and Community Development*	Thomas Kapsalis	
1979				
1980	Jane M. Byrne	Department of Planning	Martin R. Murphy	George J. Cullen
1981				
1982				
1983				Miles Berger
1984	Harold L. Washington		Elizabeth Hollander	
1985				
1986				

Planning Departments and Leadership, City of Chicago, 1955–2013			
	Mayor	Planning Department Name	Planning Commissioner	Chicago Plan Commission Chair
1987	Harold L. Washington	Department of Planning	Elizabeth Hollander	E. Wayne Robinson
1988	Eugene Sawyer			
1989				
1990			David Mosena	
1991			Charles Thurow (acting)	
1992		Department of Planning and Development	Valerie Jarrett	Reuben L. Hedlund
1993				
1994				
1995				
1996			Joseph F. Boyle Jr.	
1997				
1998			Christopher R. Hill	Peter Bynoe
1999				
2000				
2001	Richard M. Daley			
2002			Alicia Mazur Berg	
2003				
2004				
2005			Denise M. Casalino	Linda Searl
2006			Lori T. Healey	
2007				
2008			Arnold L. Randall Jr.	
2009		Department of Zoning and Land Use Planning (DZP)**	Patricia A. Scudiero	
2010				
2011		Department of Housing and Economic Development***	Andrew J. Mooney	
2012	Rahm I. Emanuel			
2013				Marin Cabrera Jr.

* Formed by merger of Department of Development and Planning and Department of Urban Renewal

** Department of Planning and Development split into DZP and Department of Community Development

*** Formed by merger of DZP, Department of Community Development, and Department of Housing

APPENDIX B
SELECTED LIST OF PLANS AND REPORTS, 1958–2012

CITY AND CENTRAL AREA REPORTS AND PLANS
1958
Annual Report, Chicago Plan Commission
Annual Report, Department of City Planning
Development Plan for the Central Area of Chicago,
        Department of City Planning

1966
The Comprehensive Plan of Chicago, Department of
Development and Planning

1966–1973
Development Area Plans:
        The Riveredge Plan of Chicago
        Illinois Center: Air Rights Development Guidelines
        South Loop New Town: Guidelines for Development
        Near South Development Area
        Southeast Development Area
        Far Southwest Development Area
        Far Southeast Development Area
        Far South Development Area
        Southwest Development Area
        Mid-South Development Area
        Northwest Development Area
        North Development Area
        Far North Development Area
        Far Northwest Development Area
        Far West Development Area

Mid-West Development Area
Near West Development Area
O'Hare Development Area

1970
A Lake Michigan Site for Chicago's Third Major Airport: Summary of Engineering Studies,
Mayor Richard J. Daley; Harza Engineering

1972
The Lakefront Plan of Chicago, Mayor Richard J. Daley; Chicago Plan Commission; City Council;
Chicago Park District

1973
Chicago 21: A Plan for the Central Area Communities, Mayor Richard J. Daley; Chicago Plan Commission; Chicago Central Area Committee; Skidmore, Owings, and Merrill

1982
Chicago Comprehensive Neighborhood Needs Analysis, Mayor Jane Byrne; Melaniphy and Associates
Chicago 1992 Comprehensive Plan, draft for discussion, Department of Planning
North Loop Guidelines for Conservation and Redevelopment, Mayor Jane M. Byrne; Chicago Plan Commission; City Council

1983
Chicago Central Area Plan, Mayor Harold Washington; Chicago Central Area Committee; Skidmore, Owings, and Merrill

1984
Chicago Works Together: 1984 Chicago Development Plan, Mayor Harold Washington; Department of Economic Development; Mayor's Development Subcabinet

1989–1990
Downtown Parking Policies; River North Urban Design Guidelines; Chicago River Urban Design Guidelines, Chicago Department of Planning

1991
Building the Future of Chicago, Chicago Central Area Committee
Planning Principles for the Central Area, Chicago Department of Planning

1993
State Street Development Plan and Urban Design Guidelines, Chicago Plan Commission; Department of Planning and Development

1997
Vision for Great State Street: Next Steps, Department of Planning and Development, with contributions from the State Street Commission and the Greater State Street Council

1998
Central Business District: A Residential Impact Study and Scenarios for Office Growth, Chicago Development Council

1999
Downtown Chicago Market Trends, Rosen Consulting Group; Chicago Development Council
Chicago River Corridor Development Plan and Guidelines, Mayor
    Richard M. Daley; Department of Planning and Development; Lambert Group; Wolff Clements and
    Associates; Skidmore, Owings, and Merrill

2000
A Vision for State Street, Wabash Avenue and Michigan Avenue:
    Chicago's Historic Downtown Core, Mayor Richard M. Daley;
    Department of Planning and Development; Skidmore, Owings, and
    Merrill; Lambert Group; Ed Zotti
Summary of Issues Facing Chicago's Central Area, Draft Report,
    Skidmore, Owings, and Merrill; Department of Planning and Development, Chicago

2001
Economic Base and Sector Analysis, Central Area, 2000–2020,
    Arthur Andersen; Department of Planning and Development

2003
Chicago Central Area Plan, Mayor Richard M. Daley; Chicago Plan Commission; Department of
    Planning and Development; Department of Transportation; Department of Environment; Skidmore,
    Owings, and Merrill; Arthur Andersen; Goodman Williams Group; Real Estate Planning Group;
    Lambert Group; Panto-Ulema; Ed Zotti; Emily J. Harris; Duncan Associates; TranSystems; DLK
    Architecture; Donald Hey

2009
Chicago Central Area Action Plan, Mayor Richard M. Daley; Chicago Plan Commission; Department of
    Zoning and Land Use Planning; URS Corporation; Site Design Group; Goodman Williams Group

INDUSTRIAL AND ECONOMIC DEVELOPMENT REPORTS AND PLANS
1986
Building on the Basics: The Final Report of the Mayor's Task Force on Steel and Southeast Chicago,
    Department of Economic Development
Business Loss or Balanced Growth: Industrial Displacement in Chicago, New City YMCA; Department of
    Economic Development

1987
Cooperation for Survival and Growth: New Designs for Apparel
    Manufacturing in Chicago, Department of Economic Development

1988
Printing in Chicago, Final Report of the Printing Industry Task Force, David Ranney and
    Wim Wiewel, Center for Urban Economic Development, University of Illinois–Chicago
Clybourn Corridor Planned Manufacturing District, Staff Report to the Chicago Plan Commission, Depart-
    ment of Economic Development

1989
Corridors of Industrial Opportunity: A Plan for Industry on Chicago's North Side, Mayor Eugene Sawyer;
    Department of Planning

1990

Keeping Jobs for Chicago's Future: A Development Impact Assessment of Goose Island, Donna Ducharme, New City YMCA

Freight Movement and Urban Congestion in the Chicago Area, Chicago Area Transportation Study, followed by annual reports of Intermodal Advisory Taskforce 1997, 2001, 2006

1992

Corridors of Industrial Opportunity: A Plan for Industry on Chicago's West Side, Mayor Richard M. Daley; Department of Planning and Development

1994

Corridors of Industrial Opportunity: A Plan for Industry on Chicago's South Side, Mayor Richard M. Daley; Department of Planning and Development

1995

Brownfields Forum: Recycling Land for Chicago's Future, Mayor Richard M. Daley; Department of Environment; Department of Planning and Development

1998

City of Chicago Industrial Market and Strategic Analysis, Department of Planning and Development; Arthur Andersen

1999

Calumet Area Implementation/Action Plan, Department of Planning and Development; Arthur Andersen

From Steeltown to Hometown: A New Era for South Chicago and South Works, Department of Planning and Development; Skidmore, Owings, and Merrill; Lambert Group; Lakota Group; Goodman Williams Group; Civiltech; Harza Engineering

Heavy Truck Weight Corridor: Economic Impact Study of the Northwest Indiana/Southeast Chicago Steel Industry, Department of Planning and Development; Arthur Andersen

Chicago Metropolis 2020: Preparing Metropolitan Chicago for the 21st Century, Elmer W. Johnson, Commercial Club of Chicago

A Joint Proposal for the Millennium Project to Ford Motor Company, Department of Commerce and Community Affairs, State of Illinois; Department of Planning and Development; Arthur Andersen; CenterPoint Properties; FCL Builders

2001

Calumet Area Land Use Plan, Department of Planning and Development; Calumet Area Industrial Commission; Department of the Environment; Openlands Project; Southeast Chicago Development Commission

2002

Revitalizing Industry: A Look to the 21st Century, Metropolitan Planning Council

Critical Cargo: A Regional Freight Action Agenda, Chicago Metropolis 2020; Chicagoland Chamber of Commerce; Metropolitan Planning Council

2005

Chicago Region Environmental and Transportation Efficiency Program, Final Feasibility Plan, Federal Highway Administration; Illinois Department of Transportation; Chicago Department of Transportation

Realizing the Vision, 2040 Regional Framework Plan, Northeastern Illinois Planning Commission

2010
Go to 2040 Comprehensive Regional Plan, Chicago Metropolitan Agency for Planning

2011
Loop Economic Study and Impact Report, Chicago Loop Alliance;
    Goodman Williams Group
Chicago Sustainable Industries, Phase One, A Manufacturing Work Plan for the 21st Century,
    Department of Housing and Economic Development

2012
Prospering in Place: Linking Jobs, Development, and Transit to Spur Chicago's Economy, Center for
    Neighborhood Technology
Chicago Forward: Action Agenda, Mayor Rahm Emanuel; Chicago Department
    of Transportation
A Plan for Economic Growth and Jobs, Mayor Rahm Emanuel, chairman, World Business Chicago
OECD Territorial Review: The Chicago Tri-State Metropolitan Area, Organisation for Economic Coopera-
    tion and Development, sponsored by Chicagoland Chamber of Commerce, Chicago Metropolitan
    Agency for Planning, and Economic Development Administration, U.S. Department of Commerce

APPENDIX C

INDUSTRIAL EMPLOYMENT TABLES

INDUSTRIAL-CORRIDOR EMPLOYMENT CHANGE, BY REGIONS WITHIN CHICAGO, 1990s–2010	
NORTH SIDE	
Industrial employment, 1989	26,273
Industrial employment, 2010	12,739
Numeric change	−13,534
Percentage change	−51.5
Average annual loss	644
WEST SIDE	
Industrial employment, 1992	79,476
Industrial employment, 2010	38,720
Numeric change	−40,756
Percentage change	−51.3
Average annual loss	2,264
SOUTH SIDE	
Industrial employment, 1994	50,109
Industrial employment, 2010	21,415
Numeric change	−28,694
Percentage change	−57.3
Average annual loss	1,793
TOTAL	
Industrial employment, initial years	155,858
Industrial employment, 2010	72,874
Numeric change	−82,984
Percentage change	−53.2

Sources: Corridors of Industrial Opportunity plans, 1989, 1992, 1994; U.S. Census Bureau; Center for Governmental Studies, Northern Illinois University

EMPLOYMENT CHANGE AND SECTOR SHARE, CHICAGO INDUSTRIAL CORRIDORS, CHICAGO, COOK COUNTY, ILLINOIS, AND THE UNITED STATES, 2002–2010			
GEOGRAPHIC AREA	**EMPLOYMENT**		
	2002	**2010**	
INDUSTRIAL CORRIDORS			
Manufacturing*	53,556	36,288	
Nonmanufacturing industrial†	41,608	36,586	
All other employment sectors	23,091	26,102	
Total employment	118,255	98,976	
CITY OF CHICAGO (including corridors)			
Manufacturing*	102,219	64,785	
Nonmanufacturing industrial†	238,083	222,324	
All other employment sectors	879,280	948,042	
Total employment	1,219,582	1,235,151	
COOK COUNTY (not including Chicago)			
Manufacturing*	185,670	131,909	
Nonmanufacturing industrial†	283,176	248,965	
All other employment sectors	786,803	802,695	
Total employment	1,255,649	1,183,569	
ILLINOIS			
Manufacturing*	755,146	567,370	
Nonmanufacturing industrial†	1,136,293	1,069,914	
All other employment sectors	3,611,321	3,829,827	
Total employment	5,502,760	5,467,111	
UNITED STATES			
Manufacturing*	15,209,192	11,487,496	
Nonmanufacturing industrial†	21,231,840	22,850,228	
All other employment sectors	74,827,383	79,245,644	
Total employment	111,268,415	113,583,368	

* NAICS code 33
† NAICS codes 22 (Utilities), 23 (Construction), 42 (Wholesale Trade), 48–49 (Transportation and Warehousing), 56 (Administrative Support and Waste Management Remediation)
Source: U.S. Census Bureau; Center for Governmental Studies, Northern Illinois University

| CHANGE | | SECTOR SHARE (%) | |
NUMBER	PERCENT	2002	2010
−17,268	−32.2	45	37
−5,022	−12.1	35	37
3,011	13.0	20	26
−19,279	−16.3	100	100
−37,434	−36.6	8	5
−15,759	−6.6	20	18
68,762	7.8	72	77
15,569	1.3	100	100
−53,761	−29.0	15	11
−34,211	−12.1	23	21
15,892	2.0	62	68
−72,080	−5.7	100	100
−187,776	−24.9	14	10
−66,379	−5.8	21	20
218,506	6.1	65	70
−35,649	−0.6	100	100
−3,721,696	−24.5	14	10
1,618,388	7.6	19	20
4,418,261	5.9	67	70
2,314,953	2.1	100	100

EMPLOYMENT CHANGE FOR CHICAGO INDUSTRIAL CORRIDORS, BY SECTOR, 2002–2010					
	Manufacturing*		Nonmanufacturing Industrial†		
Industrial Corridor	Absolute	%	Absolute	%	
Addison	56	4.2	–17	–10.1	
Armitage	–1,103	–45.4	–160	–33.3	
Brighton Park	–1,477	–70.1	–2,222	–6.4	
Burnside	–681	–77.1	–58	–74.4	
Calumet	–188	–6.8	–173	–13.2	
Elston/Armstrong	–382	–46.8	27	20.6	
Greater Southwest	687	23.6	–76	–7.3	
Harlem	–174	–22.7	–11	–3.6	
Kennedy	–352	–42.4	–25	–8.7	
Kinzie	–2,065	–42.7	3,054	72.4	
Knox	–489	–55.9	–213	–24.9	
Little Village	–695	–37.9	1,442	134.1	
North Branch	–618	–24.1	1,269	37.6	
Northwest	–1,372	–36.1	–2,014	–60.3	
Peterson	–303	–33.2	124	42.6	
Pilsen	–609	–30.5	–228	–5.4	
Pulaski	126	8.2	–1,029	–86.0	
Pullman	–40	–11.7	–430	–39.5	
Ravenswood	–928	–58.5	–8	–1.4	
Roosevelt/Cicero	–1,720	–43.4	–1,039	–30.7	
Stevenson	–361	–10.1	–1,956	–40.8	
Stockyards	–3,872	–40.5	–467	–12.4	
West Pullman	–97	–96.0	–28	–100.0	
Western/Ogden	–611	–48.3	–784	–40.1	
TOTAL	–17,268	–32.2	–5,022	–12.1	

* NAICS code 33

† NAICS codes 22 (Utilities), 23 (Construction), 42 (Wholesale Trade), 48–49 (Transportation and Warehousing), 56 (Administrative Support and Waste Management Remediation)

‡ NAICS codes 54 (Professional, Scientific, and Technical Services), 62 (Health Care and Social Assistance), 71 (Arts, Entertainment and Recreation), 72 (Accomodation and Food Services)

Source: U.S. Census Bureau; Center for Governmental Studies, Northern Illinois University

Compatible with Manufacturing[‡]		Subtotal		Other Sectors		Total Change	
Absolute	%	Absolute	%	Absolute	%	Absolute	%
-49	-37.7	-10	-0.6	-501	-53.2	-511	-20.0
-7	-3.8	-1,270	-41.0	-73	-37.8	-1,343	-40.8
63	60.6	-3,636	-61.7	108	24.1	-3,528	-55.7
90	209.3	-649	-64.6	-371	-84.7	-1,020	-70.7
18	26.5	-343	-8.3	12	20.7	-331	-7.9
39	26.4	-316	-28.9	-48	-28.2	-364	-28.8
60	23.5	671	16.0	-521	-28.9	150	2.5
143	1191.7	-42	-3.9	-10	-19.2	-52	-4.6
9	37.5	-368	-32.2	-37	-11.3	-405	-27.6
213	10.4	1,202	10.8	385	29.9	1,587	12.8
10	90.9	-692	-39.8	82	20.2	-610	-28.4
-19	-7.9	728	23.1	1	0.5	729	21.8
263	11.7	914	11.2	1,997	68.8	2,911	26.3
-831	-84.0	-4,217	-51.9	-11	-1.6	-4,228	-48.0
-6	-12.0	-185	-14.8	2	1.2	-183	-12.9
11	2.3	-826	-12.4	792	134.0	-34	-0.5
-1	-3.6	-904	-32.8	-246	-45.7	-1,150	-34.9
16	533.3	-454	-31.7	-6	-30.0	-460	-31.7
271	67.6	-665	-25.8	-144	-21.9	-809	-25.0
-241	-21.5	-3,000	-35.4	-39	-8.9	-3,039	-34.1
-48	-53.3	-2,365	-28.0	111	15.5	-2,254	-24.6
212	124.7	-4,127	-30.6	1,383	148.7	-2,744	-19.0
-5	-71.4	-130	-95.6	-3	-25.0	-133	-89.9
13	61.9	-1,382	-42.7	-76	-32.6	-1,458	-42.0
224	2.5	-22,066	-21.2	2,787	19.6	-19,279	-16.3

ENDNOTES

CHAPTER 1

1. Richard Longworth, "Chicago: City on the Brink," *Chicago Tribune*, May 10, 1981; "The City That Survives," special issue of *The Economist*, March 29–April 4, 1980, 38.

2. Richard Florida, *The Rise of the Creative Class: And How It's Transforming Work, Leisure, Community, and Everyday Life* (New York: Basic Books, 2002).

3. John Grimond, "Special Report: Chicago—A Success Story," *The Economist*, March 16, 2006.

4. A.T. Kearney, "2012 Global Cities Index and Emerging Cities Outlook," 2012, at www.atkearney.com /index.php/Publications/2012-global-cities-index-and-emerging-cities-outlook.html. A similar study by the *Economist* placed Chicago ninth. See Economist Intelligence Unit, "Hot Spots: Benchmarking Global City Competitiveness," January 2012, at www.managementthinking.eiu.com/hot-spots.html. Aaron Renn has written a critique of Chicago's Global City rank on his blog *Urbanophile* at www .urbanophile.com.

5. For a thoughtful examination of Chicago's multiple political, cultural and economic transformations, see Larry Bennett, *The Third City* (Chicago: University of Chicago Press, 2010). See also John P. Koval, Larry Bennett, Michael I. J. Bennett, Fassil Demissie, Roberta Garner, and Kiljoong Kim, eds., *The New Chicago: A Social and Cultural Analysis* (Philadelphia: Temple University Press, 2006).

6. William Julius Wilson, *The Truly Disadvantaged: the Inner City, the Underclass, and Public Policy* (Chicago: University of Chicago Press, 1987); Janet Abu-Lughod, *New York, Chicago, Los Angeles: America's Global Cities* (Minneapolis: University of Minnesota Press, 1999).

7. Interview with Laurence Msall, July 17, 2012.

8. The term "planning" as used in this book reflects current definitions in the field of professional plan-ning, including "making informed choices about the future—that is, [creating] and maintain[ing] places where people want to live, work, and conduct business" (Gary Hack, Eugenie L. Birch, Paul H. Sedway, and Mitchell J. Silver, eds. *Local Planning, Contemporary Principles and Practice* [Wash-ington, D.C.: International City/County Management Association Press, 2009], 23). Further, plan-ners "are in the change business. . . . A planner's work should be judged by the quality and depth of its influence on people's lives" (25). Planning should "meet twenty-year needs for land, housing, transportation, and public facilities . . . based on long-range population and economic projections" (70). As well, "Every plan, regardless of scope, should be grounded in data" (215). Finally, "sound implementation involves choosing the most efficient, effective, and coherent steps for making a com-prehensive plan a reality. It invariably requires both public power and private collaboration" (273).

9. Over time, the definition of the "Central Area" has changed slightly. In 2003 the Central Area was defined as North Avenue to the north, Interstate 55 on the south, the lakefront on the east, and an irregular boundary to the west that captures the Near West Side and Chinatown. The 2009 Central Area Action Plan extended the western boundary to Ashland Avenue and also included all of the Chicago Housing Authority's Cabrini-Green site.

CHAPTER 2

1. Benet Haller, comments at "Architecture for Change Summit," Roosevelt University, Chicago, Septem-ber 22, 2010; interview with Eileen Figel, October 3, 2012. Comparisons of aldermanic privilege powers across cities are rare: on the distortive effects of ward-based zoning, see David Schleicher, "City Unplanning," George Mason Law and Economics Research Paper, no. 12-26, January 23, 2012, and Yue Zhang, "Boundaries of Power: Politics of Urban Preservation in Two Chicago Neigh-borhoods," *Urban Affairs Review* 47(4) (2011): 511–40. Milwaukee and St. Louis have aldermanic privilege systems that are similar but not as entrenched as in Chicago.

2. Len O'Connor, *Clout: Mayor Daley and His City* (Chicago: Henry Regnery, 1975).

3. Gary Rivlin, *Fire on the Prairie: Chicago's Harold Washington and the Politics of Race* (New York: Holt, 1992).

4. Keith Koeneman, *First Son: The Biography of Richard M. Daley* (Chicago: University of Chicago Press, 2013).

5. Interview with Eileen Figel, October 3, 2012. See City of Chicago, "Guide to the Chicago Landscape Or-dinance," August 2000, at: https://www.cityofchicago.org/content/dam/city/depts/zlup/Code _Enforcement/ChicagoLandscapeOrdinanceGuide.pdf.

6. Interview with Lee Bey, July 12, 2011.

7. Ibid.

8. John Mollenkopf, *The Contested City* (Princeton: Princeton University Press, 1983).

9. Until 1985, the group was known as the Metropolitan Housing and Planning Council, reflecting its roots as a housing reform organization in the 1930s.

10. It should also be noted that numerous planning organizations have long been headquartered in Chicago, including the American Planning Association (APA). Many were nurtured at the University of Chicago's Public Administration Clearinghouse in the 1950s, located at 1313 East 60th Street. The "1313" groups included, among others, the American Society of Planning Officials (a forerunner of APA), the National Association of Housing Officials (today NAHRO), the Institute of Real Estate Management, the American Institute of Real Estate Appraisers, and the American Municipal Association. The National Association of Real Estate Boards and the Urban Land Institute also started in Chicago before moving to Washington. The presence of these groups facilitated cross-fertilization of ideas and research in the 1950s and 1960s, but their dispersal by the 1980s signaled the relative decline of Chicago as the center of planning ideas in the United States. See Jennifer Light, *The Nature of Cities: Ecological Visions and the American Urban Professions, 1920–1960* (Baltimore: Johns Hopkins University Press, 2009), 52, 180. Finally, the University of Illinois–Urbana-Champaign opened one of the earliest planning graduate programs in the United States in 1945 and funneled graduates to Chicago, as did the program at the University of Illinois–Chicago.

11. In 1982, the Department of Planning produced a draft comprehensive plan that listed goals and a capital plan but was not approved by the plan commission or the council. Its only significant idea was a world's fair. (See chapter 6.) City of Chicago, Department of Planning, "Chicago 1992," released October 25, 1982. The last comprehensive plan worthy of the name was released in 1966. However, no comprehensive plan covering the whole city has been approved by the city council since the Burnham Plan of 1909.

12. Department of Housing and Economic Development, "2012 Budget Message by Commissioner Andrew Mooney," October 27, 2011, at www.cityofchicago.org/dam/city/depts/obm/supp_info/2012%20Budget/2012BudgetDeptCmteDocs/HousingandEconomicDevelopment.pdf.

13. Harold Platt, *Shock Cities: The Environmental Transformation and Reform of Manchester and Chicago* (Chicago: University of Chicago Press, 2005); William Cronon, *Nature's Metropolis* (New York: Norton, 1991). Census data from James R. Grossman, Ann Durkin Keating, and Janice L. Reiff, eds., *The Encyclopedia of Chicago* (Chicago: University of Chicago Press, 2004), 1011, and U.S. Census Bureau, 2010 Census for the Chicago-Naperville-Joliet, IL-IN-WI Metropolitan Statistical Area.

14. Alan Spear, *Black Chicago: The Making of a Negro Ghetto, 1890–1920* (Chicago: University of Chicago Press, 1967).

15. Grossman et al., *Encyclopedia of Chicago*, 834–35.

PART 2

1. City of Chicago Department of Planning and Development, Department of Transportation, and Department of Environment, *The Chicago Central Area Plan: Preparing the Central City for the 21st Century*, draft report to the Chicago Plan Commission, May 2003, 19.

CHAPTER 3

1. Chicago Plan Commission, "What Kind of a City Do I Want to Live In?" 1952, Chicago Public Library, Harold Washington Library Center (hereafter HWLC); Chicago Plan Commission, "A Plan for the Central Area of Chicago," 1952, HWLC; City of Chicago, Office of the Housing and Redevelopment Coordinator, "Relocation in Chicago, 1956," April 1957, University of Chicago Library. On urban renewal in Chicago, see Arnold Hirsch, *Making the Second Ghetto: Race and Housing in Chicago, 1940–1960* (Chicago: University of Chicago Press, 1998).

2. Joel Rast, "Creating a Unified Business Elite: The Origins of the Chicago Central Area Committee," *Journal of Urban History* 37(4) (2011), 583–605.

3. City of Chicago, Department of Planning, "Annual Report," 1958, HWLC. The reorganization of planning functions took place not long after a feud over the location of a new convention hall between the Chicago Plan Commission and Robert McCormick, the imperious publisher of the *Chicago Tribune*. McCormick wanted a showcase site along the lake on the Near South Side; CPC Chairman William Spencer, along with numerous civic organizations, objected to the use of lakefront space as well as the lack of transit or hotels near the site. Daley, eager for a convention hall and averse to public spats with the *Tribune*, sided with McCormick. Spencer soon resigned. See Lois Wille, *Forever Open, Free and Clear: the Historic Struggle for Chicago's Lakefront* (Chicago: Henry Regnery, 1972), 111–13.

4. Interview with Norm Elkin, January 25, 2012; Joel Rast, "Regime Building, Institution Building: Urban Renewal Policy in Chicago, 1946–1962," *Journal of Urban Affairs* 31(2) (2009): 181.

5. Telephone interview with Dean Macris, August 17, 2012.

6. Floor Area Ratio is a measure of the intensity of development of a site. It divides the total floor area of the building by the area of the site it sits on. For example, a two-story building that covers an entire lot would have an FAR of 2.0. A six-story building (all floors equal in size) that covers one-third of a lot would also have an FAR of 2.0.

7. Joseph Schwieterman and Dana M. Caspall, *The Politics of Place: A History of Zoning in Chicago,* ed. Jane Heron (Chicago: Lake Claremont Press, 2006), 83–85; Carol Willis, "Light, Height, and Site: The Skyscraper in Chicago," in *Chicago Architecture and Design, 1923–1993,* ed. John Zukowsky (Chicago: Art Institute of Chicago, 1993), 119–39.

8. Schwieterman and Caspall, *Politics of Place,* 47–48.

9. Kenneth Halpern, *Downtown USA: Urban Design in Nine American Cities* (New York: Whitney Library of Design, 1978); City of Chicago, Department of Planning and Development, "A New Zoning Bonus System for Chicago," December 18, 1998, HWLC.

10. Frederick Aschman, "A Review for the Chicago Central Area Committee of the City of Chicago Department of City Planning's Development Plan for the Central Area of Chicago," November 1958, HWLC. For a dissenting view that suggests that the Chicago Central Area Committee dominated the 1958 plan, see Rast, "Creating a Unified Business Elite," 594–96, and Adam Cohen and Elizabeth Taylor, *American Pharaoh, Mayor Richard J. Daley: His Battle for Chicago and the Nation* (Boston: Little, Brown), 216–20.

11. City of Chicago, Department of Planning, *Development Plan for the Central Area of Chicago*, 1958; Edward Banfield, *Political Influence* (Glencoe, Ill.: Free Press, 1961), 130–45; U.S. Census Bureau, Census of 1960. Figure computed from central business tracts and the layer of tracts immediately surrounding it.

12. Rubloff was joined in the Fort Dearborn plan by leading Chicago businessmen Holman Pettibone, chairman of Chicago Title and Trust, who had been a key player in Lake Meadows, the city's first urban renewal plan in the late 1940s. See Banfield, *Political Influence*, 130.

13. The 1960 Census reported that 8,095 people lived in census tracts 135, 136, and 137, though the Fort Dearborn plan would clear only the southern portion of 137. Edward Banfield suggested that 9,469 people lived in the area in 1950 (*Political Influence*, 128).

14. Banfield, *Political Influence*, 130–45; Rast, "Creating a Unified Business Elite," 594–96; Amanda Seligman, *Block by Block: Neighborhoods and Public Policy on Chicago's West Side* (Chicago: University of Chicago Press, 2005), 249n32; Carl W. Condit, *Chicago, 1930–70: Building, Planning, and Urban Technology* (Chicago: University of Chicago Press, 1974), 271–72.

15. Before the Federal Highway Act of 1956, expressway construction costs were split evenly among the federal government and local sources, including the city, county, and state. The Congress Expressway (now the Eisenhower Expressway) led to the relocation of 3,472 families, while two other expressways into downtown forced the relocation of 9,400 more. See City of Chicago, Department of Urban Renewal, "Relocation from Expressway Routes Within Chicago," January 1962, HWLC. After 1956, the federal government absorbed 90 percent of highway costs.

16. Richard J. Daley, "Address to the Annual Meeting of the American Institute of Planners," October 14, 1957, University of Illinois–Chicago, Special Collections Library. Thanks to John Shuler at UIC for finding this document in the unprocessed collection of Richard J. Daley materials. Cohen and Taylor (*American Pharaoh*, 217) contend that "Daley's [1958] plan was focused on automobiles," but this misreads the planning trends of the previous decades and Daley's own emphasis in this speech.

17. Urban renewal hit five areas of Chicago hard, including two districts close to the central area. First, three miles south of the Loop, the 101-acre Lake Meadows (1949–1955) project began wholesale clearance of African American neighborhoods on the South Side. Second, the University of Chicago (1958–1963) used urban renewal to defend the Hyde Park area (five miles south of the Loop) from racial transition by displacing blacks and building middle-class housing to attract whites. Third, in the 1960s, the smaller 16-acre Sandberg Village (1961–1969) was closest to the Loop (1.5 miles north); it displaced hundreds of residents, gentrified the area, and served as a "buffer" between the wealthy Gold Coast and the low-income Cabrini-Green public housing community to the west. Fourth, the city used urban renewal to build the University of Illinois campus just outside the central area, only a mile southwest of the Loop; this proposal deviated from the 1958 Plan, which had called for construction of the campus on railroad land. Fifth, in 1968, the city cleared a small portion of the West Loop for the Madison-Canal project, later redeveloped as the Presidential Towers residential complex and the Social Security Administration building.

18. Igor Marjanovic and Katerina Ruedi Ray, *Marina City: Bertrand Goldberg's Urban Vision* (Princeton, N.J.: Princeton University Press, 2010).

19. Jack Meltzer, "Zoning for Residential Development in the Central Area," May 20, 1963, HWLC.

20. Garfield Park was also a suggested site, with area residents supporting the idea of a university, hoping it would serve as a buffer against African Americans. Both the Forest Preserve District of Cook County and the Chicago Park District had no interest in selling land to the university. See Seligman, *Block by Block*, chap. 4.

21. George Rosen, *Decision-Making Chicago Style: The Genesis of a University of Illinois Campus* (Urbana: University of Illinois Press, 1980).

22. Seligman, *Block by Block*, chap. 4; Rosen, *Decision-Making Chicago Style*.

23. Interview with Miles Berger, February 6, 2012.

CHAPTER 4

1. Telephone interview with Dean Macris, August 17, 2012; interview with Norm Elkin, January 25, 2012.

2. Carl Smith, *The Plan of Chicago: Daniel Burnham and the Remaking of the American City* (Chicago: University of Chicago Press, 2006); Chicago Plan Commission, *Preliminary Comprehensive City Plan of Chicago: A General Presentation of the Physical Elements of the City Plan Designed for a Population of 3,800,000 by 1965*, January 1946, HWLC.

3. City of Chicago, Department of Development and Planning, *The Comprehensive Plan of Chicago*, December 1966, 30.

4. *Comprehensive Plan of Chicago*, 107; interview with Miles Berger, February 6, 2012.

5. City of Chicago, Department of Planning, *Basic Policies for the Comprehensive Plan of Chicago*, 1964.

6. *Comprehensive Plan of Chicago*, 35. See also Edwin C. Berry and Walter W. Stafford, "The Racial Aspects of Urban Planning: Critique of the Comprehensive Plan of the City of Chicago," ed. Harold M. Baron, with commentaries by Pierre de Vise, Stanley J. Hallett, Jerome L. Kaufman, Harold M. Mayer, and Louis B. Wetmore, Chicago Urban League Research Report, 1968.

7. The South Shore neighborhood in the late 1960s attempted proactive efforts to retain whites but failed to stop transition. See Harvey Molotch, *Managed Integration: The Dilemmas of Doing Good* (Berkeley: University of California Press, 1972). The suburb of Oak Park implemented a more controversial and complex set of strategies that were ultimately successful in achieving a higher degree of sustained integration. The strategies involved managing racial balance in apartment buildings through various nonprofit entities. See Carole Goodwin, *The Oak Park Strategy: Community Control of Racial Change* (Chicago: University of Chicago Press, 1979). Later, in the Harold Washington administration, white neighborhood groups on the Northwest and Southwest sides pushed for the "Guaranteed Home Equity Program" to insure participating homes would not fall in value in the event of transition. See Paul M. Green, "SON/SOC: Organizing in White Ethnic Neighborhoods, in *After Alinsky: Community Organizing in Illinois*, ed. Peg Knoepfle (Springfield, Ill.: Sangamon State University, 1990), 23–33.

8. Interview with Norm Elkin, January 25, 2012; *Chicago Tribune*, April 9, 1967.

9. *Comprehensive Plan of Chicago*, 7; *Chicago Tribune*, November 12, 1972.

10. Telephone interview with Dean Macris, August 17, 2012.

11. Ibid.

12. Interview with Les Pollock, August 9, 2012; interview with Dennis Harder, August 3, 2011.

13. Timothy J. Gilfoyle, *Millennium Park: Creating a Chicago Landmark* (Chicago: University of Chicago Press, 2006), 39–40, 385.

14. Skidmore, Owings & Merrill; C. F. Murphy Associates; and Real Estate Research Corporation, "Lakefront Development Plan, Central Area, Chicago, IL: Outline Interim Report Prepared for the Chicago Central Area Committee and the Chicago Community Trust," March 3, 1966, HWLC.

15. City of Chicago, Department of Development and Planning, "Illinois Central Air Rights Development: Guidelines for Development of the Randolph Terminal Properties," May 1968, HWLC.

16. Interview with Miles Berger, February 6, 2012; Miles L. Berger, *They Built Chicago: Entrepreneurs Who Shaped a Great City's Architecture* (Chicago: Bonus Books, 1992), 250–58. The city, state, and developers divided the cost of the roadways, with the city funding the bottom level, the state the middle level, and the developers the top level. Interview with Miles Berger, February 6, 2012.

17. Paul Gapp, "Chicago's 1st Citizen: the Car," *Chicago Tribune*, April 14, 1983; see also Skidmore, Owings & Merrill et al., "Lakefront Development Plan."

18. Wille, *Forever Open, Clear, and Free*, 99–114; *A Lake Michigan Site for Chicago's Third Major Airport: Summary of Engineering Studies*, prepared for the City of Chicago, Department of Public Works by Harza Engineering, February 26, 1970.

19. Wille, *Forever Open, Clear, and Free*, 120.

20. Ibid., 120–26.

21. City of Chicago, Department of Development and Planning, *The Lakefront Plan of Chicago*, December 1972, 38, 47–48, HWLC.

22. Interview with Reuben Hedlund, January 20, 2012; Schwieterman and Caspall, *Politics of Place*, chap. 10.

23. The 1972 Lakefront Plan also proposed the creation of vast new offshore islands to create sheltered waters for recreation. Landfill from the Deep Tunnel and proposed rapid-transit subways would be used to create the islands, which would link up with pedestrian bridges. The expanded park acreage, both onshore and offshore, would control erosion, allow for swimming and boating, and create sheltered water areas. The costly plan, however, made little headway.

24. *Chicago Tribune*, April 21, 1973, August 6, 1978, and December 15, 1986.

25. Chicago Plan Commission, *Chicago 21: A Plan for the Central Area Communities*, September 1973, 100, HWLC.

26. City of Chicago, Department of Planning, *The Riveredge Plan of Chicago*, 1974, 17–32, HWLC. The plan inspired large corporations like IBM with headquarters along the river to pay for small but disconnected parks in available spaces between the bridges along the south bank. Most were completed by the late 1970s. See also Friends of the Chicago River, "A Brief History of the Chicago River," at www.chicagoriver.org/upload/Chicago%20River%20History.pdf.

27. *Chicago Tribune*, June 9, 1980, and August 21, 1980. In 2012, developers unveiled a proposal for three large towers on the relatively small space, though at the time of this writing aldermanic approval remained unclear. The Metropolitan Planning Council objected to the proposal's silence on incorporating elements of the 2003 Central Area Plan, especially its recommendation for a transitway to serve the site (see chapter 18).

28. *Chicago Tribune*, October 15, 1982; City of Chicago, *Journal of the City Council of Chicago*, March 31, 1983, 17095–96.

29. Telephone interview with Dean Macris, August 17, 2012.

30. The sea change in planning took place in the 1960s. Especially influential were Paul Davidoff, "Advocacy and Pluralism in Planning," *Journal of the American Institute of Planners* 31(4) (1965): 331–38; and Jane Jacobs, *The Death and Life of Great American Cities* (New York: Random House, 1961). See also Michael Neuman, "Does Planning Need the Plan?" *Journal of the American Planning Association* 64(2) (1998): 208–20.

CHAPTER 5

1. Cohen and Taylor, *American Pharaoh*, 293.

2. *Chicago Tribune*, February 26, 1965; Blair Kamin, *Why Architecture Matters: Lessons from Chicago* (Chicago: University of Chicago Press, 2001), 105–9.

3. Chicago Plan Commission, *Chicago 21: A Plan for the Central Area Communities*, 1973, HWLC. The Department of Planning was consulted throughout the creation of Chicago 21, but the plan's most important new ideas came from SOM.

4. Nicholas Bloom, *Suburban Alchemy: 1960s New Towns and the Transformation of the American Dream* (Columbus: Ohio State University Press, 2001); Ann Forsyth, *Reforming Suburbia: The Planned Communities of Irvine, Columbia, and The Woodlands* (Berkeley: University of California Press, 2005).

5. On Cedar-Riverside, see Brent D. Ryan, *Design after Decline* (Philadelphia: University of Pennsylvania Press, 2012), 2–8.

6. Interview with Norm Elkin, January 25, 2012; interview with Lawrence Okrent, January 13, 2012; Wille, *At Home in the Loop*, 51.

7. Chicago Plan Commission, *Chicago 21*; Wille, *At Home in the Loop*, 48–53.

8. The initial investors in Dearborn Park lost a good deal of their money by the end of an 18-year development odyssey. In Wille's account (*At Home in the Loop*, 48–53, 170), the key players in Dearborn Park were Ayers and two of Chicago's most experienced real estate developers, Philip Klutznick and Ferd Kramer.

9. George Halas, owner of the Chicago Bears, had acquired an option on the Baltimore & Ohio land at a bargain price in the hopes of a building a new football stadium. After Mayor Richard J. Daley would not offer public financing for a stadium, Halas, in a civic-minded gesture, gave the valuable option to his friends on the Chicago 21 board at the same price he paid for it. Ibid., 54–59.

10. Ibid., 81, 166–67; by then, developers had partially embraced the street, including row houses in Phase II that fronted State Street.

11. In an important decision, the Chicago 21 corporation avoided FHA financing, fearing regulations on nondiscrimination that might scare away potential white buyers, even as the corporation committed itself to an interracial development. Ibid., 48–53, 170.

12. The school became a community battleground, as parents from nearby public housing developments clamored to get in, while Dearborn Park residents sought to create upper-middle-class amenities and restrain levels of low-income black children. For this conflict, see ibid., chap. 12.

13. Ibid., 113–26; Robert Bruegmann, *The Architecture of Harry Weese* (New York: Norton, 2010). Printer's Row gentrification disrupted the network effects—the subcontracting of jobs and referrals— that allowed a small printing industry to survive there. Some printers found new space in the South Loop, others headed for the suburbs, and others went out of business entirely—a microcosm of the de- cline in manufacturing and blue-collar employment in the city. See Joel Rast, *Remaking Chicago: The Political Origins of Urban Industrial Change* (DeKalb, Ill.: Northern Illinois University Press, 1999), chap. 3. Also Marika Pruska-Carroll, "The Printers Row: A Case of Industrial Displacement," master's project, University of Illinois–Chicago, 1987.

14. For a survey of consumer attitudes towards State Street before construction of the State Street Transit Mall, see Perkins and Will, "Chicago '78: A Consumer Perspective, An Attitude Survey," 1978, in Box 5, Folder 1, Chicago Loop Alliance Collection, Chicago Public Library, HWLC, Special Collec- tions.

15. Historians point to Rotterdam's 1953 Lijbaan as an early example of a planned, central-city pedes- trian mall. See Lewis Mumford, *The City in History: Its Origins, Its Transformations, and Its Prospects* (New York: Harcourt, Brace & World, 1961), pl. 63. Victor Gruen soon embraced the idea, design- ing pedestrian malls for cities such as Fort Worth, Texas (1956, unbuilt), and Kalamazoo, Michigan (1959). Kennedy Lawson Smith, "Pedestrian Malls," in *Encyclopedia of American Urban History*, ed. David Goldfield (Thousand Oaks, Calif.: Sage, 2006), 561–63. On Arthur Rubloff, see "New State Street Mall Unveiled by Arthur Rubloff," September 26, 1957, Box 5, Folder 12, Chicago Loop Alliance Collection.

16. Robert Bruegmann, "Great Chicago Planning Disasters," presentation to Chicago Architecture Foun- dation, January 27, 2010; Paul Gapp, "State Street: Great Street Gets a Mall that Appalls," *Chi- cago Tribune*, July 13, 1980; Robin Amer, "The Short, Sad Life of State Street's Pedestrian Mall," October 14, 2011, at www.wbez.org/content/short-sad-life-state-streets-pedestrian-mall.

17. Kenneth McHugh, "The Little Fish Swallows the Big Fish: Financing the DePaul Center in Chicago," in *The University as Urban Developer: Case Studies and Analysis*, ed. David C. Perry and Wim Wiewel (New York: M. E. Sharpe, 2005), 240–43; Geoffrey Hewings, Fran Casey, Suzanne Fogel, J. Steven Kelly, and Gerald W. McLaughlin, "Update 2009: Higher Education in the Loop and South Loop, An Economic Impact Study," The Chicago Loop Alliance, October 2009.

CHAPTER 6

1. Norman Krumholz and Pierre Clavel, *Reinventing Cities: Equity Planners Tell Their Stories* (Philadelphia: Temple University Press, 1994).

2. Raymond Mohl, "Stop the Road: Freeway Revolts in American Cities," *Journal of Urban History* 30(5) (2004): 674–706.

3. The "maximum feasible participation" language soon became controversial due to the difficulty of implementation. See Nancy Naples, "From Maximum Feasible Participation to Disenfranchisement," *Social Justice* 25(1) (1969): 47–66; and Daniel Patrick Moynihan, *Maximum Feasible Misunderstanding: Community Action in the War on Poverty* (Free Press, 1969).

4. Wim Wiewel, "Economic Development in Chicago: The Growth Machine Meets the Neighborhood Movement," *Local Economy* 4(4) (1990): 307–16; Dan Immergluck, "Building Power, Losing Power: The Rise and Fall of a Prominent Community Economic Development Coalition," *Economic Development Quarterly* 19(3) (2005): 211–24.

5. Committee to Elect Harold Washington, "The Washington Papers," 1983, HWLC; Norman Krumholz and Pierre Clavel, *Reinventing Cities: Equity Planners Tell Their Stories* (Philadelphia: Temple University Press, 1994), 69–71; Gary Rivlin, *Fire on the Prairie: Chicago's Harold Washington and the Politics of Race* (New York: Henry Holt, 1992).

6. Pierre Clavel, *Activists in City Hall: The Progressive Response to the Reagan Era in Boston and Chicago* (Ithaca, N.Y.: Cornell University Press, 2010); Pierre Clavel and Wim Wiewel, eds., *Harold Washington and the Neighborhoods: Progressive City Government in Chicago, 1983–1987* (New Brunswick: Rutgers University Press, 1991).

7. Krumholz and Clavel, *Equity Planners*, 73.

8. Elizabeth Hollander, "The Department of Planning," 121–45 in Clavel and Wiewel, *Harold Washington and the Neighborhoods*.

9. Chicago Central Area Committee, *Chicago Central Area Plan: A Plan for the Heart of the City*, March 1983, 81.

10. In planning the fair, Graham worked closely with Chicago architects Helmet Jahn, Kim Goluska, Dirk Lohan, and Adrian Smith. Graham also engaged in charrettes with Charles Moore, Peter Eisenman, Stanley Tigerman, Robert A. M. Stern, Frank Gehry, Robert Venturi, and Denise Scott Brown. Lee Bey, "Bruce Graham and the Chicago 1992 World's Fair," March 17, 2010, at www.wbez.org /bey/2010/03/bruce-graham-and-the-chicago-1992-worlds-fair/17994.

11. Chicago Central Area Committee, *Chicago Central Area Plan*. The plan also anticipated and supported a new generation of large planned developments, including the Dock and Canal Trust Property (46 acres), the American Medical Association properties (12 blocks), and portions of Wolf Point. Each reinforced the goals of the 1958 Development Plan for the Central Area to bring residents downtown.

12. *New York Times*, July 28, 1984.

13. Chicago Central Area Committee, *Chicago Central Area Plan*, 1983, 7, 81, and cover letter.

14. Chicago 1992 Committee, "Employment and the 1992 Chicago World's Fair," September 1984, HWLC.

15. City of Chicago, *Chicago Works Together: 1984 Development Plan*, May 1984, HWLC.

16. Ibid.

17. *New York Times*, June 25, 1985.

18. *Chicago Reader*, April 20, 1990.

19. Krumholz and Clavel, *Reinventing Cities*, 73.

20. John Kretzmann, "The Affirmative Information Policy," 201–16 in Clavel and Wiewel, *Harold Washington and the Neighborhoods*.

21. Robert Mier and Kari Moe, "The Department of Economic Development: Decentralized Development from Theory to Practice," in Clavel and Wiewel, *Harold Washington and the Neighborhoods*, 68–69.

22. Hollander, "The Department of Planning," 123; Rowan A. Miranda, "The Geographic Distribution of Community Development Block Grant Spending in the City of Chicago, 1982–1986," 1987, HWLC; Robert Mier, "Some Observations on Race in Planning," *Journal of the American Planning Association* 60(2) (1994): 235–40.

23. Mier, "Some Observations on Race in Planning"; Rivlin, *Fire on the Prairie*.

24. Hollander, "Department of Planning," 127–28; Clavel and Wiewel, *Harold Washington and the Neighborhoods*, 280.

25. Ellen Casale, "Linking Development Benefits to Neighborhoods: A Manual of Community-Based Strategies," Community Information Exchange, 1989, HWLC.

26. City of Chicago, *Chicago Works Together*, 16.

27. Hollander, "Department of Planning," 133; *Chicago Tribune*, February 27, 1986.

28. Larry Bennett, "The Dilemmas of Building a Progressive Urban Coalition: The Linked Development Debate in Chicago," *Journal of Urban Affairs*, 9(3) (1987): 263–76; Hollander, "Department of Planning," 134.

29. Robert Brehm, "The City and the Neighborhoods: Was It Really a Two-Way Street?" in Clavel and Wiewel, *Harold Washington and the Neighborhoods*, 238-269.

30. Hollander, "Department of Planning," 135.

31. John McCarron, "Chicago on Hold: The New Politics of Poverty," *Chicago Tribune*, series, August 28–September 4, 1988; for review, see *Chicago Reader*, September 15, 1988.

CHAPTER 7

1. Gerald Suttles, *Man-Made City: The Land Use Confidence Game in Chicago* (Chicago: University of Chicago Press, 1990), 123; Gregory D. Squires, Larry Bennett, Kathleen McCourt, and Philip Nyden, *Chicago: Race, Class, and the Response to Urban Decline* (Philadelphia: Temple University Press, 1987), 170–71.

2. Ross Miller, *Here's the Deal: The Making and Breaking of a Great American City* (New York: Alfred A. Knopf, 1996).

3. Miller, *Here's the Deal*, 186.

4. North Loop Redevelopment, "Mayor's Architectural Advisory Committee," report, January 11, 1980, HWLC.

5. Squires et al., *Chicago*, 172; Miller, *Here's the Deal*, 184.

6. Interview with Norm Elkin, January 25, 2012; The Chicago Theatre had not been a bastion of segregation. Elkin's argument was political: a black mayor allowing the destruction of an icon would be perceived as evidence of a general antipathy toward downtown. Interview with Doris Holleb, February 3, 2012. Marshall Holleb, Doris's husband, led the preservation group that raised $10 million as part of a $25 million package to save the Chicago Theater. See *Chicago Tribune*, October 30, 1985.

7. Interview with Miles Berger, February 6, 2012; Miller, *Here's the Deal*. Miller's description implies broad-based corruption among politicians and developers, but instead the story of the North Loop is the chaos that occurs when planning is grossly inadequate. See chapter 18.

8. The Near South Side had the second-highest concentration of subsidized housing of the city's community areas, and less than one percent of residents owned their homes. Melaniphy and Associates, "Chicago Comprehensive Neighborhood Needs Analysis, Vol. 33, Near South Side Community Area," 1982, HWLC.

9. Chicago Plan Commission, "Special Meeting Re: Central Station Development Guidelines, Revised Draft," February 15, 1990, HWLC.

10. See Gerald W. Fogelson with Joe Marconi, *Central Station: Realizing a Vision* (Evanston, Ill: Racom Communications, 2003).

11. *Chicago Tribune*, June 2, 1998; Joint Task Force on Burnham Park Planning, "Report on the McCormick Place Expansion Project," June 1990, HWLC. The 1990 plan also included a domed stadium for the Chicago Bears near McCormick Place, a plan later dropped.

12. Interview with Reuben Hedlund, January 20, 2012.

13. City of Chicago, "Central Station Development Guidelines," adopted by the Chicago Plan Commission, March 1, 1990, HWLC.

14. Chicago Plan Commission, "Special Meeting Re: Central Station Development Guidelines, Revised Draft," February 15, 1990, HWLC.

15. Ibid.

16. The Harold Washington Library Center contains a draft plan for the Central Station TIF from May 1990 that estimated public costs at $196 million, most of which went to roadways, site acquisition, and developer subsidies. But the approved TIF scaled back that figure considerably to $40 million (though again with few details). In 1994, the Central Station TIF plan was amended with an expected price tag of $105 million. A year later, the TIF was reorganized and expanded into the Near South TIF. See City of Chicago, "Central Station Tax Increment Financing Redevelopment Project and Plan," December 1990, HWLC; City of Chicago, "Central Station Tax Increment Financing Redevelopment Project and Plan, Draft 3," May 11, 1990, HWLC; City of Chicago, "Amended Central Station Tax Increment Financing Redevelopment Project and Plan," April 9, 1994, HWLC.

17. Chicago Chapter ADPSR, Architects/Designers/Planners for Social Responsibility, "Community Planning Forum," January 28, 1995, HWLC.

18. Ibid.

19. The amount of TIF money spent on developer subsidies is not possible to ascertain from publicly available reports, which describe spending only in vague categories such as "costs of property assembly" or "cost of construction of public improvements." TIF reports in Chicago have been maddeningly nontransparent until recently. See City of Chicago, "Near South Redevelopment Project Area," annual reports for 1996–2008, HWLC; Ben Joravsky, "The Poor Pay Again," *Chicago Reader*, November 18, 2010.

20. Interview with Lawrence Okrent, January 13, 2012.

21. U.S. Census Bureau, 2010 Census Special Reports, *Patterns of Metropolitan and Micropolitan Population Change: 2000 to 2010*, C2010SR-01 (Washington, D.C.: U.S. Government Printing Office, 2012), 28.

CHAPTER 8

1. Martin Bulmer, *The Chicago School of Sociology: Institutionalization, Diversity, and the Rise of Sociological Research* (Chicago: University of Chicago Press, 1986); Light, *Nature of Cities*. For more recent criticism, see Sudhir Venkatesh, "Chicago's Pragmatic Planners: American Sociology and the Myth of Community," *Social Science History* 25(2) (2001): 275–317.

2. South Side Planning Board, "An Opportunity for Private and Public Investment in Rebuilding Chicago," 1947, HWLC; on urban renewal, see Arnold Hirsch, *Making the Second Ghetto: Race and Housing in Chicago, 1940–1960* (Cambridge: Cambridge University Press, 1983), and Sarah Whiting, "Bas-Relief Urbanism: Chicago's Figured Field," in *Mies in America*, ed. Phyllis Lambert, Werner Oechslin, Detlef Mertins, Peter Eisenman, and Rem Koolhaas (New York: Harry N. Abrams, 2001), 642–91.

3. In other contexts, conservation became an effort to resist racial change. As Amanda Seligman explained in *Block By Block*, residents of Garfield Park sought to use code enforcement, spot clearance, a new university campus, and later urban renewal to avoid an influx of African Americans.

4. The housing rehabilitation effort involved working with local savings and loans, while the Back of the Yards newspaper published lists of owners who repaired their property, spurring others through peer pressure. Within 16 months, 32 percent of structures had completed at least some remodeling or significant repair, with much of the work done by owner-occupants and community tradesmen. See Gurney Breckenfeld, "Chicago: Back of the Yards," 179–219 in Martin Millspaugh, Gurney Breckenfeld, and Miles L. Colean, *The Human Side of Urban Renewal: A Study of the Attitude Changes Produced by Neighborhood Rehabilitation* (New York: Ives Washburn, 1960).

5. There is a large literature on the Community Action Program and Model Cities. In Chicago, especially the city's Woodlawn neighborhood, see John Hall Fish, *Black Power / White Control: The Struggle of the Woodlawn Organization in Chicago* (Princeton: Princeton University Press, 1973). For an overview of the history of Community Development programs, see Alexander Von Hoffman, *Fuel Lines for the Urban Revival Engine: Neighborhoods, Community Development Corporations, and Financial Intermediaries* (Washington, D.C.: Fannie Mae Foundation, 2001).

6. Von Hoffman, *Fuel Lines for the Urban Revival*, 11–24; interview with Ted Wysocki, September 14, 2012.

7. Squires et al., *Chicago*, 140–41. A change in Illinois banking law also spurred this change. Before 1985, Illinois banks could have only one drive-up facility within 1,500 feet of the main branch. As a result, most Chicago banks had one large office downtown (which also had the effect of benefitting downtown real estate). By 1993, all restrictions were lifted on branches, so long as they were within the state. New branches, however, required not only state but also federal approval, placing their community lending practices under the scrutiny of CRA regulations. See Tara Rice and Erin Davis, "The Branch Banking Boom in Illinois: A Byproduct of Restrictive Branching Laws," *Chicago Fed Letter*, Chicago Federal Reserve Bank of Chicago, May 2007.

8. Paul Brophy, "Re-engineering Community Development Housing Sector for Increased Effectiveness and Long-Term Sustainability," *Living Cities*, September 2009, at www.surdna.org/images/stories /content_img/docs/pubs/re-engineering_final.pdf.

9. Interview with Les Pollock, August 9, 2012; telephone interview with Patrick Barry, August 17, 2012. Barry and Pollock wrote and produced LISC Chicago's New Community Program "Planning Handbook" available at www.newcommunities.org/cmadocs/NCPPlanningHandbook.pdf.

10. *Chicago Tribune*, May 19, 2005. Andrew Mooney was appointed Chicago's Commissioner of Housing and Economic Development by Mayor Richard M. Daley in November 2010. Previously, he served as executive director and then chairman of the Chicago Housing Authority (1981–1983).

11. The scribes included experienced journalists Patrick Barry, formerly with the *Chicago Sun-Times*, and John McCarron, formerly of the *Chicago Tribune*.

12. Telephone interview with Patrick Barry, August 17, 2012.

13. In one instance, LISC pulled out of a community after two strong neighborhood organizations could not agree which would be the lead agency. Ibid.

14. Robert J. Sampson, *Great American City: Chicago and the Enduring Neighborhood Effect* (Chicago: University of Chicago Press, 2012), chap.8.

15. Ibid., 422–23.

CHAPTER 9

1. Robert Bruegmann, "Schaumburg, Oak Brook, Rosemont, and the Recentering of the Chicago Metropolitan Area," in John Zukowsky, *Chicago Architecture and Design, 1923–1993* (Chicago: Art Institute of Chicago, 1993), 164.

2. Richard Lawrence Nelson and Frederick T. Aschman, "Conservation and Rehabilitation of Major Shopping Districts," Technical Bulletin No. 22, Urban Land Institute, February 1954, 5.

3. Nelson and Aschman, "Conservation and Rehabilitation of Major Shopping Districts," 24–26; Elsa C. Beck, "Redevelopment of Urban Shopping Centers," American Bar Association, Section on Real Property, *Problems and Transcript of Proceedings* 39 (1953); Englewood Shopping Concourse Commission, Annual Report, 1974, HWLC.

4. Victor Gruen, "Dynamic Planning for Retail Areas," *Harvard Business Review*, November–December 1954.

5. Hirsch, *Making the Second Ghetto*, 37–38.

6. Central Englewood Urban Renewal Project, IL R-47, 1965, HWLC.

7. Chicago Department of Urban Renewal, "Information for Tenants and Property Owners of the Englewood Conservation Project," 1963, HWLC.

8. Compare the City of Chicago, Department of Planning, "Studies of the Englewood Conservation Area, Preliminary Draft," May 1960, HWLC, with City of Chicago, Department of Planning, *Englewood Community Area Proposal: The Conservation Plan*, 1962, HWLC.

9. Central Englewood Urban Renewal Project, IL R-47, 1965. For community opposition, see James O. Stampley, "Challenges with Changes: A Documentary of Englewood," 1979, HWLC.

10. City of Chicago, *Englewood Mall Area TIF Redevelopment Plan and Project*, August 1989, HWLC.

11. Chicago Department of Development and Planning, *Mid-South Development Area*, September 1968, 9.

12. "Englewood Concourse Revitalization Strategy," May 1987, HWLC.

13. "A Brief History of Englewood," *Chicago Reporter*, December 1999.

14. Teamwork Englewood, *Englewood: Making a Difference, Quality-of-Life Plan*, December 2005; interview with Eileen Figel, October 3, 2012.

15. Interview with Les Pollock, August 9, 2012.

16. Under the plan's goal 4.3 to "develop or expand housing and support-service programs tailored to the needs of specific populations," it lists 11 "potential partner organizations," several of which are not explained in the text, while others are social service agencies. The housing element is the least developed in the plan.

17. Analysis of data from the Illinois Assisted Housing Action Research Project at the University of Illinois–Chicago, at www.uic.edu/cuppa/voorheesctr/iharp_home.html. Englewood ranked fourth in the percentage of households with a Housing Choice Voucher. Data on affordable housing projects by community area are not available, but data by zip codes strongly suggest that only Washington Park, South Shore, and Woodlawn had more subsidized housing developments—as well as more Housing Choice Vouchers—than Englewood.

18. See City of Chicago Police Department website on Block Clubs. On Englewood community capacity, see Rebekah Levin, Lise McKean, and Susan Shapiro, "Community Organizing in Three South Side Communities: Leadership, Activities, and Prospects," Center for Impact Research and the Woods Fund of Chicago, September 2004.

19. *Chicago Tribune*, May 6, 2004.

20. Tamara E. Holmes, "Urban Revitalization Projects Bring Economic Challenges: Will Local Communities Be Left Out of Development Efforts?" *Black Enterprise*, October 2006.

CHAPTER 10

1. Roger Guy, *From Diversity to Unity: Southern and Appalachian Migrants in Uptown Chicago, 1950–1970* (Lanham, Md.: Lexington Books, 2007).

2. Chicago Commission on Human Relations, "The Uptown Community Area and the Southern White In-Migrant," May 1957, HWLC.

3. Uptown Chicago Commission, "Experimental Pilot Center for Newcomers in Uptown," October 27, 1958, HWLC.

4. "Code Enforcement and the Rehabilitation of Converted Properties," Uptown Chicago Commission, November 19, 1958, HWLC.

5. Albert N. Votaw to Edmund G. Pabst, "Relationship of Privately-Financed Planning to Federally-Supported Programs of Urban Renewal in Chicago Neighborhoods," January 25, 1960, Uptown Chicago Commission papers, box 14, folder 5, Chicago History Museum (hereafter cited as UCC Papers).

6. Larry Bennett, *Neighborhood Politics: Chicago and Sheffield* (New York: Taylor & Francis, 1997), 78–80; Uptown Chicago Commission, "Uptown: A Planning Report," prepared by Jack Meltzer Associates, 1962.

7. Bennett, *Neighborhood Politics*, 82–84; Todd Gitlin and Nancy Hollander, *Uptown: Poor Whites in Chicago* (New York: Harper and Row, 1970).

8. City of Chicago, Model Cities Program, "North Model Area: Problem Analysis, Goals and Objectives, Draft for Discussion," n.d., HWLC.

9. Uptown People's Planning Coalition, "A Community Plans," n.d., UCC Papers, box 16, folder 5; telephone interview with Rodney Wright, March 23, 2012; Paul B. Siegel, "Uptown, Chicago: The Origins and Emergence of a Movement Against Displacement, 1947–1972," PhD diss., University of Illinois–Chicago, 2002, 290–93.

10. "Neighborhood and Community Planning," 1971, UCC Papers, box 16, folder 5; telephone interview with Rodney Wright, March 23, 2012.

11. "Proposal for 'Hank Williams Village,' submitted by Voice of the People Ad Hoc Committee," n.d., UCC Papers, box 16, folder 3.

12. Urania P. Damofle, Chairman, Uptown Conservation Community Council, to Gerald Smith, Executive Secretary, IL Junior College Board, March 12, 1970, UCC Papers, box 48, folder 9.

13. Siegel, "Uptown, Chicago," 294.

14. Estimates of actual displacement by the construction of Truman College are difficult to come by. The community college site shrank from an original proposal of 13 acres to seven acres. A 1969 canvas by the city Department of Urban Renewal covering the 13-acre site found 1,765 persons including 33 minors. Presumably, the smaller site resulted in far less displacement. H. Nelson and S. Messinger, "Analysis of Proposed Site for a City College, Uptown Conservation Area," February 17, 1969, Department of Urban Renewal, UCC papers, box 48, folder 11.

15. "Save Our Neighborhoods," UCC Papers, box 47, folder 1; Bennett, *Neighborhood Politics*, 176–81, Elizabeth Warren, "Chicago's Uptown: Public Policy, Neighborhood Decay, and Citizen Action in an Urban Community," Center for Urban Policy, Loyola University, 1979, 8. Estimates of the number of subsidized units in Uptown in the 1980s range from 5,000 (Warren) to 9,000 ("Save Our Neighborhoods").

16. Bennett, *Neighborhood Politics*, 168.

17. John E. Eisendrath, "Slim Coleman: The Poet, the Politician, and the Punk," *Chicago Reader*, December 21, 1983, quoted in Bennett, *Neighborhood Politics*, 169.

18. Flora Johnson, "In Order to Save It?" *Chicago Magazine* 25(12) (1976): 165–74; Jack Hafferkamp, "Uptown Revisited," *Chicago Magazine* 29(7) (1980), 124–26; Richard Sander, "The Future of Uptown/Edgewater: An In-depth Look at Neighborhood Change," report sponsored by the Organization of the North East (ONE), rev. ed., 1986, Chicago History Museum.

19. Bennett, *Neighborhood Politics*, 171–73.

20. "Section 221(d)(3) New Construction Projects, Uptown Community Area, as of December 1, 1967," UCC Collection, box 16, folder 1; Warren, "Chicago's Uptown," 89–91.

21. Bennett, *Neighborhood Politics*, 93.

22. "Wilson Yard Redevelopment Project Area, 2001 Annual Report," June 30, 2002, HWLC, 10–13; *Chicago Tribune*, November 12, 2000.

23. Ben Joravsky, "Helen's Voters," *Chicago Reader*, March 30, 2007.

24. Ben Joravksy, "The Right Fight," *Chicago Reader*, December 11, 2008.

25. Prominent TIF critic Ben Joravsky was ambivalent about the lawsuit against Wilson Yards, agreeing that the city regularly skirted the "but for" clause but commending Shiller for her skill in utilizing the TIF (the "only game in town") for affordable housing. See Joravsky, "The Right Fight." On Uptown opposition to affordable housing, see Angela Caputo, "Taking on TIFs," *Progress Illinois*, December 4, 2008; Alby Gallun, "Residents Sue to Stop Wilson Yard Project, Claim TIF Abuse," *Crain's Chicago Business*, December 3, 2008; Jake Malooley, "Fixed Wilson Yard," *TimeOut Chicago*, July 21, 2010.

26. LISC Chicago, "'Yard' Work Rewarded in Uptown," n.d., at www.lisc-chicago.org/Our-programs /Grants-and-Loans/-Yard-Work-Rewarded-in-Uptown1.html.

CHAPTER 11

1. Evelyn Mae Kitagawa and Karl E. Taeuber, "Local Community Fact Book: Chicago Metropolitan Area," 1960.

2. Census data from *Local Community Fact Book for 1960 and 1980*; U.S. Census, 2000 Census, Table DP-1.

3. Joseph Boyce, "All Politics Is Local: Hispanic Influx Spurs Legislator to Practice Multiethnic Diplomacy" *Wall Street Journal*, May 7, 1997.

4. Little Village Community Development Corporation, "Little Village Quality of Life Plan," May 2005, 2.

5. Eric Klinenberg, *Heat Wave: A Social Autopsy of Disaster in Chicago* (Chicago: University of Chicago Press, 2003).

6. Chicago Department of City Planning, *Comprehensive Plan of Chicago: Mid-West Development Area*, 1967, HWLC.

7. See Teresa Cordova, "Harold Washington and the Rise of Latino Electoral Politics in Chicago, 1982–1987," in David Montejano, *Chicano Politics and Society in the Late Twentieth Century* (Austin: University of Texas Press, 1999), 31–57.

8. David K. Fremon, *Chicago Politics, Ward by Ward* (Bloomington: Indiana University Press, 1988).

9. Gabriel A. Cortez, "Education, Politics, and a Hunger Strike: A Social Movement's Struggle for Education in Chicago's Little Village Community," PhD diss., University of Illinois–Urbana-Champaign, 2008, 91–105.

10. Trkla, Pettigrew, Allen & Payne, "Little Village," June 19, 1990, HWLC; interview with Jesus Garcia, April 26, 2012.

11. Little Village Community Development Corporation, "Little Village Quality of Life Plan"; interview with Jesus Garcia, April 26, 2012.

12. The Little Village High School campus contains four schools under one roof: the Multicultural Academy of Scholarship High School; the Infinity Math, Science, and Technology High School, the World Language High School; and the Social Justice High School; interview with Jesus Garcia, April 26, 2012.

13. Interview with Jesus Garcia, April 26, 2012.

14. Little Village Community Development Corporation, "Little Village Quality of Life Plan." When looking at parks within a half-mile of Little Village, the figure is 2.2 acres per 1,000 residents, still a minimal figure. (Douglas Park is on the community's northeast border.)

15. Little Village Community Development Corporation, *Little Village Quality of Life Plan*, 19–20.

16. Larry Bennet, John Koval, and Spirou Costas, "Latinos and Neo-Regionalism in Metropolitan Chicago," in *Latinos in Chicago: Reflections of an American Landscape*, white paper series, Institute of Latino Studies, Notre Dame University, June 2010.

17. Alexandra Solomon, "EPA Begins Clean Up in Little Village," WBEZ radio, September 9, 2008; *Chi-Town Daily News*, September 10, 2008.

18. Blair Kamin, *CityScapes* blog, October 14, 2011, at http://featuresblogs.chicagotribune.com /theskyline/2011/10/how-to-correct-chicagos-open-space-shortage-10-ideas-that-could-help-citys-park-poor-neighborhoods-a.html.

19. Little Village Environmental Justice Organization, press release, October 25, 2011.

20. In September 2012, a diverse task force, funded by the Joyce Foundation and the Sierra Club, issued a report on principles and recommendations to guide redevelopment of the power plants, most of which focused on economic development and encouraging collaboration among community stakeholders. See City of Chicago, "Fisk and Crawford Reuse Task Force: Process, Principles and Recommendations," final report, September 2012.

21. *Chicago Reader*, December 22, 2011.

CHAPTER 12

1. Bureau of the Census, Report CPHL-188, "The 100 Poorest Tracts in the United States: 1989," Census Bureau Library, Suitland, Md.; Sudhir Venkatesh, *Off the Books: The Underground Economy of Urban Poor* (Cambridge, Mass.: Harvard University Press, 2006); Sudhir Venkatesh, *American Project: The Rise and Fall of a Modern Ghetto*, 2000); Susan J. Popkin, Victoria E. Gwiasda, Lynn M. Olson, Dennis P. Rosenbaum, and Larry Buron, *The Hidden War: Crime and the Tragedy of Public Housing in Chicago* (New Brunswick, N.J.: Rutgers University Press, 2000).

2. D. Bradford Hunt, *Blueprint for Disaster: The Unraveling of Chicago Public Housing* (Chicago: University of Chicago Press, 2008).

3. Ibid., chap. 7; Popkin et al., *Hidden War*; Rhonda Williams, *The Politics of Public Housing: Black Women's Struggles Against Urban Inequality* (New York: Oxford University Press, 2004); Roberta Feldman and Susan Stall, *The Dignity of Resistance: Women Residents' Activism in Chicago Public Housing* (New York : Cambridge University Press, 2004); Mindy Turbov, "Public Housing Redevelopment as a Tool for Revitalizing Neighborhoods: How and Why Did it Happen and What Have We Learned?" *Northwestern Journal of Law and Social Policy* 1(1) (2006).

4. The ACLU lawyers, led by Alexander Polikoff, chose Dorothy Gautreaux, a public housing resident of Altgeld Gardens, as their lead plaintiff in a suit. A federal judge ruled in favor of the *Gautreaux* plaintiffs in 1969, and the CHA was ordered to build public housing in white neighborhoods. But the city and the CHA engaged in more than a decade of legal obstruction and foot-dragging, building only 2,000 scattered site units by 1983, few of them in white neighborhoods. See Alexander Polikoff, *Waiting for Gautreaux: A Story of Segregation, Housing, and the Black Ghetto* (Evanston, Ill.: Northwestern University Press, 2006), and Leonard S. Rubinowitz and James E. Rosenbaum, *Crossing the Class and Color Lines From Public Housing to White Suburbia* (Chicago: University of Chicago Press, 2000). For a dissenting view on the effects of voucher moves to the suburbs, see Jens Ludwig, Jeffrey B. Liebman, Jeffrey R. Kling, Greg J. Duncan, Lawrence F. Katz, Ronald C. Kessler, and Lisa Sanbonmatsu, "What Can We Learn about Neighborhood Effects from the Moving to Opportunity Experiment?" *American Journal of Sociology* 114(1) (2008): 144–88.

5. Hunt, *Blueprint for Disaster*, 277–78.

6. James E. Rosenbaum, Linda K. Stroh, and Cathy A. Flynn, "Lake Parc Place: A Study of Mixed-Income Housing," *Housing Policy Debate* 9(4) (1998): 703–40; Philip Nyden, "Comment," *Housing Policy Debate* 9(4) (1998): 741–48.

7. Turbov, "Public Housing Redevelopment as a Tool for Revitalizing Neighborhoods."

8. In phase I of the Horner Homes redevelopment (before repeal of the "one-for-one" rule), 466 public housing units were demolished and replaced with 461 apartments, all for public-housing eligible families. In phase II, only 32.5 percent of newly constructed units were for public housing families. Over the two phases, the 1,775 units in the original Henry Horner complex were replaced with 1,325 new apartments and townhomes, of which 822 were reserved for former public housing residents with the remainder market rate or lightly subsidized (a category confusingly called "afford-able"). Roughly 75 percent of eligible residents in the original Henry Horner Homes elected to return, with the remainder taking housing vouchers. See William P. Wilen, "The Horner Model: Successfully Redeveloping Public Housing," *Northwestern Journal of Law and Social Policy* 1(1) (2006): 62–95.

9. Matthew F. Gebhardt, "Politics, Planning and Power: Reorganizing and Redeveloping Public Housing in Chicago," PhD diss., Columbia University, New York, 2009, 174.

10. *Chicago Tribune*, June 28, 1996; Gebhardt, "Politics, Planning and Power," 174–78.

11. Chicago Housing Authority, *Plan for Transformation*, January 6, 2000, HWLC. It should be noted that an unknown number of squatters—hundreds, perhaps thousands—occupied CHA units without a lease and would receive no assistance under the Plan for Transformation.

12. Chicago Housing Authority, "1984/85 Statistical Report," HWLC. For a critique of the *Plan for Trans-formation*, see Janet L. Smith, "The Chicago Housing Authority's Plan for Transformation," 93–123 in *Where Are Poor People to Live? Transforming Public Housing Communities*, ed. Larry Bennett, Janet L. Smith, and Patricia A. Wright (Armonk, N.Y.: M. E. Sharpe, 2006).

13. Jamie Kalven, a longtime observer and activist, says that the MacArthur Foundation has spent $65 million in support of the *Plan for Transformation*. However, a portion of this figure likely includes loan guarantees. See Jamie Kalven, "Bite the Hand That Feeds: The Chicago News Cooperative and the Tricky Nonprofit Terrain," *Columbia Journalism Review*, May–June 2010, at www.cjr.org/feature/bite_the_hand_that_feeds.php; Arthur M. Sussman, "Making Grants to Governments," *Foundation News & Commentary* 47(4) (2006), at www.foundationnews.org/CME/article.cfm?ID=3735.

14. Lawrence Vale, *Purging the Poorest: Public Housing and the Design Politics of Twice-Cleared Commu-nities* (Chicago: University of Chicago Press, 2013). The idea of a "total mix" of residents had been implemented in 1998 with success at North Town Village, the first phase of Cabrini redevelopment that preceded the Plan for Transformation.

15. Alex Kotlowitz, "Where Is Everyone Going?" *Chicago Tribune*, March 10, 2002; Business and Professional People in the Public Interest, "The Third Side: A Mid-Course Report on Chicago's Trans-formation of Public Housing," September 2009, 30–33; David Thigpen and Maggie Sieger, "The Long Way Home," *Time*, August 5, 2002. On crime rates in receiving communities, see Susan Popkin, Michael J. Rich, Leah Hendey, Chris Hayes, and Joe Parilla, "Public Housing Transformation and Crime: Making the Case for Responsible Relocation," Urban Institute, April 2012.

16. Michael Sosin, Christine George, Susan Grossman, Julie Hilvers, and Koonal Patel, "Final Wave Survey Results: A Preliminary Evaluation of Chicago's Ten Year Plan to End Homelessness," Alliance to End Homelessness, 2011.

17. Business and Professional People in the Public Interest, "The Third Side," 33–36; Susan J. Popkin, Brett Theodos, Liza Getsinger, and Joe Parilla, "An Overview of the Chicago Family Case Management Demonstration," Urban Institute, December 2010; Opportunity Chicago, "A Partnership for Change: How Opportunity Chicago Helped Create New Workforce Pathways for Public Housing Residents," June 2012. The Opportunity Chicago jobs effort, funded largely by the MacArthur Foundation, is undergoing an independent evaluation by researchers at the University of Illinois–Chicago.

18. Susan J. Popkin, Diane K. Levy, Larry Buron, Megan Gallagher, and David J. Price, "The CHA's Plan for Transformation: How Have Residents Fared?" Urban Institute, August 2010.

19. Popkin et al., "CHA's Plan for Transformation."

20. Mark L. Joseph, Robert J. Chaskin, and Henry S. Webber, "The Theoretical Basis for Addressing Poverty Through Mixed-Income Development," *Urban Affairs Review* 42(3) (2007): 369–409.

21. Mark Joseph and Robert Chaskin, "Living in a Mixed-Income Development: Resident Perceptions of the Benefits and Disadvantages of Two Developments in Chicago," *Urban Studies* 47(11) (2010): 2347–66; Robert Chaskin and Mark Joseph, "Social Interaction in Mixed-Income Developments: Relational Expectations and Emerging Reality," *Journal of Urban Affairs* 33(2) (2011): 209–37; Naomi J. McCormick, Mark Joseph, and Robert Chaskin, "The New Stigma of Relocated Public Housing Residents: Challenges to Social Identity in Mixed-Income Developments," *City & Community* 11(3) (2012): 285–308.

22. Specifically, the early versions of the Plan for Transformation included rehabilitation of three low-rise projects now considered for demolition and mixed-income redevelopment: Lathrop Homes, Cabrini Homes, and Altgeld-Murray. See Chicago Housing Authority, "Proposed FY2013 Moving to Work Annual Plan, Submitted for HUD Approval," October 18, 2012.

23. Data here from Lawrence Vale and Erin Graves, "The Chicago Housing Authority's Plan for Transformation: What Does the Research Show So Far?" Final report to the MacArthur Foundation, June 8, 2010, 8–9.

PART 4

1. See Guian A. McKee, *The Problem of Jobs: Liberalism, Race, and Deindustrialization in Philadelphia* (Chicago: University of Chicago Press, 2008); Joseph Heathcott and Maire Agnes Murphy, "Corridors of Flight, Zones of Renewal: Industry, Planning, and Policy in the Making of Metropolitan St. Louis, 1940–1980," *Journal of Urban History* 31(1) (2005): 151–89; Robert O. Self, *American Babylon: Race and Struggle for Postwar Oakland* (Princeton, N.J.: Princeton University Press, 2003).

2. *Chicago Tribune*, August 10, 1987; Richard Longworth, "Holding Actions," *Chicago Tribune*, April 14, 1984.

CHAPTER 13

1. The task force was chaired by M. Leanne Lachman, president of the Real Estate Research Corporation, and staffed by Robert Mier, the newly appointed commissioner of the Department of Economic Development. U.S. Steel, the largest steel producer in the city and region, declined to join, although it later participated in conferences and meetings. Mayor's Task Force on Steel and Southeast Chicago (MTFSSC), "Building on the Basics: The Final Report of the Mayor's Task Force on Steel and Southeast Chicago," 1986, HWLC.

2. MTFSSC, "Building on the Basics," 20.

3. MTFSSC, "Building on the Basics," 26–27.

4. Ibid., 28. In 1992, the city proposed a large new airport in southeast Chicago surrounding Lake Calumet, but space limitations, environmental concerns, and the objection of several neighborhoods led Mayor Daley to abandon the idea.

5. Robert Giloth and Joshua Lerner, "Chicago's Industry Task Forces: Joint Problem Solving for Local Economic Development," *Economic Development Quarterly* 1(4) (1987): 356. The Apparel and Fashion Industry Task Force was chaired by Dorothy Fuller, executive vice president of Merchandise Mart Properties, and involved more than 40 leaders from industry, retailers, and unions collaborating in six working groups, with a final report issued in 1987.

6. University of Illinois–Chicago, Printing Industry Task Force, "Printing in Chicago: The Final Report of the Printing Industry Task Force," May 1988; Rast, *Remaking Chicago.*

7. Robert Giloth, "Community Economic Development: Strategies and Practices of the 1980s," *Economic Development Quarterly* 2(4) (1988): 343–50. On the importance of manufacturing, see Stephen S. Cohen and John Zysman, *Manufacturing Matters: The Myth of the Post-Industrial Economy* (New York: Basic Books, 1987).

8. Rast, *Remaking Chicago,* 111–16.

9. John F. McDonald and Daniel P. McMillen, "Land Values, Land Use, and the First Chicago Zoning Ordinance," *Journal of Real Estate Finance and Economics* 16(2) (1998): 135–50; Rast, *Remaking Chicago,* 115.

10. City of Chicago, Zoning Ordinance, chap. 17-6-0400.

11. Rast, *Remaking Chicago,* 134–40.

12. Donna Ducharme, Robert Giloth, and Lynn McCormick, "Business Loss or Balanced Growth: Industrial Displacement in Chicago," New City YMCA, City of Chicago Department of Economic Development, and University of Illinois–Chicago, Center for Urban Economic Development, 1986, HWLC.

13. Donna Ducharme, "Keeping Jobs for Chicago's Future: A Development Impact Assessment of Goose Island," New City YMCA LEED Council, 1990; interview with Donna Ducharme, 1998.

14. Interview with Kathleen Nelson, May 30, 2012.

15. Chicago Department of Planning and Development, *Corridors of Industrial Opportunity: A Plan for Industry in Chicago's West Side*, December 1991, rev. March 1992; *Corridors of Industrial Opportunity: A Plan for Industry in Chicago's North Side*, December 1992, rev. October 1993; and *Corridors of Industrial Opportunity: A Plan for Industry in Chicago's South Side*, March 1995, all at HWLC, Municipal Reference Collection (MRC).

16. The area had been home to the 475-acre Union Stock Yards, which closed in 1970, as well as the site of the first planned manufacturing district in the United States—a 265-acre industrial park created in 1905. With federal assistance, the city had begun adding a street grid to the site in the 1960s, which evolved into the Stockyards Industrial Corridor.

17. Exelon has built a 10-megawatt facility on 41 acres in the West Pullman industrial park, calling it the "largest urban solar installation in the United States." See "Exelon City Solar," at www.exeloncorp.com/assets/energy/powerplants/docs/pdf_ExelonCitySolarFact.pdf.

18. Interview with Eric Strickland, October 22, 2012; interview with Ed Lewis, October 18, 2012.

CHAPTER 14

1. Due to changes in classification, employment categories are not strictly comparable over time. In 1997, the federal government switched from the Standard Industrial Classification (SIC) system to the North American Industry Classification System (NAICS). The State of Illinois made the same switch in 2001. "Industrial Workers" are defined here by the following NAICS categories: construction, manufacturing, wholesale trade, and transportation and warehousing. The 155,858 figure is based on SIC codes. See Chicago Department of Planning and Development, *Corridors of Industrial Opportunity: A Plan for Industry in Chicago's West Side*, December 1991, rev. March 1992; *Corridors of Industrial Opportunity: A Plan for Industry in Chicago's North Side*, December 1992, rev. October 1993; and *Corridors of Industrial Opportunity: A Plan for Industry in Chicago's South Side*, March 1995, all at HWLC.

2. This table was developed in consultation with the City Department of Housing and Economic Development. Special thanks to Kathleen E. Dickhut, deputy commissioner of the department, and Sherrie Taylor, research associate and demographer, Center for Governmental Studies, Northern Illinois University, DeKalb, Ill.

3. The corridors represent only a small slice of total employment in the city. In 2010, 8.0 percent of all jobs were in the corridors, down from 9.7 percent in 2002. Nearly half of manufacturing jobs in Chicago are outside of the corridors. Further, while suburban Cook County had a slightly smaller percentage decline in manufacturing employment than the city of Chicago and its industrial corridors, suburban Cook's losses were from a higher base and therefore were felt more acutely. Chicago and suburban Cook have roughly the same total employment (1.2 million jobs), but suburban Cook lost 53,761 manufacturing jobs from 2002 to 2010, while the city of Chicago lost 37,434, according to census data. See Appendix C

4. William Strauss, "Is Manufacturing Disappearing?" Federal Reserve Bank of Chicago, August 19, 2010; at http://midwest.chicagofedblogs.org/archives/2010/08/bill_strauss_mf.html.

5. Interview with Ted Wysocki, September 14, 2012.

6. City of Chicago, Department of Housing and Economic Development, "Staff Report to the Community Development Commission Requesting Developer Designation," April 12, 2011; City of Chicago, Office of the Mayor, press release, July 27, 2012. Finkl's business increased in 2012, and it maintained production at its North Branch facility while expanding into the new Burnside campus.

7. City of Chicago, Chicago Sustainable Industries (CSI), Land Use Task Force, "Contemporary Industrial Zoning Policies," September 22, 2011; Bay Area Economics, "Industrial Land Use Analysis, Baltimore, Maryland," City of Baltimore Development Corporation, 2004; City of Portland, Oregon, "Central Eastside Industrial Zoning Study," 2003.

8. City of Chicago, Department of Housing and Economic Development, *Chicago Sustainable Industries: Phase One: A Manufacturing Work Plan for the 21st Century*, March 2011, at www.cityofchicago.org/city/en/depts/dcd/supp_info/chicago_sustainableindustries.html.

9. This work, by economist John McDonald and the Metro Chicago Information Center, characterizes industrial employment as manufacturing, wholesale trade, transportation, and waste management.

10. CSI, Land Use Task Force, "Report of the Data Analysis Subcommittee," July 11, 2011. Further, just over half of the jobs in industrial corridors were found to be held by city residents, and only 40 percent in the goods-producing sectors.

CHAPTER 15

1. "City of Chicago Industrial Market and Strategic Analysis," Department of Planning and Development, Arthur Andersen, March 1998, HWLC.

2. Ibid. The Calumet area had organized an industry advocacy group, the Calumet Area Industrial Commission, in 1967 and was planned as an industrial corridor in the Corridors of Industrial Opportunity report (1995). But major new development had not followed. Earlier, hopes had been high that the St. Lawrence Seaway, opened in 1959, would bring significant traffic to the Port of the City of Chicago on Lake Calumet, but this did not materialize.

3. "Calumet Area Implementation / Action Plan," Department of Planning and Development, Arthur Andersen, May 1999.

4. City of Chicago, Department of Planning and Development, *Calumet Area Land Use Plan*, 2002.

5. Interview with Doris Holleb, February 3, 2012.

6. Interview with Tony Reinhart, July 19, 2012.

7. Interview with Mary Culler, May 22, 2012.

8. Under direction from Mayor Daley and Governor Ryan, who had promised Ford seamless city and state cooperation, there was daily coordination between Pam McDonough, director of the Illinois Department of Commerce and Community Affairs, and Andy Norman, deputy commissioner of planning for the City. Interview with Mary Culler, May 22, 2012.

9. Some of the infrastructure projects included a new 126th Street, built to heavy truck standards to link Torrence Avenue and Avenue O, providing access to the supplier park and to new areas for redevelopment. Torrence Avenue was also shifted to open the east side of the Ford Assembly Plant to truck access, and the intersection of 130th and Torrence eventually underwent grade separation projects for two railroads.

10. Data from Corporate Accountability for Tax Expenditures Act, Annual Project Progress Reports, 2007–2011, available at: www.ilcorpacct.com/corpacct; Illinois Department of Commerce and Economic Opportunity, DCEO Agreements Reports, 2001–2006.

CHAPTER 16

1. Chicago Metropolitan Agency for Planning, *Metropolitan Chicago's Freight Cluster: A Drill-Down Report on Infrastructure, Innovation, and Workforce*, June 2012, at www.cmap.illinois.gov/freight-drill-down.

2. See, e.g., Chicago Regional Planning Association, *Planning the Region of Chicago*, 1956, 98–105.

3. The freight railroads already had a relationship with CATS because of its close connection to the Regional Transit Authority, which had taken over the railroads' passenger commuter services in 1974.

4. Interview with Gerald Rawling, August 2, 2012.

5. Chicago City Council, Committee on Finance Report, November 19, 1997. In Illinois, property taxes paid by railroads were collected by the state and redistributed to municipalities according to the amount of railroad mileage located within them, not by the value of the underlying land.

6. Interview with Gerald Rawling, August 2, 2012.

7. E-mail from Joe Schacter, Illinois Department of Transportation, July 19, 2012.

8. Ibid.

9. CREATE, "63rd and State (Englewood) Flyover: Fact Sheet" at www.createprogram.org/factsheets/P1.pdf.

10. *Metropolitan Chicago's Freight Cluster: A Drill-Down Report on Infrastructure, Innovation, and Workforce*, June 2012.

PART 5

1. The Burnham Plan Centennial, "Vision and Theme," 2009, at http://burnhamplan100.lib.uchicago.edu/about.

CHAPTER 17

1. Visitor data from Chicago Loop Alliance, "Loop Economic Study and Impact Report," February 2011, at http://chicagoloopalliance.com/Resources/business/2011_Loop_Economic_Study_FINAL.pdf.

2. Marc V. Levine, "Downtown Redevelopment as an Urban Growth Strategy: A Critical Appraisal of the Baltimore Renaissance," *Journal of Urban Affairs* 9(2): 103–23.

3. In the 1950s, the city extended heavy-rail lines onto the pier and added a southern exterior promenade to allow unloading of large ship cargoes that were expected via the St. Lawrence Seaway. But the traffic never reached expected levels, and the line—which might have been used for transit to the pier—was ripped up sometime in the 1970s. For a history of Navy Pier, see Douglas Bukowski, *Navy Pier: A Chicago Landmark* (Chicago: Ivan Dee, 1966).

4. *Chicago Tribune*, May 4, 1978, March 15, 1979, and November 2, 1980; *Chicago Sun-Times*, May 10, 1979.

5. *Crain's Chicago Business*, June 5, 1989; *Chicago Tribune*, January 27, 1984, February 13, 1984; *All Chicago City News*, February 18, 1984; *Chicago Sun-Times*, November 6, 1988, clipping files, HWLC.

6. *Chicago Tribune*, August 23, 1985, September 22, 1985, February 16, 1986, and July 10, 1990. On the evolution of this deal, see *Crain's Chicago Business*, June 5, 1989.

7. *Chicago Tribune*, January 23, 1991, April 12, 1992, and May 3, 1992; *Crain's Chicago Business*, February 11, 1991. McPier Vice Chairman Patrick Daly, a developer, resigned over the choice of designer. Several architectural firms were upset that the competition allowed their ideas to be used in the final product, but fees for the competition were minimal.

8. *Chicago Sun-Times*, September 28, 1988; Metropolitan Planning Council, "A Light-Rail Transit System for Chicago's Central Area," 1989.

9. *Chicago Reader*, October 18, 1991.

10. State Street merchants wanted access to convention-goers and tourists as well, leading planners to plan a single north-south line that ran from McCormick Place to North Michigan Avenue, taking a circuitous route through downtown rather than moving directly along spacious Columbus Drive. Interview with Steve Schlickman, November 16, 2011.

11. *Chicago Sun-Times*, November 13, 1992; *Inside*, November 1, 1995; *North Loop News*, June 11, 1993, clipping files, HWLC.

12. Streeterville Organization of Active Residents (SOAR) worked actively to kill the Circulator. The organization objected to light rail down Illinois and Grand Avenues, saying it would disrupt traffic entering Lake Shore Drive, yet these were overbuilt, four-lane, one-way roads that could easily accommodate light rail. SOAR feared greater development and greater traffic of all sorts. It did support a new subway tunnel through Streeterville, knowing that this option was prohibitively costly. See *North Loop News*, September 22, 1993.

13. *Chicago Reader*, May 29, 1992.

14. Interview with Steve Schlickman, November 16, 2011.

15. See McCormick Place, "History," at www.mccormickplace.com/about-us/history.php.

16. McCormick Place, "History"; Choose Chicago, "Convention Attendance," at www.choosechicago.com/articles/view/convention-attendance/70; *Chicago Tribune*, June 27, 2012.

17. *Chicago Tribune*, May 6, 1990.

18. Recent announcement for a music venue and a microbrewery suggest a desire by entrepreneurs to make Motor Row into "Music Row" rather than one catering directly to convention goers. See *Chicago Sun Times*, November 9, 2011 and Chicago *Sun Times*, August 15, 2012.

19. *Chicago Journal*, May 30, 2012. The $50 million for the new CTA Green Line Station at Cermak Road and 23rd Street will come from the Near South TIF, filled with tax revenues generated by the Central Station development described in chapter 7. The *Chicago Journal* reports that: "One reason the station is budgeted to be so expensive is because the city is accelerating the project's timeline, hoping to have it done by the end of 2014. That's when the Near South TIF fund expires."

20. See *Chicago Tribune*, June 27, 2012. Orlando's center is hardly a model of urban planning, yet the proximity of hotels and restaurants is superior to Chicago's. On October 30, McPier CEO Jim Reilly gave a speech acknowledging that McCormick Place needed to focus more on its surroundings, but he continued the "bubble" thinking that pervades McCormick Place planning, rather than embracing an urban-themed entertainment district centered on the existing Motor Row: "What Las Vegas has that we don't have is a megahotel complex where 3,000 people can meet, eat, be entertained and sleep without ever going outside." See *Chicago Tribune*, October 31, 2012.

21. Timothy J. Gilfoyle, *Millennium Park: Creating a Chicago Landmark* (Chicago: University of Chicago Press, 2006), 75–82.

22. Ibid., 170. Estimates on parking garage revenue proved optimistic, and the city sold the garage to private investors in 2006 for $563 million, half of which went to retire earlier debt on the garages and Millennium Park. *Chicago Tribune*, October 31, 2006.

23. Gilfoyle, *Millennium Park*, 81–181.

24. Ibid., 124.

25. Goodman Williams Group, "Millennium Park: Economic Impact Study," April 21, 2005. See also Edward Uhlir, "The Millennium Park Effect, Creating a Cultural Venue with an Economic Impact," *Economic Development Journal* 4(2) (2005).

CHAPTER 18

1. Interview with Reuben Hedlund, January 20, 2012.

2. Interview with Ley Bey, July 12, 2011.

3. Chicago Department of Planning, "Planning Principles for the Central Area," 1991, HWLC.

4. Rosen Consulting Group, "Downtown Chicago Market Trends," May 1999.

5. Interview with Lee Bey, July 12, 2011.

6. City of Chicago, Department of Planning and Development, Department of Transportation, and Department of the Environment, *The Chicago Central Area Plan: Preparing the Central City for the 21st Century*, draft report to the CPC, May 2003, hereafter cited as "City of Chicago, *Chicago Central Area Plan*"; Bruce Nussbaum, "Chicago Blues," *Business Week*, October 15, 2000.

7. Arthur Andersen LLP and Goodman Williams Group, "An Economic Base and Sector Analysis, Central Area, Chicago, Illinois, 2000–2020," prepared for the City of Chicago Department of Planning and Development, March 2001; City of Chicago, *Chicago Central Area Plan*, chap. 2.

8. City of Chicago, *Chicago Central Area Plan*, chap. 2. The total annual demand for office, residential, institutional, and retail amounted to 4.0–6.0 million square feet per year (80–120 million over 20 years), in line with the Department of Planning and Development estimates in 1999. At densities equal to or exceeding current zoning standards, this resulted in a need for 10–20 acres of sites per year or 120–180 acres for 20 years. The land-supply analysis indicated a site capacity of 215 million square feet of building space—or a 35–40-year supply. Thus, there was enough land for all the major land uses in the central area.

9. Ibid.

10. Ibid., chap. 4.

11. The 2003 *Central Area Plan* was the first to credit authorship to three different departments (Planning and Development, CDOT, and the Environment), with major policy and project input coming from all three. This multidepartment investment gave added impetus to coordinated action among departments on plan goals.

12. City of Chicago, *Chicago Central Area Plan*, 139.

13. Interview with Lee Bey, July 12, 2011.

14. Larry Bennett, Michael Bennett, and Stephen Alexander, "Chicago and the 2016 Olympics: Why Host the Games? How Should We Host the Games? What Should We Accomplish by Hosting the Games?" Egan Urban Center, DePaul University, November 2008.

15. *Chicago Tribune*, March 12, 2004, and June 12, 2008. The CTA originally thought that the airport express "superstation" would go somewhere in the South Loop; see *Chicago Tribune*, August 22, 2001.

16. In February 2005, the CTA advertised "for bids by consulting firms to flesh out the airport-express concept and create a business plan that includes recommended fare structures, train schedules, financing and other operating details." See *Chicago Tribune*, February 18, 2005.

17. Interview with Terry Haymaker, August 31, 2012; *Chicago Tribune*, June 12, 2008.

18. City of Chicago, *Central Area Action Plan*, adopted by the CPC, August 20, 2009.

19. Ibid., 2–8.

20. Jeffrey Sriver, "Bus Rapid Transit and the Future of Transit Service in Chicago," November 27, 2011.

CHAPTER 19

1. Chicago Civic Federation, "City of Chicago, FY 2012 Proposed Budget: Analysis and Recommendations," November 2, 2011, 101–4; *Chicago Sun-Times*, April 4, 2012.

2. There was an advantage, however, to city financed infrastructure projects such as the Skyway, as it allowed Mayor Richard M. Daley to distribute contracts and jobs.

3. Louise Nelson Dyble, "Tolls and Control: The Chicago Skyway and the Pennsylvania Turnpike," *Journal of Planning History* 11(4) (2012): 70–88.

4. Ben Joravsky and Mick Dumke, "FAIL, Part One: Chicago's Parking Meter Lease Deal," *Chicago Reader*, April 9, 2009. On why parking rates are usually undervalued, see Donald Shoup, FAICP, *The High Cost of Free Parking* (Chicago: APA Planners Press, 2005).

5. Nathan Hellman, "Chicago Is Blowing Its Future on Current Spending, Analysts Say," *Medill Reports*, February 25, 2010, at http://news.medill.northwestern.edu/chicago/news.aspx?id=158464.

6. *New York Times*, November 19, 2009.

7. "Findings and Recommendations for Reforming the Use of Tax Increment Financing in Chicago: Creating Greater Efficiency, Transparency, and Accountability," report of the TIF Reform Panel, August 23, 2011, 3.

8. Interview with Les Pollock, August 9, 2012.

9. See Mick Dumke and Ben Joravsky, "The Shadow Budget: Who Wins in Daley's TIF Game," *Chicago Reader*, May 20, 2010; Ben Joravksy, "Chicago Property Tax 101," *Chicago Reader*, October 27, 2011.

10. "Findings and Recommendations for Reforming the Use of Tax Increment Financing in Chicago: Creating Greater Efficiency, Transparency, and Accountability," report of the TIF Reform Panel, August 23, 2011.

11. The Infrastructure Trust Fund does allow the city to avoid assuming the risks of cost overruns or revenue shortfalls, which will instead be borne by the private investors. *New York Times*, March 29, 2012.

CHAPTER 20

1. Schwieterman and Caspall, *Politics of Place*, chaps. 7 and 12; City of Chicago, Department of Planning and Development, "A New Zoning Bonus System for Chicago," December 18, 1998, HWLC.

2. Schwieterman and Caspall, *Politics of Place*, chaps. 9 and 13.

3. Interview with Dennis Harder, August 3, 2011; Schwieterman and Caspall, *Politics of Place*, 90–95; 119–24.

4. City of Chicago, Mayor's Zoning Reform Commission, "Principles for Chicago's New Zoning Ordinance: Recommendations for Preserving, Protecting, and Strengthening Chicago's Neighborhoods," May 2002; comments of Kirk R. Bishop at the Gerald Fogelson Forum on Real Estate, "The 2004 Zoning Reform: Is it Working for Chicago?" Roosevelt University, September 27, 2012; Schwieterman and Caspall, *Politics of Place*, 125–26.

5. Schwieterman and Caspall, *Politics of Place*, 128–29.

6. Interview with Lawrence Okrent, January 12, 2012.

7. Interview with Jack Guthman, January 27, 2012; Michael Ibrahem, "Update: Zoning and Affordable Housing," *We the People Media*, November 30, 2004, at http://wethepeoplemedia.org/uncategorized/update-zoning-and-affordable-housing.

8. Department of Planning and Friends of the Chicago River, "Chicago River Urban Design Guidelines: Downtown Corridor," Adopted by the Chicago Plan Commission, June 14, 1990; *Chicago Tribune*, March 13, 1990, and March 24, 1990.

9. See, e.g., *Chicago Tribune*, April 23, 1985, August 12, 2004, and January 28, 2008; Paul H. Gobster and Lynne M. Westphal, eds., "People and the River: Perception and Use of Chicago Waterways for Recreation (Chicago Rivers Demonstration Project Report)," Milwaukee, U.S. Department of the Interior, National Park Service, Rivers, Trails, and Conservation Assistance Program.

10. *Chicago Tribune*, September 8, 1995; Chicago Department of Planning, "Chicago River Corridor Development Plan," 1999, HWLC. See also Felix Weickmann, "Riverfront Planning: Case study of the Chicago River Corridor Development Plan," March 2006, Network for European and U.S. Regional and Urban Studies.

11. *Chicago Tribune*, June 28, 2009.

12. City of Chicago, Office of the Mayor, "Mayor Emanuel Announces Plans to Complete Chicago Riverwalk," press release, October 8, 2012. The city says it will look to the U.S. Department of Transportation to fund the Riverwalk.

13. *Chicago Tribune*, March 11, 1996, March 18, 1996, July 3, 1996, and December 6, 2001; "History of Meigs Field," *Friends of Meigs Field* at http://friendsofmeigs.org/html/history/meigs_history.htm.

14. *Chicago Tribune*, April 1, 2003, and April 2, 2003.

15. *Chicago Tribune*, April 6, 2003, and June 23, 2005.

16. *Chicago Tribune*, December 2, 2010; SmithGroupJJR and Studio Gang Architects, "Northerly Island Framework Plan," May 2011.

17. *Chicago Tribune*, August 16, 2012; U.S. Army Corps of Engineering, "Northerly Island Great Lakes Fishery and Ecosystem Restoration (GLFER) Project," presentation by Kirston Buczak, June 26, 2012. The Corps can fund only restoration activities, not recreational ones.

18. City of Chicago, Mayor's Bicycle Advisory Council, "The Bike 2000 Plan," May 1992.

19. Ben Gomberg and Randy Neufeld, "Chicago Bike Parking," in "Improving Conditions for Bicycling and Walking: A Best Practices Report," prepared for the Federal Highway Administration by the Rails-to-Trails Conservancy and the Association of Pedestrian and Bicycle Professionals, January 1998.

20. City of Chicago, Mayor's Bicycle Advisory Council, "Bike 2015 Plan," January 2006; Mike Amsden, Mark de la Vergne, and John Wirtz, "Chicago's Protected Bike Lane Initiative," n.d., at www.transportchicago.org.

21. Amsden, de la Vergne, and Wirtz, "Chicago's Protected Bike Lane Initiative"; City of Chicago, Department of Transportation, "Chicago Forward: Department of Transportation Action Agenda," May 2012.

22. League of American Bicyclists, "2010 Bike Commuting Data Released," at http://blog.bikeleague.org/blog/2011/09/2010-bike-commuting-data-released.

23. Carl Smith, *The Plan of Chicago: Daniel Burnham and the Remaking of the American City* (Chicago: University of Chicago Press, 2006).

CHAPTER 21

1. World Business Chicago, "A Plan for Economic Growth and Jobs," March 2012, 14; OECD Territorial Reviews, *The Chicago Tri-State Metropolitan Area*, 2012, 15–31; Aaron M. Renn, "Chicago Takes a Census Shellacking," *New Geography*, February 16, 2011; Rob Paral, "What Does the 2010 Census Tell Us About Metropolitan Chicago?" Chicago Community Trust, May 2011.

2. *Chicago Tribune*, February 29, 2012.

3. For example, South Shore saw an uptick in the 2000 census only to lose 19 percent of its population by 2010. Paral and Associates, "What Does the 2010 Census Tell Us about Metropolitan Chicago?"; Renn, "Chicago Takes a Census Shellacking."

4. For example, the largest absolute losses were from three community areas affected by deep poverty and the Plan for Transformation: Austin (−21,500), South Shore (−12,100), and West Englewood (−10,100) accounted for a quarter of the black losses. See Beauty Turner and Brian J. Rogal, "Deadly Moves: Moving at their Own Risk," *Residents' Journal* series, at http://wethepeoplemedia.org /uncategorized/deadly-moves-moving-at-their-own-risk-2; *Chicago Sun Times*, September 9, 2004.

5. For this analysis, the Central Area is Community Area 8 (Near North), 28 (Near West), 32 (Loop), and 33 (Near South). North side neighborhoods are Community Areas 1 (Rogers Park), 3 (Uptown), 4, (Lincoln Square), 5 (North Center), 6 (Lakeview), 7 (Lincoln Park), 22 (Logan Square), 24 (West Town), and 77 (Edgewater). On Latino trends in Chicago, see Jeffrey Passel, D'Vera Cohn, and Ana Gonzalez-Barrera, "Net Migration from Mexico Falls to Zero—and Perhaps Less," Pew Hispanic Center, April 23, 2012.

6. Alan Ehrenhalt makes a similar argument in *The Great Inversion and the Future of the American City* (New York: Alfred A. Knopf, 2012).

7. Among large cities, Chicago is the most segregated in the nation. Segregation is measured by a "dissimilarity index" which describes the proportion of the population that would have to move to achieve a balanced racial distribution. In 1980, the city's dissimilarity index was 90.6, and by 2010 it had dropped to 82.5; sociologists consider ratings above 60 to indicate high levels of segregation. The Chicago metro area had the second-highest percentage drop between 2000 and 2010 but also remains at the top of the dissimilarity index, followed distantly by New York and Philadelphia. Data on City of Chicago from Brown University, American Communities Project, US2010, at www.s4.brown .edu/us2010/index.htm. For metro area data, see Edward Glaeser and Jacob Vigdor, "The End of the Segregated Century: Racial Separation in America's Neighborhoods, 1890–2010," Manhattan Institute, Civic Report no. 66, January 2012. Glaeser and Vigdor take a more optimistic view of the data than most commentators.

8. Aaron Renn, "State of Chicago: The New Century Struggle," *Urbanophile*, July 2, 2012, at www .urbanophile.com/2012/07/02/state-of-chicago-the-new-century-struggle.

9. Woodstock Institute, "Struggling to Stay Afloat: Negative Equity in Communities of Color in the Chicago Six County Region," March 2012.

10. City of Chicago, Office of the Mayor, press release, October 23, 2012.

11. World Business Chicago, "A Plan for Economic Growth and Jobs," March 2012; interview with Ted Wysocki, September 14, 2012.

12. OECD, *Chicago Tri-state Metropolitan Area*, 2012; Aaron Renn, "The OECD Reviews Chicago," *Urbanophile*, May 6, 2012, at www.urbanophile.com/2012/05/06/the-oecd-reviews-chicago.

CHAPTER 22

1. Chicago Public Library, "CPL 2010: A Vision for Our Future," 2010. According to the Mayor's office, during Mayor Daley's tenure (1989–2009), 56 libraries were built or completely renovated, roughly two-thirds of the total of 79 libraries. City of Chicago, Office of the Mayor, press release, July 28, 2011.

2. Interview with Laurence Msall, July 17, 2012.

Notes on Interviews

In the course of their research, the authors interviewed the people listed below. The conclusions drawn by the authors from those interviews are their own.

Miles Berger, former chairman, Chicago Plan Commission*

Lee Bey, executive director, Chicago Central Area Committee

Mary Culler, director, state and local government relations, Ford Motor Company

Norman Elkin, AICP, former staff member, Department of City Planning, City of Chicago*

Marilyn Engwall, coordinator of economic development, Department of Housing and Economic Development, City of Chicago*

Eileen Figel, AICP, director, Institute for Comprehensive Community Development

Jesus G. Garcia, Cook County Commissioner, Seventh District

Jack Guthman, partner, Shefsky and Froelich; former chairman, Chicago Zoning Board of Appeals*

Dennis Harder, former staff member, Department of Planning and Development, City of Chicago

Terri Haymaker, AICP, director of planning, Public Building Commission of Chicago*

Reuben L. Hedlund, attorney at law, McGuire Woods; former chairman, Chicago Plan Commission*

Doris Holleb, AICP, member, Chicago Plan Commission*

Edward Lewis, coordinator, economic development, Department of Housing and Economic Development, City of Chicago

Dean L. Macris, FAICP, former staff member, Department of Development and Planning, City of Chicago*

Laurence J. Msall, president, the Civic Federation, Chicago

Kathleen A. Nelson, senior director, Cushman and Wakefield; former staff member, Department of Planning and Development, City of Chicago*

Larry Okrent, president, Okrent Associates*

Leslie Pollock, FAICP, principal consultant, Camiros*

Gerald Rawling, former staff member, Chicago Area Transportation Study and Intermodal Advisory Taskforce

Tony Reinhart, regional manager of governmental affairs, Ford Motor Company

Hipolito (Paul) Roldan, president and CEO, Hispanic Housing Development Corporation

Steve Schlickman, executive director, Urban Transportation Center, University of Illinois–Chicago

Ted Wysocki, president and CEO, North Branch Works (formerly the Local Economic and Employment Development Council)

*Member of Lambda Alpha International

CREDITS

Maps Dennis McClendon, Chicago CartoGraphics

I.1, 5.3, 5.5, 7.2, 7.6, 9.3, 9.5, 12.3–4, 13.2, 17.4–5 Larry Okrent

1.1 Wikipedia Commons

1.2, III.1, 9.4, 9.6, 10.2, 11.1–2 Lee Bey

2.1, 6.1, 7.2, 11.6, 13.1, 15.3, V.1 *Chicago Tribune*

2.2–3, 12.1, 12.6, 19.1 D. Bradford Hunt

2.4 Newberry Library

2.5, 3.6, 6.2 Chicago History Museum, ICHi-05776, HB-23215-F, ICHi-67270

2.6 Library of Congress, LC-USW36-603

II.1, 3.2, 10.4–5 *Chicago Sun-Times*

3.1, 3.3–5, 4.1–3, 4.5–6, 5.1–2, 7.4, 8.2, 13.3, 13.5, 15.1, 17.2, 20.1 City of Chicago

3.7–8 University of Illinois–Chicago

4.4 City of Chicago and Harza Engineering Company

5.4 Ron Gordon

6.3 Chicago Public Library, Special Collections and Preservation Division, HWAC 1987-11-25

7.1 Okrent Associates

7.3 Ross Miller

7.7 Central Station Development Corporation

7.8 Anne Evans, Archicenter

8.1, 12.2 Chicago Housing Authority

8.3 Associated Press

8.4 Historic Pullman Foundation

8.5, 9.7–8, 11.5 LISC Chicago

9.1, 18.4, 22.1 Chicago Transit Authority

9.2 Urban Land Institute

10.1 Jon Lidolt

10.3 Chicago History Museum, ICHi-67264 and Rodney and Sydney Wright

10.6 Jason Reblando

10.7 Holsten Real Estate Development

11.3, 11.8 Blanca R. Soto

11.4 Madilyn Strantz

11.7 Little Village Environmental Justice Organization

12.5 Chicago Alliance to End Homelessness

12.7 Lawrence Vale, Yonah Freemark, and D. Bradford Hunt

IV.1, 14.1 Resolute Consulting

13.4 istockphoto/Steve Geer

15.2 Studio Gang Architects

15.4 FCL Builders

16.1 U.S. Department of Transportation

16.2 BNSF

17.1 David Bjorgen

17.3 Andrew Jameson

18.1 Appraisal Research Counselors and D. Bradford Hunt

18.2a–b City of Chicago, URS Corporation, and Goodman Williams Group

18.3 City of Chicago, Skidmore, Owings and Merrill, and DLK Civic Design

18.5 Union Station Civic Advisory Committee and TranSystems

18.6 City of Chicago and URS Corporation

19.2 Cook County Clerk's Office

20.2 City of Chicago and Skidmore, Owings and Merrill

20.3 Studio Gang Architects, SmithGroupJJR, Studio V Design, and the Chicago Park District

20.4 Chicago Bicycle Program

21.1–2 Christopher Winters, University of Chicago Library

21.3 Reuters

INDEX

A. Finkl and Sons, 166–67, 177, 190–91

Active Transportation Alliance, 264

Adler Planetarium, 86, 88.

African Americans. *See also race*
>   in Chicago 21 plan, 61
>   deindustrialization affecting, 5
>   discrimination against, 16, 18
>   displacement of, 26, 98, 153
>   in Englewood redevelopment, 111, 113–14
>   home equity data, 271
>   in politics, 12, 13, 69
>   population trends, 16, 17, 18, 267–69
>   public housing survey results, 163
>   rioting by, 68
>   in South Side industry, 182, 194
>   in Uptown, 126, 135

air rights projects
>   downtown residential, 31, 35
>   early use, 20
>   Illinois Center, 45–46
>   Outer Drive East, 36
>   Union Station, 242

aldermanic privilege, 11–12, 20, 29, 134, 175

Alinsky, Saul, 68, 100–101

American Indians, in Uptown, 126

apparel industry, 172–73, 179, 190

Architects/Designers/Planners for Social
>   Responsibility (ADPSR), 91

Arthur Andersen, 193, 197, 200, 275

Aschman, Frederick T., 30, 112

Asian Americans. *See also race*
>   in Chicago 21 plan, 61
>   population trends, 17, 18, 268, 269
>   assets, sale of, 248–49

Ayers, Thomas, 61, 72

Babcock, Richard, 60

Bach, Ruth, 125

Back of the Yards Coalition, 68, 100

Baird, John W., 62–63

barrier islands, 50, 262

Bauhaus modernism, 6–7

Bennett, Edward, 6, 8, 19, 42

Bennett, Larry, 130, 132

Berg, Alicia, 274, 275

Berger, Miles, 38, 47–48, 83, 86

Bey, Lee, 14, 246

bike planning, 263–66, 280

Bike 2000 Plan, 263

Bilandic, Michael, 76, 168

blight. *See also specific areas*

 abandoned steel mills, 174

 in city's history, 3

 migration and, 125

 stopping approach of, 97, 99, 126

 as threat, 7

 TIF based on, 250

Block 37, 85, 86, 239–40

Blucher, Walter, 98

Boeing, 5, 271, 274–75

Bryan, John, 226

Building Owners and Managers Association, 14

Burke, Ed, 13, 74

Burlington Northern Santa Fe RR, 205, 206–7

Burnham, Daniel, 6, 8, 19, 42, 261

Burnham Park, 88, 89

Burnham Plan, 26, 212, 246

bus rapid transit (BRT), 242, 245–46

business interests, in growth coalitions, 14

business parks, 183–84

Butler, Jerry, 216

Byrne, Jane

 on CBDOs, 68

 criticism of, 76

 on economic development, 168

 elections and, 12, 13, 69

 federal funding use by, 74

 on Navy Pier project, 216

 on North Loop redevelopment, 83

 on riverfront plans, 53, 54

Cabrini-Green, 133, 156, 157, 161, 232

Calumet Area plans, 194, 195, 196, 198

Calumet district brownfields, 193–96, 197

Campaign Against the North Loop Tax Break, 83

capital improvements, 27, 42, 252, 279

Center Pointe Properties, 197, 200

Central America, migration from, 18

central area. *See also downtown; Loop*

 capital budget for, 252

 future of, 273, 276, 279–80

 lack of planning for, 229–30

 models of, 22–23, 93

 planning reorganization, 38–39

 railroads and, 19–20

Central Area Action Plan (CAAP), 212–13, 241–46, 273, 280

Central Area Circulator, 218–21, 241, 244, 246

Central Area Committee (CAC)

 in Chicago Works Together plan, 70

 plan leadership by, 58, 230

 planning request from, 29–30

 on riverfront plan, 51–52

 role of, 14, 26

 on World's Fair, 71, 72, 73

Central Area Plan (1973), 230

Central Area Plan (1983), 70, 225, 230, 261

Central Area Plan (2003)

 events leading up to, 230–31

 gathering data for, 231, 234–36

 implementation and planning decline, 212–13, 237–40

 praise for, 280

 retail growth plan, 232–33

 transit in, 236–37

Central Loop Alliance, 14

Central Station, 89, 90, 91–92

Chicago Affordable Housing Coalition, 90

Chicago Alliance to End Homelessness, 158

Chicago Area Transportation Study (CATS), 205

Chicago Assembly Plant, 197

Chicago Association of Neighborhood Development Organizations (CANDO), 14–15, 68, 101

Chicago Children's Museum, 218

Chicago Department of Transportation (CDOT)

on bike planning, 263, 264, 265, 266

Block 37 plan, 239, 240

on CAAP, 241

central area planning, 236–37

Union Station plan, 242

Chicago Development Council, 14, 230, 231

Chicago Economic Development Commission, 168

Chicago Historic Resources Survey, 80

Chicago Housing Authority (CHA). *See also housing; Plan for Transformation*

within city government, 27

current status of, 162–65

history of, 152–54

McCormick Place affected by, 224

mixed-income housing, 151–52, 154–56

progress chart, 164

Chicago Land Clearance Commission, 27

Chicago Landmarks Commission, 81

Chicago Manufacturing Campus, 198, 201

Chicago Neighborhood Initiatives, 103

Chicago & Northwestern Railroad, 35

Chicago Park District, 225–26, 261

Chicago Plan Commission (CPC)

conservation approach, 99

history of, 16, 26

Illinois Center plan, 47–48, 54

McCormick Place project, 222

in Near South redevelopment, 90

Northerly Island, 261

waterfront plans, 51, 53, 54, 258

Chicago Public Schools (CPS), 142–43

Chicago Regional Environmental and Transportation Efficiency (CREATE), 208–9

Chicago Reinvestment Alliance, 101

Chicago River

in Comprehensive Plan of Chicago, 51–54

Corridor Development Plan, 258–59

Friends of the, 52–53, 54, 258–59

in Illinois Center plan, 47, 48

North Branch employment district, 175

postindustrial housing plans along, 31

River City development on, 64

riverfront modernization, 177, 258–60

Chicago Riverwalk Main Branch Framework Plan, 259–60

Chicago School model, 97–100

Chicago Skyway lease, 248–49

Chicago Stock Exchange, 80

Chicago Sustainable Industries, 182, 191–92

Chicago Theatre, 83, 84, 85

Chicago Transit Authority, 116, 117, 180, 220, 239, 240. *See also transit; specific areas*

Chicago 21 plan, 58–64, 215

Chicago Union Station Master Study, 242

Chicago Works Together plan, 70–73

Chicagoland Bicycle Federation, 263, 264

Cincotta, Gail, 101

citizen involvement

bike planning, 264–65

Chicago 21 plan, 60–61

comprehensive plan (1966), 43

displacement protests, 38

Englewood redevelopment, 117, 119

equity planning, 15, 68

future planning success, 228, 278

historic preservation, 84, 85, 102

history of, 106–7

LISC effort, 104, 105, 108

Little Village high school plan, 142–46

Little Village park plan, 146–50

Near South redevelopment, 91

public housing redevelopment, 161

tradition of, 100–101

zoning reform, 256–57

City Beautiful movement, 6

City Hall, 38, 93, 232, 237, 242

Cityfront Center (Dock and Canal project), 48

civil rights movement, 106

class

affecting industrial development, 194

in Chicago 21 plan, 61

planning affected by, 9, 36, 224

population trends, 269, 270

as Uptown conflict, 123

in urban renewal, 26

Clybourn PMD, 177, 179, 233

Coalition of Central Area Communities, 60

Coleman, Walter "Slim," 129, 130–31

Coleman-Shiller movement, 130–31, 132, 134

Columbia College, 65

Commercial Club of Chicago, 171

Commercial District Development Commission, 83

Commission on Chicago Landmarks, 80

Committee for Gov't. Buildings Downtown, 31

Common Operational Picture system, 208

Commonwealth Edison, 197, 200

community conservation, 9, 99, 114

Community Development Block Grants, 74, 102

community development corporations (CDCs)

in employment district strategy, 175

funding for, 15, 101, 104

Little Village, 140–41

origin of, 101

Community Reinvestment Act (1977), 9, 101

Community Workshop on Economic Development
(CWED), 69

community-based development organizations
(CBDOs), 15, 68, 69

Comprehensive Plan of Chicago (1966)

conservation approach in, 100

effectiveness of, 54–55

elements in, 41–45

Englewood redevelopment in, 115

Illinois Center in, 45–48

lakefront plan in, 48–51

main goal of, 230

origin of, 15–16, 27

race and, 139

recreation and parks in, 43, 44

riverfront plan in, 51–54

and tourism, 215

Congestion Mitigation and Air Quality (CMAQ)
Improvement Program, 264

conservation, in Uptown, 125–26, 128

conservation approach, 97–100

Continuum of Care plan, 158

Corridors of Industrial Opportunity, 177, 179, 205

Council Wars, 13, 74, 76, 216

crime

deindustrialization affecting, 5–6

politicians committing, 12

public housing and, 152–53, 162, 224

reduction efforts, 109

sense of community and, 139

Crosstown Expressway, 68

Culler, Mary, 197, 200

Daley, Richard J.

on Chicago 21 plan, 58

on comprehensive plan, 41–42, 43, 47–48

on Crosstown Expressway, 68

on lakefront plans, 49, 50, 261

leadership of, 11, 12

in McCormick Place project, 222

on Model Cities program, 101

planning reorganization by, 15, 25–28

postindustrial city model and, 22–23

on riverfront plans, 51

on transit plans, 33

on urban university, 38

on zoning reform, 256

Daley, Richard M.

bidding for industry, 200, 274, 275

bike planning, 263

on Block 37 plan, 239

city asset sales, 249
on comprehensive planning, 229
economic development policy, 77, 278
on Englewood redevelopment, 116
on environmental protection, 237
on historic preservation, 80–81
on industry policy, 176–77, 179, 190
Latino political connection, 140
leadership of, 7–8, 11, 12, 13–14
Meigs field closing, 261
on Millennium Park, 226
on Near South redevelopment, 88, 90–91
on sheltering the homeless, 158
on TIF control, 133
on tourism, 218, 221
on 2003 Central Area Plan, 237
on Uptown redevelopment, 127
Damofle, Urania, 128
Dearborn Park, 61–64, 66, 86, 87
debt, city's level of, 247–48
deindustrialization, 3, 5–6, 16
Democratic Party, 13, 68, 69, 101.
demographics, change in, 16–18
density, 29, 46, 153, 159, 256
Dept. of Development and Planning, 241
Dept. of Economic Development, 168
Dept. of Housing and Economic Development, 81
Dept. of Housing and Urban Development (HUD)
control of CHA, 154, 156
funding CHA plan, 160
in park planning, 183, 184
in Uptown redevelopment, 131, 132
Dept. of Planning
central area development, 30
Chicago 21 plan and, 58
granting bonuses, 29
Illinois Center, 46, 48
lack of urgency, 230
Lakefront Plan of Chicago, 50, 51

in North Loop redevelopment, 83, 85
Riveredge Plan, 52–54
role of, 16, 26, 41
on Uptown renewal, 126
Dept. of Planning and Development, 177, 191, 194, 196, 231, 239
Dept. of Public Works, 48–49
Dept. of the Environment, 196
Dept. of Urban Renewal, 83, 114, 126
Dept. of Zoning and Land Use Planning, 241
design, versus planning, 13–14
Development Plan for the Central Area of Chicago
after deindustrialization, 22–23, 24, 29–33
main goal of, 230
railroad yard redevelopment, 45
riverfront plan in, 51
discrimination, racial, 16, 18, 42. See also race
displacement. See also CHA; housing
development without, 123
of industry with housing, 175
postindustrial, 25–26
protests, 38
results of, 153, 162, 164
voucher program, 151, 154, 155, 165
Distributor subway plan, 218, 246
district strategy, 174–75, 182–83
downtown. See also central area; Loop
early housing plans in, 33–36
Near South redevelopment and, 92–93
neighborhoods vs., 7, 67, 74, 277, 278
zoning bonus system, 257
drug trade, unemployment affecting, 5–6
Ducharme, Donna, 177, 179
Duncan, Arne, 143
Elkin, Norm, 43, 45, 60, 85, 232
Emanuel, Rahm
on business planning, 14
goals of, 213
on historic landmarks, 81

Infrastructure Trust Fund, 254
  on lost decade, 267
  on riverfront protection, 260
  TIF reform, 252–53
Empowerment Zone program, 106
Englewood
  history of, 111–12
  lack of planning in, 115–18
  Perimeter Plan in, 112–15
  planning problems in, 96, 111, 278
  Quality of Life Plan in, 118–22
  railroad in, 205
environmental protection
  Calumet district, 196
  Chicago River, 258–59
  city's goal for, 237
  Little Village, 147, 149
  open space and industry, 193, 198–99
  solar energy farm, 183
equity planning movement, 7, 12, 13, 45
  Chicago Works Together plan, 70–73
  growth planning versus, 14, 15, 67
  implementing, 73–74
  industrial policy in, 169
  legacy of, 76–77
  linked development in, 74–76
  rise of, 67–70
exaction tax, 75–76
FamilyWorks program, 162
Far-South Development Area Plan (1966), 102
Federal Highway Administration, 263–64
Federal Housing Administration (FHA), 35–36, 114
Federal Transportation Administration, 221
Field Museum, 86, 88. See also Museum Campus
Figel, Eileen, 12, 13–14
floor area ratio (FAR), 28–29, 256, 257
Fogelson, Gerald, 87–88, 89, 90
Ford Calumet Environmental Center, 199
Ford Motor Company, 193, 194, 196, 197–202

Fort Dearborn Urban Renewal plan, 31–32, 64
Freeway Revolts, 49, 68
freight industry. See also industrial policy; railroads
  CREATE program, 208–9
  intermodal capacity, 203–4
  intermodal growth plans, 187, 204–8
funding. See also grants; LISC; TIF; specific projects
  asset sales, 248–49
  debt levels, 247–48
  fickle nature of, 278, 279
  historic preservation, 102–3
  linked development, 74–76
  in postindustrial economy, 27–28, 35–36
  transit, 220–21, 224
Gapp, Paul, 48, 65, 217, 218, 222
Garcia, Jesus, 140–41, 146
Gautreaux program, 154, 156, 160, 163
Gehry, Frank, 226, 227
gentrification, 7
  conservation inspiring, 100
  Printer's Row, 61–64, 80, 173
  tax revenue from, 24
  of Uptown, 129–32
Gilfoyle, Timothy, 225
Giloth, Robert, 174
"global cities," 4–5, 9, 10
GO TO 2040 plan, 243, 273
Gold Coast, 31, 36, 57, 80
Goldberg, Bertrand, 35–36, 64, 81
Goose Island PMD, 176, 177, 179, 180–81
Graham, Bruce, 58, 71, 225
Grant Park, 72, 86, 88
grants, 8–9, 15, 74. See also funding
Greater North Michigan Avenue Association, 14
Greater North Pulaski Development Corp., 174
grocery stores, 232
Gropius, Walter, 6–7, 98
growth coalition
  Chicago 21 and Dearborn Park, 58–64, 66

equity planning vs., 14, 15, 67, 71

history of, 14–16

increased effort of, 57–58

in Near South redevelopment, 91–93

in postindustrial economy, 26, 28–29

resistance to, 9

role of, 7, 9

State Street transit mall, 64–66

Gruen, Victor, 33, 113

Hammond Lakes Area Project, 198

Hank Williams Village, 128

Harder, Dennis, 45, 256

Healey, Lori, 14, 241

Heart of Uptown Coalition, 130

Hedlund, Reuben, 51, 88, 229

Henry Horner Homes, 155, 156

highways. *See roads*

Hispanics or Latinos. *See also race*

    in Chicago 21 plan, 61

    city's entry point for, 18, 96, 137

    home equity data, 271

    in Pilsen district, 60, 138

    politics and, 13, 140–43, 146

    population trends, 17, 18, 268, 269

    in Uptown, 126

historic preservation

    North Loop redevelopment, 82–86

    Pullman community, 80, 102–3

    regulation enactment, 80–81

Historic Pullman Foundation (HPF), 102

Hollander, Elizabeth, 76, 85, 175

Holleb, Doris, 90, 196

HOPE VI program, 155

housing

    beginning of downtown, 7, 30–31, 33–36

    central area data, 93, 233, 235, 236

    Chicago 21 plan, 58–64

    development without displacement, 123

    displacement protests, 38

    in Englewood, 114, 116, 117, 118–21

    fair housing ordinance, 42

    historic, 103

    for homeless, 158–59

    inclusionary zoning, 258

    industrial buildings converted to, 175

    Little Village, 138

    mixed income, 151–52, 154–56, 163

    in Near South redevelopment, 91–92

    poverty and, 6, 86, 97–99, 104

    for senior citizens, 61, 91, 133, 160

    in Uptown, 125, 127, 128, 129–33,

        132–35

    voluntary rehabilitation of, 114

Housing Act (1954), 28

Hyde Park, 49–50, 126

Ida B. Wells Homes, 161

Illinois, University of, 31, 36–38, 39, 216

Illinois Center, 45–48, 54, 219

Illinois Central Railroad

    in Illinois Center plan, 45–46

    Millennium Park and, 72, 225–26

    in Near South redevelopment, 87

    rail yard plans, 21, 31

Illinois Historic Preservation Agency (IHPA), 102

Illinois Institute of Technology, 6–7

immigration, 18, 135, 137–39

impact fees, 75

income. *See class*

industrial corridors

    district strategy for, 176–79, 182–83

    employment in, 185–89, 191–92

    zoning reform, 191–92

industrial parks, 183–84

industrial policy

    brownfield planning, 193–96, 197

    district strategy, 174–75, 182–83

    and Ford, 197–202

    future of, 273, 279–80

history of, 10, 68
nature in, 193, 198–99
sector strategy, 171–74
industry task forces, 171–74
Infrastructure Trust Fund, 254
integration, racial, 42, 61. See also race
Intermodal Advisory Task Force (IATF), 205, 209
Intermodal Surface Transportation Efficiency Act
    (ISTEA), 204, 208, 264
Jane Addams Hull House, 37
Jarrett, Valerie, 14, 177
Jewelers Row, 80
jobs. See also deindustrialization; industrial policy
    creating, 68–69, 70, 168, 278
    decline in private-sector, 269, 271, 272
    employment data, 186, 188–89, 190–91
    FamilyWorks program, 162
    future of, 271
    in industrial corridors, 185–89
John Hancock Tower, 4–5, 57
Johnson, Johnson & Roy, 50
Kapoor, Anish, 226, 227
Kennedy-King Community College, 116–17
Kenwood-Oakland Community Organization
    (KOCO), 75
King, Martin Luther, Jr., 42
Kinzie Industrial Corridor, 182, 187, 188
Klein, Gabe, 264, 266
Lake Point Tower, 49, 50
Lake Shore Drive, 49, 50, 86, 87, 89, 90
lakefront planning, policies guiding, 48–51
Lakefront Protection Ordinance, 51, 54, 256
land banks, 131
Landmark Preservation Ordinance, 80, 256
Lawndale area, 106, 111, 137–39, 146
Lincoln Park, 99, 100, 126, 175
linked development, 74–76
Little Village
    in Empowerment Zone Program, 106
    fight for high school, 142–46
    as Latino entry point, 18, 96, 137
    planning problems in, 278
    politics and action in, 140–43, 146
    Quality of Life Plan, 144–45, 146–50
    sense of community in, 138–39
    streetscape, 94–95
Little Village Community Development Corporation
    (LVCDC), 140–41, 143, 146, 147, 150
Little Village Environmental Justice Organization
    (LVEJO), 147, 148, 149–50
Little Village Industrial Corridor, 187, 189
Local Industrial Retention Initiative (LIRI), 179, 184
Local Initiatives Support Corporation (LISC), 15,
    101, 104–8, 146
Loop. See also central area; downtown; South Loop
    Central Loop Alliance, 14
    development of, 9, 57–58
    North Loop, 79, 82–86
    protecting size of, 31
    railroads and, 19, 20
    retail revival, 232–33
    West Loop, 58, 64
Low Income Housing Trust Fund, 158
MacArthur Foundation, 15, 104, 108, 160–62
machine politics, 11–14, 68, 69. See also politics
Macris, Dean, 28, 41, 45
manufacturing districts, 174–75, 182–83
Marina City, 35–36, 51
McCarron, John, 76
McCormick, Robert, 49, 222
McCormick Place
    Navy Pier control and, 217
    in Near South redevelopment, 88, 89
    tourism and, 222–25
    transit to, 218, 219
McKinney Act (1987), 158
Meigs Field, 49, 210–11, 261–62
Meltzer, Jack, 126

Merchandise Mart, 20, 53

Metra, 208, 220–21, 241, 242

Metropolitan Housing Council, 53

Metropolitan Pier and Exposition Authority (McPier), 88, 89, 217, 222

Metropolitan Planning Council, 15, 90, 208, 218, 256

Metropolitan Water Reclamation District, 54

Mexico, migration from, 18, 137, 138, 150

Michigan Avenue

    historic street wall, 80

    Millennium Park and, 225

    Navy Pier and, 216

    North, 20, 31, 57, 64, 219, 221

    retail and restaurant development, 232

Mid-South Development Area Plan (1968), 115

Midway airport, 245, 249

Mier, Rob, 69–70, 72, 101, 174, 175

migration. See also immigration

    1950s–1970s, 111–12, 139

    out of the city, 267, 268, 269

    of southern whites, 123, 125

    war production increasing, 16

Millennium Park, 4, 5, 225–28

    land use before, 20, 21, 72

    parking garage lease, 249

    road under, 223

    transit to, 218, 242

Millennium Reserve, 198, 199

mixed-income housing model, 151–52, 154–56, 163. See also CHA

Model Cities, 45, 68, 101, 106, 126, 127

Moe, Kari, 69, 72

Mosena, David, 14, 177

Motor Row, 80, 223–25

Msall, Laurence, 8, 279

Munoz, Ricardo, 140, 141

Museum Campus, 88, 89, 90, 91, 227

Navy Pier, 36–37, 215–18, 219

Near South, redevelopment in, 86–96

Neighborhood Capital Budget Group, 279

neighborhood effects, 109–10

Neighborhood Investment Fund, 205

neighborhoods. See also specific

    activists defending, 60, 68, 127

    Chicago Neighborhood Initiatives, 103

    civic pride in, 138–39

    conservation of, 97–100

    displacement and, 38, 39, 68

    downtown versus, 7, 67, 74, 277, 278

    on North Loop redevelopment, 83

    planning history, 9–10

    saving historic landmarks, 80

    "Washington Papers" on, 68–70

    on World's Fair proposal, 72

    zoning and character of, 257

Netsch, Walter, 37

New Communities Program (NCP)

    in Englewood, 108, 111, 118–19

    focus of, 104, 105

    future expansion of, 279

    inspiration for, 45

    in Little Village project, 108

    success of, 277, 280–81

Norfolk Southern, 196, 205, 209

North Branch Industrial Corridor, 179, 187, 189

North Lawndale, 106, 139, 146

North Loop, redevelopment in, 79, 82–86

North Side, industrial development, 174, 175, 177–79, 183, 185. See also specific areas

Northerly Island, 48–49, 71, 260–63, 280

Northwestern University, 81, 220

office growth

    boom in, 4, 7

    location of, 32

    in Loop, 24, 234, 236

    skyscrapers and, 18

O'Hare airport, 239–40, 245, 261

Okrent, Lawrence, 60, 257

Olympics Plan (2009), 5, 15, 238, 246

open space, and industry, 193, 198–99

Operation Ceasefire, 109

Organisation for Economic Co-operation and Development (OECD), 273, 276

outmigration, 267, 268, 269

parking. See also roads; vehicles
    in Englewood redevelopment plan, 112–15
    meter privatization, 249
    Millennium Park lease, 249
    Navy Pier, 216, 217, 218
    in postindustrial city, 26, 33

parks. See also specific
    business/industrial parks, 183–84
    in comprehensive plan (1966), 43, 44
    Little Village plans for, 146–50
    National Park Service, 103
    supplier parks, 194–96

pedestrians
    design accommodating, 64–66, 196
    in Englewood design plan, 113, 114
    in Illinois Center plan, 46, 48
    in Near South redevelopment, 89
    zoning to accommodate, 29, 257

Perkins + Will, 149

permanent supportive housing, 158–59

Pilsen district, 60–61, 106, 138

Plan for Transformation. See also CHA
    drafting, 156–57, 160–61
    implementation of, 161–62
    population affected by, 267, 269
    praise for, 96, 277
    results of, 162–65

Plan of Chicago (1909), 6, 19–20, 42, 48, 100
    anniversary of, 212
    Millennium Park project and, 226
    Northerly Island in, 260

Plan to End Homelessness, 158

Planned Development (PD) process, 28–29
    Illinois Center and, 46, 48
    in Near South redevelopment, 89–90
    in riverfront planning, 52, 54
    zoning reform, 256, 257, 258

Planned Manufacturing Districts (PMDs), 175, 177

planners, professional
    on city staff, 15–16, 26–28, 280
    in growth coalitions, 14, 15–16

planning
    bringing back, 277–81
    erosion of, 10
    politics versus, 9, 16, 278–79, 280, 281
    in postindustrial economy, 25–28

planning departments, 8–9, 14
    changing role of, 55, 241
    project funding, 7, 27–28
    strength of, 280

politics, 73
    aldermanic privilege, 11–12, 20, 29, 134
    backing CHA, 160–61
    in Circulator plan, 220, 221
    growth and, 7–8, 14
    Latino, 140–43, 146
    mayoral succession, 12–14
    in Meigs Field closure, 261
    on Navy Pier project, 216
    neighborhood groups and, 68
    planning vs., 9, 16, 278–79, 280, 281
    in Uptown planning, 134–35

Pollock, Les, 45, 252

Popkin, Susan, 162, 163

population. See also immigration; migration
    changes in, 3, 16–18, 137, 150
    recent decline in, 267–69

Port of Chicago, 216

postindustrial economy
    benefiting central area, 24
    central area planning, 29–33

downtown living, 33–36

planning reorganization in, 25–28, 38–39

urban university plans, 36–38

zoning reform and growth coalition, 28–29

poverty, 5–6, 130–32

Preliminary Comprehensive Plan (1946), 42

Prentice Women's Hospital, 81

Printer's Row, 61–64, 80, 173

printing industry, 173, 174, 190

Prudential Building, 28, 45

Public Buildings Commission of Chicago, 27

public housing. *See CHA; housing; urban renewal*

Pulaski Avenue, as employment district, 174–75

Pullman, historic preservation in, 80, 102–3

Quality of Life Plan, 104, 105, 107, 108

Englewood, 118–22

Little Village, 144–45, 146–50

race; racial change. *See also specific*

civil rights movement, 106

in comprehensive plan (1966), 42–43,
54–55

in Council Wars, 74

integration, 42, 61 (*see also segregation*)

in Little Village growth, 138, 146

in redevelopment, 85, 86

planning affected by, 9, 36, 57

politics and, 12, 13

population trends, 16–18, 267, 269, 270

as public housing issue, 154, 224

sense of community and, 139

in Uptown planning, 123–24, 126

railroads. *See also freight industry; transit*

heavy-rail capacity, 203–4

history of, 18–20, 21, 203

in Millennium Park project, 72, 225

in Near South redevelopment, 87

in urban university planning, 38

Ratner, Albert, 87–88, 89, 90

real estate developers, in growth coalitions, 14

recreation, in comprehensive plan (1966), 43, 44

Republic Steel, 174, 194

retail business

Englewood, 112–15

growth estimate, 236

Little Village, 138–39, 140–41

Loop revival, 57, 64–66, 232–33

postindustrial location of, 30–31

River City, 64

Riveredge Plan, 52–53, 258

Riverwalk Framework Plan, 280

roads. *See also parking; vehicles; specific roads*

central area plan for, 32–33

Freeway Revolts, 49, 68

in Illinois Center plan, 46–48

McPier building exclusive, 223

national highway system, 204

Robert Brooks Homes, 152–53, 154

Robert Taylor Homes, 69

Roosevelt Road, 62, 86, 89, 90

Roosevelt/California Business Park, 183–84

Rouse, James, 215, 216

Rubloff, Arthur, 31, 57, 64, 82–83

Rust Belt, 5, 24

Ryan, George H., 200, 261

Sawyer, Eugene, 76, 175, 177

schools, 97–100, 114, 142–46.

Sears Corporation, 58, 115

Sears Tower (Willis Tower), 29, 58, 274

Second Great Migration, 111–12

sector strategy, 171–74

segregation, 18, 146, 159, 269. *See also race*

senior citizen housing for, 61, 91, 133, 160

service connector program, 160, 162

Shaw, Charles, 83

Shedd Aquarium, 86, 88

Shiller, Helen, 130–31, 133, 135

Shuldiner, Joseph, 154

Single Resident Occupancy (SRO) apartments, 159

Skidmore, Owings & Merrill (SOM), 15
    Central Area Plan (1983), 70
    Chicago 21 plan, 58, 59–60
    Crosstown Expressway design, 68
    Fort Dearborn project, 32
    Illinois Center, 46, 48
    Millennium Park plan, 225, 226–27
    in Olympic bid process, 58, 59–60
    riverfront design, 259–60
skyscrapers, birth of, 18, 28
slums, 3, 97–99, 152–53
Smith, Adrian, 88, 226–27
solar energy farming, 183
South Chicago, 108
South Lawndale area, 137–39
South Loop
    New Town, 59–61, 64
    universities in, 36, 38, 39, 65
South Side. See also specific areas
    industrial development, 182–83, 185, 194
    perceived border of, 86
    race issues, 16, 18
    urban renewal, 98
Southtown Planning Association, 113
State Street, 64–66, 82, 232, 242
State Street Mall Commission, 65
steel industry, 171–72, 190
Streets for Cycling Plan, 2020, 264
Students for a Democratic Society (SDS), 126
Studio Gang Architects, 199, 262
suburbs, 6, 7, 16. See also neighborhoods
Sullivan, Louis, 80, 232
Superfund site, 147
supplier parks, 194–96.
Swibel, Charles, 35–36
Tax Increment Financing (TIF), 250–51
    Calumet district, 194, 196
    Central Area, 252
    current use of, 8–9, 212, 250–54

distribution of, 7, 278
    Englewood redevelopment, 117, 118
    Goose Island redevelopment, 180
    LaSalle Street, 252
    Little Village proposals, 141, 150
    Near South redevelopment, 90, 91
    North Loop, 82, 85
    Uptown redevelopment, 132–33
taxes, 75–76, 80–81
technology, changing manufacturing, 190
Theater District redevelopment, 83–85
Thompson, Jim, 217, 218
tourism. See also Millennium Park
    boom in, 4
    Central Area Circulator, 218–21
    hotel growth estimate, 236
    McCormick Place, 88–89, 222–25
    Navy Pier, 36–37, 215–18
traffic, intermodal, 187, 203–8.
transit. See also railroads
    airports, 49, 210–11, 239–40
    bicycles as, 263–66, 280
    Block 37 plan, 239–40
    central area need for, 212, 236–37
    the Circulator, 218–21
    elevated, 18–19
    increased capacity for, 279
    to McCormick Place, 223
    to Navy Pier, 216, 218
    passenger trains, 208, 209, 218–21
    postindustrial plans for, 32–33
    State Street transit mall, 64–66
    Union Station, 241, 242–43
transitway system, 241, 244–45, 246
Truman Community College, 128–29
Union Pacific, 205
Union Station, 241, 242–43
United Auto Workers, 197, 200–201
United Neighborhood Organization (UNO), 140

University Center, 65–66

Uptown
    citizen planning coalition, 126–29, 130
    conservation, 125–26
    gentrification, 129–32
    planning problems, 96, 278
    Wilson Yards, 132–35, 251

Uptown Chicago Commission (UCC), 125–26, 128–29, 132

Uptown Community Conservation Council, 128

Uptown People's organizations, 130

Urban Development Action Grant, 83, 102

urban renewal
    class in, 26
    department leading, 83, 114, 126
    Fort Dearborn proposal, 31–32, 64
    postindustrial, 33, 34
    slum clearance, 97–99, 152–53
    in university planning, 38, 39

U.S. Army Corps of Engineers, 263

U.S. Department of Transportation, 208–9

U.S. Environmental Protection Agency (EPA), 147

U.S. Steel; USX, 172, 174, 194

U.S. Supreme Court, 38

van der Rohe, Mies, 6–7, 29, 36

vehicles. *See also parking; roads*
    in Englewood redesign, 113, 114, 116
    in Illinois Center plan, 48
    in postindustrial planning, 32

Voice of the People, 132

Vrdolyak, Ed, 13, 74, 216

Wacker Drive, 48, 51

warehouse space, 204

Washington, Harold
    death and legacy of, 76–77
    election of, 12–13
    focus on employment, 171, 278
    on linked development, 75–76
    on Navy Pier, 216

    on North Loop redevelopment, 83, 85
    political position, 12–13, 67, 68, 69
    on World's Fair proposal, 72, 73

Washington Park, 106

Weese, Harry, 62–63, 216

West Loop, 58, 64

West Loop Transportation Center (WLTC), 236–37, 238–39, 243

West Side, industrial development, 182, 183, 184, 185.

whites. *See also race*
    in Chicago 21 plan, 60, 61
    displacement of, 25–26
    in Englewood, 111–12
    home equity data, 271
    low-income southern, 123, 125, 126
    moving to suburbs, 3, 18, 25, 43, 55
    population trends, 16, 17, 18, 268, 269

Wilson, William Julius, 5

Wilson Yards, 132–35, 251

Wisconsin Steel, 174, 194

Wislow, Robert, 230, 231

Wolf Point, 53

Woodlawn area, 106, 111, 126

World Business Chicago (WBC), 14, 271, 273, 274, 276, 280

World's Fair proposal, 71–73

Wright, Rodney and Sydney, 127–28

Wrigley Building, 21, 181

Wrigley Global Innovation Center, 179, 180–81

Wysocki, Ted, 190, 273

zoning
    central area change in, 230
    code updates, 191–92, 255–58
    lakefront protection, 51
    in postindustrial economy, 28–29, 36
    in sheltering the homeless, 159

Zoning Ordinance (1957), 28–29

Zoning Reform Commission, 256

ABOUT THE AUTHORS

D. Bradford Hunt is associate professor of social science and history at Roosevelt University in Chicago. He received his PhD in history from the University of California–Berkeley in 2000. His history of the Chicago Housing Authority, *Blueprint for Disaster: The Unraveling of Chicago Public Housing* won the 2009 Lewis Mumford Prize from the Society of American City and Regional Planning History. He is a series editor of the Chicago Architecture and Urbanism series published by the University of Chicago Press.*

Jon B. DeVries, AICP, is founding director of the Marshall Bennett Institute of Real Estate at Roosevelt University. He has over 35 years of planning and economic consulting experience at URS, Arthur Andersen, and Goodkin Research. He worked on numerous plans for Chicago including the Central Area Plan (2003) and the Central Area Action Plan (2009). In 2008 he received the Holleb Community Service Award from Lambda Alpha International/Ely Chapter.*

Contributors

Kathleen E. Dickhut is deputy commissioner of the Sustainable Development Division in Chicago's Department of Housing and Economic Development, Bureau of Planning and Zoning.

Charles Hoch teaches in the Department of Urban Planning and Policy at the University of Illinois–Chicago. He studies ways to remedy the homeless problem and serves on the board of Mercy Housing Lakefront, a nonprofit that builds affordable supportive housing.

Larry E. Lund is principal of the Real Estate Planning Group and former international president of Lambda Alpha International.*

Paul O'Connor is an urban strategist in the City Design Practice of Skidmore, Owings and Merrill. He was the founding executive director of World Business Chicago.

James E. Peters, AICP, is a historic preservation consultant and adjunct professor at the School of the Art Institute of Chicago and the University of Illinois–Chicago. He is a former president of Landmarks Illinois and a former staff , director of the Commission on Chicago Landmarks.*

Leslie S. Pollock, FAICP, is principal consultant at Camiros, a Chicago-based planning firm, and former international president of Lambda Alpha International. He is an adjunct professor at University of Illinois–Urbana-Champaign and University of Illinois–Chicago.*

Michael A. Shymanski is a former associate of McDonough Associates, president of the Historic Pullman Foundation, director of the Dunes National Park Association, and director of the Bielenberg Historic Pullman House Foundation.*

Jeffrey T. Sriver is a projects administrator at the Chicago Department of Transportation. He was formerly general manager of strategic planning with the Chicago Transit Authority.*

William J. Trumbull is general manager, real estate and asset management, for the Chicago Transit Authority, and former deputy commissioner, Industrial Division, Chicago Department of Planning.*

* Member, Lambda Alpha International